PROVERBS

•

ECCLESIASTES

THE ANCHOR BIBLE is a fresh approach to the world's greatest classic. Its object is to make the Bible accessible to the modern reader; its method is to arrive at the meaning of biblical literature through exact translation and extended exposition, and to reconstruct the ancient setting of the biblical story, as well as the circumstances of its transcription and the characteristics of its transcribers.

THE ANCHOR BIBLE is a project of international and interfaith scope. Protestant, Catholic, and Jewish scholars from many countries contribute individual volumes. The project is not sponsored by any ecclesiastical organization and is not intended to reflect any particular theological doctrine. Prepared under our joint supervision, THE ANCHOR BIBLE is an effort to make available all the significant historical and linguistic knowledge which bears on the interpretation of the biblical record.

THE ANCHOR BIBLE is aimed at the general reader with no special formal training in biblical studies; yet, it is written with the most exacting standards of scholarship, reflecting the highest technical accomplishment.

This project marks the beginning of a new era of co-operation among scholars in biblical research, thus forming a common body of knowledge to be shared by all.

William Foxwell Albright
David Noel Freedman
GENERAL EDITORS

Following the death of senior editor W. F. Albright, The Anchor Bible Editorial Board was established to advise and assist David Noel Freedman in his continuing capacity as general editor. The three members of the Editorial Board are among the contributors to The Anchor Bible. They have been associated with the series for a number of years and are familiar with its methods and objectives. Each is a distinguished authority in his area of specialization, and in concert with the others, will provide counsel and judgment as the series continues.

EDITORIAL BOARD

Frank M. Cross   Old Testament
Raymond E. Brown   New Testament
Jonas C. Greenfield   Apocrypha

THE ANCHOR BIBLE

PROVERBS

·

ECCLESIASTES

INTRODUCTION, TRANSLATION, AND NOTES

BY

R. B. Y. SCOTT

Doubleday & Company, Inc.

Garden City, New York

ISBN 0-385-02177-1
Library of Congress Catalog Card Number 65–13988
Copyright © 1965 by Doubleday & Company, Inc.
All Rights Reserved
Printed in the United States of America
Second Edition
Sixth Printing

FOREWORD

This book is indebted to "many men, many minds," as will be evident to the observant reader. The author is grateful, in particular, to the editors of this series: Dr. William F. Albright, who with characteristic generosity has offered valued suggestions from his rich treasury of learning, and Dr. David Noel Freedman, whose meticulous scholarship and friendly counsel have greatly improved the original draft. The weaknesses which remain are the author's own; no doubt they will be pointed out faithfully by the reviewers.

R. B. Y. Scott

Princeton, New Jersey

To Kathleen, with love

CONTENTS

II. THE FIRST COLLECTION OF SOLOMONIC PROVERBS

III. THE THIRTY PRECEPTS OF THE SAGES

IV. THE SECOND COLLECTION OF SOLOMONIC PROVERBS

V. THE FOUR APPENDIXES

ECCLESIASTES (QOHELETH)

PRINCIPAL ABBREVIATIONS

1. PUBLICATIONS

AJSL	American Journal of Semitic Languages and Literatures
ANET	*Ancient Near Eastern Texts Relating to the Old Testament,* ed. J. B. Pritchard, 2d ed.
BWL	W. G. Lambert, *Babylonian Wisdom Literature*
Gordis	Robert Gordis, *Koheleth, the Man and His World*
Gordon	E. I. Gordon, *Sumerian Proverbs*
PNWSP	M. Dahood, *Proverbs and Northwest Semitic Philology*
VT	Vetus Testamentum
WIANE	*Wisdom in Israel and the Ancient Near East,* eds. M. Noth and D. W. Thomas

2. VERSIONS

Aq.	Ancient Greek translation of the Old Testament by Aquila
EV, EVV	English version(s)
KJ	The Authorized Version of 1611, or the King James Bible
LXX	The Septuagint
MT	Masoretic Text
RSV	The Revised Standard Version
Symm.	Ancient Greek translation of the Old Testament by Symmachus
Syr.	Syriac version, the Peshitta
Syro-Hex.	Syro-Hexaplar, the Syriac version of the Old Testament by Paul of Tella
Targ.	Targum, Aramaic translation or paraphrase
Theod.	Ancient Greek translation of the Old Testament by Theodotion
Vulg.	The Vulgate

3. OTHER ABBREVIATIONS

Fr.   French
Gr.   Greek
Heb.   Hebrew
Lat.   Latin
OT   Old Testament

General Introduction

THE WISDOM MOVEMENT AND ITS LITERATURE

THE WISE MEN AND THEIR WRITINGS IN ANCIENT ISRAEL

The prophet Jeremiah was regarded by some of the leading men of Jerusalem in his day as a dangerously subversive influence. On one occasion his adversaries are reported as saying, "Come, let us make a plot against Jeremiah! For the priest's giving of instruction [torāh] must not cease, nor the wise man's counsel, nor the prophet's message!" (Jer xviii 18.) The roles of the priest and of the prophet are well known. But who was the "wise man," and why should his function in the community be correlated with theirs? Is there any connection between these three kinds of authoritative guidance and the fact that the Hebrew Bible is in three parts, known as "the Law ["instruction," torāh], the Prophets, and the Writings"?

The Torāh or "Law of Moses" was the first "canon" (corpus of authoritative sacred literature) of Judaism, and is still its primary and basic standard. It comprises four books, Exodus to Deuteronomy, which deal with the constitutive period of Moses, prefaced by Genesis which fills in the background for this and traces its antecedents back to the creation of the world and man. Its narratives and law codes set forth the fundamental beliefs and obligations of Israel as the covenant people of Yahweh.[1] There is abundant evidence that to teach these was one of the functions of the priesthood.[2] The second division, "The Prophets," in turn comprises collections of the oracular messages or "words" of Israel's prophets, preceded by a "prophetic" interpretation of Israel's history in the books Joshua to II Kings.

[1] "Yahweh" is probably the original pronunciation of the *proper name* of Israel's God, represented in English versions as "Jehovah" or "the Lord."
[2] Cf. Deut xxvi 1–11, xxxiii 10; II Chron xv 3; Mal ii 4–7, etc.

The third part of the Hebrew Bible, "the Writings" [Hagiographa] is more miscellaneous in content. It is the part of the Old Testament least dominated by priestly and prophetic interests, and in which "the wise man's counsel" is most prominent. Three of its major works, Proverbs, Job, and Ecclesiastes-Qoheleth are "Wisdom books," as the Psalms and the Song of Songs are also, according to the ancient reckoning.[3] Of the remainder, Lamentations contains five additional psalms of a particular kind, Ruth is a parable, Esther and Daniel turn in part on the superior wisdom of Jewish piety, and the priest-scribe Ezra of Ezra-Nehemiah is described as endowed with divine wisdom (Ezra vii 25).

We thus have preliminary evidence from two sides that the wise men and their writings were a kind of "third force" in the religious and social life of the people of the Old Testament. Whereas the prophets often found themselves opposed to the priests at the point where institutional religion had become an end in itself, they shared with the priests the conviction that Israel was the chosen people of Yahweh and had special obligations arising from that relationship. Their theologies and immediate concerns might differ, but they were united in believing that Israel had a unique relationship to her unique God. Yahweh had revealed himself to her through his spokesmen and through her historical experiences. He had laid upon her his commandments, and continually concerned himself with her response and with her welfare. The wise men, on the other hand, have almost nothing to say about institutional religion, or about this special relationship of Yahweh and Israel, past or present. They do not address Israel as such, at all. They make no direct appeal to the authority of a revealed religion, though their occasional exhortations to piety toward Yahweh (e.g., Prov xvi) presuppose an accepted belief. They speak to and about men primarily as individuals. The authority to which they chiefly appeal is the disciplined intelligence and moral experience of good men.

Hence, on the one hand, the content of a book like Proverbs is closer to life in the secular world, and to the day-to-day problems of the ordinary man who is content to leave traditional theology to the experts. On the other hand, because of their independent approach, some of the Wisdom writers were able to raise ultimate

---

[3] Presumably because of the tradition that Solomon's wisdom led to his composing of songs as well as of proverbs (cf. I Kings iv 32 EV).

philosophic and theological problems and discuss them without the restraints of orthodoxy (e.g., Job and Qoheleth). Wisdom taught a practical religious philosophy through which a good man might find satisfaction in life, in a moral order which had established itself through experience. As part of this drive toward a vital equilibrium it sought further to find satisfaction for the tortured mind, through probing the problems of human freedom under divine sovereignty, of reward and retribution, and of the anomalies of suffering and injustice. The wise men sought for a unified structural principle in life. By generalizing from experience they propounded rules as indicators of this moral structure of life, and as guideposts on its way. Through reflection and debate they attempted to reach, within a general religious framework, rational explanations of man's existence and his intellectual and moral problems.

The wise man [*ḥākām*]—to the extent that he was indeed wise —personified, and sought to impart to others, Wisdom [*ḥokmāh*], a quality and principle of life. The constant enrichment of the meaning of this word tells the story of the Wisdom movement in Israel. The primary reference of *ḥokmāh* is to unusual skill or ability, to expertness of a particular kind, attained by training and experience added to special gifts. This was the secret of the true craftsman, like Bezalel who was "filled with divine power [literally "spirit"], in wisdom, intelligence, knowledge, and craftsmanship to design and make objects of gold, silver, and bronze . . ." (Exod xxxv 30–35; cf. Hiram of Tyre, I Kings vii 13–14). We hear of the special "wisdom" of warriors, sailors, farmers, and soothsayers, as well as of priests, scribes, counselors, judges, and kings. *Ḥokmāh* was especially necessary for kings, like David to whom was ascribed "wisdom like that of the 'messenger' of God who knows everything on earth" (II Sam xiv 20). Solomon became the legendary paragon of Wisdom. Of the ideal king of Isa xi 1–2 it is said that "Yahweh's spirit will rest on him, a power [literally "spirit"] of wisdom and discernment, a power of counsel and performance, a power of knowledge and religion [literally "fear of Yahweh"].

Thus *ḥokmāh* gained the sense of "skill in living," the trained ability to live in equilibrium with the moral order of the world. At one level it is intelligence or shrewdness. At the next it is good sense, sound judgment, and moral understanding. "A clever man's wisdom makes him behave intelligently" (Prov xiv 8). A third level is the capacity to consider profounder problems of human life and destiny. "Buy truth, and do not sell wisdom, instruction, and understanding" (Prov xxiii 23). Wisdom thus becomes the fruit of the unending quest for the meaning of man's experience of life and religion. "Where shall wisdom be found?" asks the Book of Job. "Man does not know the way to it. It is hidden from the eyes of all living things. God understands the way to it" (Job xxviii 12, 21, 23). "All wisdom comes from the Lord, and is with him forever," affirms Sirach (i 1). The search for the higher wisdom led to the twin convictions that, in the last analysis, wisdom comes to man only as a divine gift, and that it belongs to the very nature of God himself.

The different levels of understanding of what wisdom means point to the fact that the Wisdom literature of the Old Testament came into existence over a long period of time. It is the product of what—for want of a better term—may be called the "Wisdom movement." Reference to the historical narratives confirms this, though these indications are largely incidental because the narratives were written chiefly from the standpoint of the priests and prophets. As a result, the materials for the history of the Wisdom movement are far from complete, and we must rely to a great extent on what can be inferred from the Wisdom books themselves as to the time and circumstances of their origin. One remarkable fact is evident from study of these works, as well as from specific statements in other parts of the Old Testament: that Israelite Wisdom was similar to that of neighboring peoples like the Edomites, and had antecedents and counterparts in the much older cultures of Phoenicia, Egypt, and Mesopotamia. It was in fact part of an international, intercultural, and interreligious school of thought whose beginnings can be traced to early times in Sumer and Egypt, and which was to make its impress eventually on the New Testament and the Talmud. In order to understand it we must (a) examine the elements in the Old Testament which represent the thought and way of speaking of the Wisdom school; (b) reconstruct so far as possible the history of the Wisdom movement in pre-Exilic Israel and post-Exilic Judaism; and (c) compare with these the corresponding phenomena in the surrounding cultures of the ancient Near East.

In the neighboring cultures and also in Israel the Wisdom literature was of two main types that apparently represented divergent tendencies among the sages. The first is represented in the Bible by the Book of Proverbs (except for viii 22–31 and xxx 1–4), the second by Job and Ecclesiastes (Qoheleth). The spirit of the former is conservative, practical, didactic, optimistic, and worldly wise. The latter type is critical, even radical, in its attitude to conventional beliefs; it is speculative, individualistic, and (broadly speaking) pessimistic. The former expresses itself characteristically in brief rhythmic adages and maxims suited to instruction, as well as in longer admonitions; the latter, chiefly in soliloquy and dialogue.

The Book of Proverbs is a source book of materials for the instruction of youth and the more advanced study of their elders, in the wisdom which conduces to a satisfying life (cf. i 2–6). Its introductory section, chapters i–ix, comprises a series of admonitory discourses, together with two metaphorical poems in which personified Wisdom addresses mankind, and some more miscellaneous materials. In x 1–xxii 16 and again in chapters xxv–xxix we have collections of proverbs in poetic parallelism, for the most part two-line adages and maxims arranged, with slight exceptions, in no discernible order. The first of these collections is followed in xxii 17–xxiv 22 by a compendium of thirty precepts, with a supplement, modeled on the Egyptian *Instruction of Amen-em-ope*. Chapters 30–31 contain four short appendixes. The content ranges from folk proverbs to lofty speculations on the ultimate nature of Wisdom and its relationship to God, man, and the universe (Prov viii[4]).

The Book of Job belongs to the second type of literature produced by the Wisdom movement, the speculative and radical. It is in fact, among other things, a searching criticism of the doctrine of reward and punishment as taught by the conservative sages. The recurrent problem of the suffering of a just man is presented dramatically in a prose introduction which tells how Yahweh permitted Job's piety to be put to the test of personal disaster and loathsome

[4] See further the Introduction to Proverbs, below.

disease. The problem is then explored in a poetic colloquy between Job and three friends who represent the traditional viewpoint, culminating in the intervention of God to challenge Job's impugning of the divine wisdom and justice. The subject of the Book of Job, however, is not simply the moral problem of the suffering of the innocent, though it begins from this. Nor is it the intellectual problem of theodicy—whether God's government of man's world be just. Its theme is the riddle of the nature of man and the nature of God, and the possibility of man's knowledge of God—and hence the meaning of true religion.

The many literary and historical questions posed by the present form of the book need not concern us here. Clearly the book is not a literary unity as it stands. The third cycle of the debate has suffered disarrangement, apparently as a result of the intrusion of supplementary material, like the speeches of Elihu in chapters xxxii–xxxvii. There is room for difference of opinion about the relationship of the prose prologue to the poetic colloquy, and how it is that the "voice out of the storm" brings Job to humility without having answered his questions on which the whole debate has turned. Nor is it possible to say much more about the dating of the work than that it must be later than the rise to influence of the views of which it is so profoundly critical. The period of Jeremiah seems a likely time. The shocking death in 609 B.C. of the reforming King Josiah may have stirred the debate out of which the Book of Job was written.

THE THIRD BIBLICAL WORK of the Wisdom schools is again from the radical wing. Ecclesiastes (Qoheleth) comprises a series of soliloquies on the theme that man's earthly existence and his struggles to achieve and to understand are as futile and ephemeral as a breath of air, because the conditions and experiences of his life are determined inexorably by an inscrutable power. The only possible value or "good" for man is the enjoyment to be derived from each experience as it passes. On the basis of this philosophy, the Qoheleth ("the Teacher" [?]) counsels moderation, reserve, avoidance of fretful anxiety and fruitless ambition, and the enjoyment of such temporary happiness as is possible through facing facts and accepting the conditions under which life must be lived. Qoheleth denies the possibility of man's knowing God either through revelation or by reason. He goes beyond the author of the Book of Job in his dogmatic rationalism; his concern is primarily intellectual, where Job's is moral and religious. Whereas Job denounces the traditional doctrine that the reward of virtue and the punishment of vice can explain such suffering as his, Qoheleth declares that the doctrine is totally false, since man's fate is simply that of an animal. His break with the conservative Wisdom teachers is thus even more far-reaching than Job's. To Job, God has temporarily and incomprehensibly withdrawn into the mystery of his being; to Qoheleth, God is no more than a name for the incomprehensible power which has created the unalterable conditions of man's existence and determines his fate.[5]

AMONG THE ONE HUNDRED AND FIFTY poetic compositions which make up the Book of Psalms, there are about a dozen which exhibit the distinctive ideas and language of the Wisdom schools. Needless to say, none of them resemble Qoheleth, for the Psalms breathe the spirit of worship and personal religious devotion. There is more resemblance to the Book of Job in such anguished outcries against the prosperity of the wicked as are found for example, in Ps lxxiii; it is noteworthy that anguish here gives way to understanding, in an act of worship. The writer of Ps xlix reflects on the fact that pride of wealth cannot save a man from death, in language reminiscent of Proverbs and Job, and even of Qoheleth. Psalms xxxiv and xxxvii might have been composed by the authors of the more pious elements in Proverbs. The motto of that book, "The fear of the Lord is the beginning of wisdom" is quoted at Ps cxi 10. In Psalms such as i, xxxvii, cxii the changes are rung on the contrasting fortunes and fate of the righteous and the wicked, as in Prov x–xi and in the speeches of Job's counselors. Finally, the theological identification of the divine wisdom with the content of the Torah or written Law (Deut iv 6–8; Sirach xxiv 23–29; Baruch iv 1) underlies the Torah Psalms i, xix 7–14 EV, and cxix. The Wisdom psalms thus represent what may be called the pious wing of the Wisdom movement, as distinct from the worldly wisdom of many (but not all) of the proverbs, and from the heterodoxy of Job and Qoheleth.

Two other types of material in the Hebrew Bible related to the Wisdom movement must be mentioned. The first is a motif in the

[5] See further the Introduction to Ecclesiastes (Qoheleth) below.

Joseph narratives in Gen xxxvii ff. and the Daniel stories in Dan
i, ii, iv, and v: the Hebrew at a foreign court who displays a skill
or "wisdom" in the interpretation of dreams and signs which have
baffled the professional wise men of Egypt and Babylon respectively. In addition, Joseph is portrayed as exhibiting the prudence,
fidelity, and generosity which Proverbs holds up as characteristic of
the man who orders his life wisely. The story as a whole is an
object lesson in belief in divine providence. Daniel, too, is exemplary
in his courage and piety, and the tales about him imply that his
wisdom is of a higher order than that of the magicians and as-
trologers of Babylon.

Attention must be drawn also to the references in mythological
material in Gen iii and Ezek xxviii to a secret divine wisdom
possessed by archetypal man in "Eden, the garden of God." This
can be correlated with the idea, in non-mythological Wisdom writings, that ultimately the meaning of Wisdom is known only to God
(Job xxviii 12–13, 21, 23, xlii 3; Eccles iii 11; Ps cxxxix 6 EV;
cf. I Cor ii 7). In the background of these ideas are the gods and
goddesses of Wisdom in the ancient mythologies of Egypt, Canaan,
and Mesopotamia (cf. Proverbs, NOTES on Sec. 9, below).

Two major Wisdom works, Ecclesiasticus (Sirach) and the Wisdom of Solomon, and others containing "Wisdom" elements, Tobit,
I Esdras, and Baruch, are found in the Greek and Latin Bibles
(Septuagint and Vulgate), but not in the Hebrew Bible. The reason
is that these were included in the larger and more loosely defined
collection of sacred books of the Jews of Alexandria, which became the Old Testament in the earliest Christian Bible.

SIRACH[6] came into use in the Christian Church in its Greek form,
but it was written originally in Hebrew, as the translator tells us
in his prologue. Fragments of the Hebrew version came to light in
Egypt early in the present century, and further fragments have appeared recently in the Qumran scrolls and at Masada. It is the work
of a sage of Jerusalem, translated by his grandson in 132 B.C. and
hence to be dated in its original form early in the second century B.C.

---

[6] The full name of the work in the Greek Bible is "The Wisdom of Jesus,
son of Sirach." For a reason which is not entirely clear it came to be known
in the Latin-speaking Church as *liber ecclesiasticus*, "the ecclesiastical book."
The use of the title in English is unfortunate, since it leads to confusion with
Ecclesiastes (Qoheleth).

The author, like many of his predecessors, was a scholar and teacher of "Wisdom" who gathered pupils or disciples in his own school (Sirach li 23). He had traveled widely, in keeping with the international tradition of the Wisdom movement (xxxix 4, li 13). His book resembles the Book of Proverbs in its use of adages, maxims, and exhortations, and builds on Prov viii its theological treatment of the nature of Wisdom in chapter xxiv. The virtues it commends and the vices it condemns are similar, though with less emphasis on the sins of the flesh. There is, however, a basic difference, in that Sirach speaks of himself as the heir of the Law and the Prophets, as well as of the Wisdom teachers. He goes far beyond the assertion that true religion is the basis of wisdom, and makes the religious life a subject in itself. Sirach is primarily a theologian. For him wisdom is the revealed wisdom embodied in Israel's Torah. His ethical precepts are interspersed with devotional meditations and prayers, and the main part of his book concludes with a paean of praise—of God, the Lord of creation, of the past heroes of Israel's faith, and of worship as conducted in the temple of Jerusalem by the contemporary high priest Simon "the Righteous."

THE WORK ENTITLED The Wisdom of Solomon (or, the Book of Wisdom) was composed, not in Hebrew but in Greek, and apparently at Alexandria in the first century B.C. Its author, like Qoheleth, assumes the role of Solomon the all-wise ruler. He addresses himself in imagination to the rulers of the earth, on the assumption that wisdom is prerequisite to all such exercise of authority. But wisdom as he sees it is not so much perspicacity as righteousness. So he proceeds to state the case for Judaism before the Gentile world, and at the same time, to confirm his fellow Jews in their faith, and to provide them with an apologetic. He does this not in traditional terms; rather, he builds a bridge between Hebrew religious ideas and Greek philosophical thought. It is righteousness, he says, which teaches the four cardinal virtues of Plato and the Stoics: self-control, prudence, justice, and courage (viii 7). The spirit of Wisdom is described in terms of the universal reason (vii 17–viii 1). From Platonism he draws his doctrine of the creation of the world out of formless matter (xi 17), and the view that the soul of man, temporarily burdened by the body, is pre-existent and immortal, (viii 19–20, ix 15). "The souls of the righteous

are in the hands of God" (iii 1), who created man to be immortal
(i 13–15); death is the result of sin and the lot of the adherents of
the devil, who introduced it into the world (i 16, ii 24, v 13–14).
The Jewishness of the author is more evident in the second part of
the work, where he discourses on the guidance of Israel's unique
history by divine wisdom, and on the nature and folly of idolatry.
The concluding homiletic midrash on the plagues and miracles of
the Exodus is less significant.

TOBIT is a very different kind of book from either of the fore-
going. It is a romantic tale of the vicissitudes which befell Tobit, a
pious Jewish exile in Assyria, and his son Tobias, and it was told
to illustrate the deliverance of such sufferers through divine Providence. The story incorporates elements from pagan folklore, and
introduces the far-famed Assyrian sage Ahiqar[7] as Tobit's nephew.
Its Wisdom features are evident, partly in its resumption of the
theme of the suffering just man (Tobit is deprived of his property
and is accidentally blinded as a result of his pious burying of the
dead), and partly in two collections of precepts and aphorisms put
in the mouths of Tobit and the angel Raphael respectively (iv 3–
19, xii 6–10). The book seems to have been composed in Aramaic in the late Persian period. Fragments of it in *both* Aramaic
and Hebrew have been found at Qumran.

I ESDRAS is not a distinct work but an alternative recension in
the Old Greek version of the concluding chapters of II Chronicles,
the Book of Ezra, and a short section from Nehemiah as these appear in the Hebrew Bible. The Greek form inserts in iii 1–iv 62 a
romantic tale about one of three young guardsmen who won the
favor of Darius by triumphing in a debate about the relative strengths
of wine, the king, women, and (climactically) of truth. The story
seems to have been Persian in origin. It is connected with Jewish
history by the device of identifying the third guardsman with
Zerubbabel, who became governor of Judah, and by describing his
reward as permission to rebuild Jerusalem. Its connection with Jewish Wisdom is slight; no more, in fact, than its illustration of the
motif (found also in Daniel) of the superiority in wisdom displayed by pious Jews at the courts of oriental monarchs.

BARUCH purports to be a work from the pen of the companion-

---

[7] On Ahiqar, see below, pp. LI–LII.

secretary of the prophet Jeremiah (Jer xxxvi 4). It is not, however, a literary unit, and the indications are that it was composed in Hebrew (though preserved in Greek) in the second and first centuries B.C., and thus has no authentic connection with the Baruch of history. It comprises a prayer of confession, with an introduction, and two poems, of which the first, iii 9–iv 4, concerns us here. This is in the form of a summons to Israel to relearn the wisdom whose neglect has resulted in her exile in a foreign land; it echoes the thought of earlier Wisdom writings such as Job xxviii and Ecclesiasticus xxiv, as well as the language of Deut xxx 12–13.

THE HISTORY OF HEBREW WISDOM IN THE OLD TESTAMENT PERIOD

The difficulty in dating the Wisdom writings of pre-Exilic Israel and of the scattered Jewish community centered at Jerusalem after the Babylonian Exile is compounded by the uncertainties which beset the reconstruction of the history into which these must be fitted.[8] There are great gaps in the narrative after the end of the succession of Judean kings, so that for long periods in the Babylonian, Persian, and early Hellenistic periods we know very little of the sequence of events. Even for the pre-Exilic period our historical resources are rather meager, except for the years of the single monarchy from Saul to Solomon, and certain other times when events occurred which the religious historians considered particularly significant. The corpus of "historical" works from Joshua to II Kings contains much factual and reliable material, but it is highly selective and is dominated by the theological views of its editors. Their purpose is to tell the story of Yahweh's chosen people in the land of promise, and to show how the national vicissitudes were determined by the loyalty or disloyalty of Israel and her leaders to the Mosaic covenant formulated in the Book of Deuteronomy. The second historical corpus, Chronicles-Ezra-Nehemiah, repeats, summarizes, and supplements the same story; but its special interest in the temple

[8] The latest and most successful attempt to integrate the biblical materials, the results of Palestinian archaeology, and what is known of the history and culture of the ancient Near East prior to and contemporary with this history, is John Bright, *A History of Israel,* Philadelphia, 1959.

cult, its personnel, and the connection of King David with cultic origins makes its treatment even more selective and prone to distortion. This does not mean that these two histories are to be discarded as unreliable, but simply that the objective historian must approach them in full awareness of the historical methods and special interests of the writers and editors. Fortunately it is possible to check and supplement the material of the biblical histories, at many points, from other books of the Old Testament, notably the records of prophecy; and also from archaeological evidence and the historical records of contemporary peoples like the Egyptians, where these impinge upon the life of Israel.

The defectiveness of the biblical histories and prophetic records which matters most for our present purpose is that, because of their special historico-theological interests, they largely leave out of account the Wisdom movement, with its international orientation, and its personal and practical concerns. The chief exceptions to this are the legendary glorification of Solomon's wisdom inserted in the First Book of Kings and the mainly hostile references to wise men by the prophets. Yet enough evidence can be gleaned from these and other sources, and from the Wisdom writings themselves, to reconstruct on broad lines the history of Israel's Wisdom teachers.

FOLK WISDOM is a perennial phenomenon in coherent traditional societies. It appears early,[9] and continues alongside the developing sophistication of literate circles. Moreover, it underlies and supports that development. There is more than enough evidence of the existence of Israelite folk wisdom, in proverbial sayings quoted incidentally in the narratives and in the prophetic books, to say nothing of those incorporated in the Wisdom literature itself. Such folk sayings are brief and pointed comments on human behavior and recurrent situations. They make frequent use of metaphor and comparison. Sometimes they take the form of rhetorical questions to show that something is absurd or impossible. A large proportion of Old Testament colloquial proverbs have a distinctly scornful tone, implying a deviation from social norms:

[9] Cf. the Phoenician and Canaanite proverbs of the fourteenth century B.C., quoted in *Ancient Near Eastern Texts Relating to the Old Testament* (abbr. ANET), ed. James B. Pritchard, 2d ed., Princeton University Press, 1955, p. 426a.

"Is even Saul among the prophets? And who is *their* father?" [i.e., unlike Saul, they are "nobodies"] (I Sam x 11–12);
"One who is girding himself [for battle] should not boast like one ungirding himself [afterwards]" (I Kings xx 11);
"Can an Ethiopian change [the color of] his skin, or a leopard his spots?" (Jer xiii 23);
"From the wicked comes wickedness" (I Sam xxiv 13 EV).

The last example is expressly identified as "a wise saying of the ancient(s)," "an old saying." In Gen x 9 the proverb "Like Nimrod, a master hunter in Yahweh's sight!" is introduced with the phrase "As the saying is" [literally "therefore it is said"]. The contemptuous saying about Saul (above) is said afterwards to have *become* a proverb. These are examples of adages connected with particular persons or episodes, historical or legendary, famous for some particular thing, like Caesar's wife who must be above suspicion, or the disastrous victory of Pyrrhus.[10] Places, too, have special associations which perpetuate their names in proverbial comparisons and metaphors. The reputation of the town of Abel for wisdom had existed from former times, the wise woman told Joab (II Sam xx 18); "They always would say in former times, 'The place to ask questions is at Abel'": which reminds us of the deliberately acquired reputation of the English Gotham as a town inhabited by fools. What may be an obscure allusion to the name of Jerusalem in Gen xxii 14 is quoted as a common saying. In I Kings ix 7 Israel is threatened with becoming "a proverb and a byword" and her temple a ruin, if she lapses into idolatry.

The prophets quote a number of sayings which may be of remote antiquity, and which in any case are sufficiently familiar to their hearers to give force to their use in support of what the prophets are saying. Jeremiah (xxxi 29) and Ezekiel (xviii 2) both refer to a proverb-of-consequence: "When the fathers have eaten un-

[10] In II Sam v 8 the common saying "The blind and the lame shall not come into the house" is connected with the defiance of the defenders on the occasion of David's capture of Jerusalem. It is far-fetched to suggest that the proverb *originated* in these circumstances (since Jerusalem was not a "house"); all the more so if it be interpreted as a cultic regulation. Perhaps the saying was older than this time and was derived from the taunt in a children's game like (cf. "I'm the king of the castle / You're the dirty rascal!").

ripe grapes, the children's teeth are set on edge" [literally "blunted", i.e., they are unable to eat at all. A man's greed or haste harms others even more than himself, so his children pay for his folly]. In Amos iii 3–6a, 8a occurs a series of rhetorical questions quite unlike the other oracles of this prophet, and which also have the form of proverbs-of-consequence, for example, "Do two go in company [or, "act together"] unless they are in agreement?" (vs. 3). This looks like the Israelite equivalent of our "A man is known by the company he keeps." With the remaining questions it wins the consent of the audience prior to Amos' climactic conclusion[11]: "When a lion roars, who is not afraid? / When Lord Yahweh speaks, who can help prophesying?" (vs. 8).

The proverb-of-analogy "Like mother, like daughter" is said in Ezek xvi 44 to be of a kind familiar to "those who use proverbs." It appears again in Hosea's "Like people, like priest" (iv 9), and in the taunt of the Midianite kings, "As the man, so his strength" [i.e., "if you dare!"] (Judg viii 21). Ezekiel, in fact, complains that he himself is dismissed as a mere maker or user of "proverbs" (xx 49 EV), a description no doubt prompted by his highly figurative language and symbolic actions.[12] Jeremiah alludes to colloquial sayings, for example,

"What has straw in common with wheat?" (xxiii 28);
"He who grows rich through injustice is [like] a partridge
hatching eggs it has not laid" (xvii 11);
"Can one break iron, iron from the north, and bronze?"
(xv 12).

Isaiah's outcry against instruments which (figuratively personified) consider themselves more important than their users (x 15) may or may not be based on popular sayings, but it is significant that the same motif appears in the Assyrian-Aramaic sayings of *Ahiqar* vii (ANET, p. 429a): "Why should wood strive with fire, flesh with a knife, a man with (a king)?"

A further source of Israelite popular sayings is the Wisdom literature itself, especially, as might be expected, the Book of Proverbs.

---

[11] The same rhetorical technique is used in Amos chs. i–ii in the series of denunciations of Israel's enemies culminating in a similar denunciation of Israel.

[12] Cf. Ezek iv 1–v 4, xvi 1–xvii 10, xxiii 1–35, etc. In xxxiii 32 the people pay no more heed to him than if he were a wandering minstrel.

The latter incorporates some of these in its literary adages. They can be recognized with some degree of probability from certain formal characteristics, as well as by their divergence from the predominantly catechetical tone of their contexts. The traditional sayings are compact, pointed, picturesque, complete in themselves, and often are marked by alliteration and assonance. Examples are:

> *bā' zādōn, bā' qālōn,* (literally) "Comes insolence, comes disgrace" (xi 2);
>
> *šōmēr miṣwāh šōmēr napšō,* "To observe the law is to preserve yourself" (xix 16);
>
> *rō'eh kᵉsīlīm yērōᵃ',* "The fellow of fools will fare ill" (xiii 20);
>
> *nepeš 'āmēl 'āmlāh lō,* "The toiler's appetite toils for him" (xvi 26a).

A second genre of folk wisdom is the riddle. The contest of wits was a favorite form of entertainment; Solomon's success in solving the riddles propounded by the Queen of Sheba (I Kings x 1–3), and the debate of the three guardsmen at Darius' court (I Esdras iii 1–iv 47) are well-known examples. The story of Samson's wager with the wedding guests (Judg xiv 10–18) carries this type of wisdom-play into humbler surroundings and into the pre-monarchical period. It seems improbable that "Out of the eater came something to eat, / Out of the strong came something sweet" would suggest to the hearers wild honey found in a lion's carcass, and the failure to guess the answer is not surprising. The curious thing is that the answer, when obtained by a stratagem, should itself be in the form of a riddle, "What is sweeter than honey? What is stronger than a lion?" The answer would be "love between the sexes" (cf. Song of Sol viii 6–7), which makes this a more appropriate riddle for the occasion.

The fable combines features of the riddle and of the parable. A "fable" in the strict sense is an imaginative tale in which the actors are animals or inanimate objects such as trees (which may seem alive because of movement and sound when a wind is blowing) endowed with human speech. Often, as in Aesop's fables, the story conveys a message or carries a moral for human behavior. In addition to stories with fabulous features such as the talking ass of Balaam (Num xxii 21–35) and the "riddle-proverb" of the

Eagle, the Cedar, and the Vine in Ezek xvii 1–10, two full-blown fables occur in the Old Testament. The first is told by Jotham about the trees' election of a king (Judg ix 7–15), the second by Jehoash about the impertinence of a thistle who wanted to marry the daughter of a cedar of Lebanon (II Kings xiv 9). The antiquity of such fables in Sumer and Egypt, together with the fact that the first of these is set in the period of the Judges, supports the view that this genre was found early in Israel's life in Canaan.

WITH THE ESTABLISHMENT of the monarchy and the increasingly elaborate organization of the royal courts of David and Solomon a new era began which had far-reaching effects on the development of Hebrew Wisdom. The succession of temporary charismatic leaders of the tribes, thrown up to meet recurrent crises, had finally failed when Saul was unable to cope with the organized campaign of the Philistines to dominate the whole of Palestine. In David, the most commanding personal leadership since Moses was combined with personal military power on a continuing basis, and with the capacity for political initiative. The result was the creation of a nation state with executive power centered in a monarch, as it had never been before in Israel. One result of this, in turn, was the necessary establishment of an administrative system to carry out the king's policies, and to enforce his edicts throughout the wide territory he eventually controlled. David's private fortress of Jerusalem became a political capital, as well as the successor of the amphictyonic shrine at Shiloh, through the king's bringing to it the Ark of the Covenant.

Thus, quite suddenly, Israel became a kingdom whose subjects were of diverse origins and religions,[13] where formerly it had been a federation of tribes of related physical stock giving allegiance to a common religious tradition. While it cannot be proved, the probability is that the new situation resulting from the location of the Ark at Jerusalem gave an impetus to the writing down of the distinctive religious traditions of Israel. Most scholars agree that the narrative of David's own reign and the succession of Solomon (II Sam ix–xx;

---

[13] Hebrews as distinct from Israelites (I Sam xiv 21), Jebusites (II Sam v 6–7), and other Canaanites (Judg i 27–33), Amorites (Judg i 34–36; II Sam xxi 2), Hittites (I Sam xxvi 6; II Sam xi 3), in addition to David's private army of Cretans and Philistines (II Sam xv 18), etc.

I Kings i–ii) is an almost contemporary account. Scribes are listed among the court officials of both kings (II Sam viii 17, xx 25; I Kings iv 3). The national vigor during the greater part of their combined reigns of about eighty years is the most natural explanation of the beginnings of a consecutive literary narrative of Israel's past. The fact that the *E* document in the Pentateuch shows evidences of origin in North Israel after the division of the kingdom at Solomon's death, but follows the outline of the Judean *J* document which it later was used to supplement, indicates that both stem from a common source before the kingdom split in two.[14]

The significance of these developments for our present subject is this. Both documents in Genesis contain the story of Joseph in Egypt, which differs from the other tales of the patriarchs in its length, and in its form as a historical novel centered at the Egyptian court. Another distinction has been pointed out by von Rad[15]: Joseph is pictured as the ideal wise man, not only in his capacity as counselor and ruler, but in his personal qualities of modesty, decorum, intelligence, goodness, and self-control. This portrait could have been drawn only by someone imbued with the views of the Wisdom schools, such as we find in Prov x–xxix, and in the more ancient Egyptian "Instructions."[16] Thus already before the death of Solomon there were such men at work in Israel, presumably at the royal court, just as in later times "the men of Hezekiah" edited and published one of the collections of Solomonic proverbs (Prov xxv 1).

The records indeed provide glimpses of sages at the courts of David and Solomon. Although nothing is said of their having been engaged in literary composition, it is a reasonable assumption that they belonged to the same circle as the author of the Joseph story, an assumption which underlies both existing versions of it. The king's scribe or secretary (*sōpēr*) is named among the high officers of David's entourage, (II Sam viii 17, xx 25); one of the two men named as having held this office has an Egyptian name, as has also his son who served in the same capacity under Solomon (I Kings iv 3). Such an official would keep records, read documents to the

---

[14] On the documentary sources of the Pentateuch, see E. A. Speiser, *Genesis*, 1964, Introduction.

[15] G. von Rad, "Josephgeschichte und ältere Chokma," *Supplements to Vetus Testamentum* 1 (1953), 120–27.

[16] See below, pp. XLII–XLV.

king (II Kings xxii 8–10), and conduct the king's correspondence with other monarchs. He would have a staff of scribes working under his direction, in an administrative organization large enough for a kingdom and empire like that of David and Solomon. The important position of scribes in such circumstances is evident from Egyptian, Sumerian, Babylonian, and Assyrian records.

A second group of what were in effect "professional" wise men (or women!) of the time were the royal counselors, and their counterparts whose services were available to men of lesser rank.[17] Chief among the former was one with the special title "the King's Friend" (II Sam xv 37; I Kings iv 5; cf. Gen xxvi 26), a title in use also at the courts of the pharaohs.

The existence of scribes and wise men in influential posts at the royal court is thus demonstrated. The fact is particularly important in considering the later reputation of Solomon as the wisest of all men, the author of proverbs and Wisdom poetry, and the fountain-head of Wisdom. The narratives about Solomon in I Kings ii–xi are not all of one piece and must be separately evaluated. In the famous story of the young king's dream the wisdom for which he prays and which is promised him is the ability to distinguish right from wrong, and hence to administer justice (iii 9–12). This gift is then illustrated by the appended story of Solomon's decision between the two mothers claiming the same baby (iii 16–28), a folk tale to which there are many parallels. In other contexts what is meant by the king's wisdom is his competence as a ruler (cf. ii 9; v 1–12 EV). Quite different is the picture given in iv 29–34 EV; x 1–10, 13, 23–24. Here Solomon's wisdom is one element in a description of his superlative magnificence—the vast extent of his dominions, the power of his chariot force, the incomparable splendor of his court, his wealth in silver and gold and exotic imports, his pre-eminence in wisdom beyond that of Egypt and of the Arabs, his universal reputation to which all peoples and kings paid tribute. Not only is the language extravagant but its vocabulary is that of some of the latest books in the Old Testament, as detailed examination will show. Yet it is this late and essentially legendary picture which is our only specific evidence that "Solomon uttered three

[17] For the former, cf. II Sam xv 12, 31, xvi 20, 23, xvii 14; I Kings xii 6; for the latter, cf. II Sam xiv 2, xx 16–22; I Kings i 12.

thousand proverbs, and his songs [Wisdom poems] were a thousand and five" (iv 32 EV).

This does not, however, eliminate the probability that the Wisdom movement flourished at the court of Solomon and under his patronage. As we have seen, scribes and sages were among his high officers. His orientation toward the Egyptian court, from which came his principal wife and possibly his state secretary with the Egyptian name, seems apparent, and court Wisdom was an old tradition in Egypt. The Joseph story with its Egyptian setting and embodiment of the Wisdom spirit is in keeping with this. Moreover, Alt[18] has drawn attention to a curious point: the subject matter of the proverbs attributed to Solomon in iv 32–33 EV is the non-human natural world, whereas it might be expected from the "Solomonic" proverbs in Prov x 1–xxii 16, xxv–xxix, that it would be human character and behavior. Sayings about trees, birds, animals, reptiles, and fish suggest rather a connection with the Egyptian *onomastika,* or classification lists of nature-wisdom. Although the accounts of Solomon's power, wealth, and wisdom have been exaggerated in legend, his temple, palaces, and garrison cities endured as evidence of his power and wealth, and there is undoubtedly some substance to the tradition that associated with his name the flourishing of the early Wisdom movement. How far this centered in the king himself, and how far it was the activity of scribes and sages under his patronage, it is impossible to say. A similar claim that the Assyrian king Ashurbanipal had himself written the tablets in his library does not carry conviction. It may be that the truth in the Solomonic tradition is that Solomon was responsible for introducing into Israel a school of Wisdom teachers on the Egyptian model, and possibly also for the distinctive bilinear *poetic form* of the proverbs in the two collections associated particularly with his name.[19]

WHEN WE NEXT have evidence of the Wisdom movement in the eighth and seventh centuries B.C.,[20] it is again associated with the

[18] Abrecht Alt, "Die Weisheit Salomos," *Theologische Literaturzeitung* 76 (1951), 139–44.

[19] Prov x 1–xxii 16 and xxv–xxix. See further the Introduction to Proverbs below.

[20] There may have been a connection between this renewed activity of Wisdom teachers in Judah and a Phoenician literary renascence posited by Albright at about the same time; cf. W. F. Albright, *From the Stone Age to Christianity,* 2d ed., 1957, p. 318.

royal court, though probably not exclusively so. The heading in
Prov xxv 1 to the second collection of "Solomonic" proverbs asserts
that this was transmitted or published by "the men of Hezekiah,
king of Judah." Hezekiah (c. 715–687 B.C.) was the first Judean
king since Solomon to reign without a rival king of North Israel,
and he seems to have undertaken to bring together the historical
and religious writings of the two peoples, including Wisdom materials. In fact, according to II Chron xxix–xxxii, he fostered a national revival, with Solomon as his model. The contemporary testimony of the prophecies of Isaiah supports this view. The ruling
circles of Jerusalem were then in close contact with Egypt and under strong Egyptian political and cultural influence.[21] They counted
on the pharaoh's support in a general revolt against Assyrian domination. Isaiah bitterly denounced the self-styled "wise men" of the
court with their calculated pro-Egyptian political policy, which, in
his view, implied distrust of the power of Israel's God. "Yet he too
is *wise!*"[22] he warned them ironically. Again, he poured scorn on
the sages of Egypt on whom the wise men of Judah were modeling
themselves (xix 11–15). It seems clear that the reference is to the
royal counselors, the official, politically minded wing of the Wisdom movement of the time. On the other hand, Isaiah himself
adopts the style and thought of the Wisdom teacher in his parable
of the farmer, whose special skill "comes from Yahweh of hosts,
who is wonderful in counsel and excellent in wisdom" (xxviii
23–29). Other prophets of the eighth century show the influence
of some of the characteristic stylistic marks of the Wisdom books,
for example, the progressive numerical formula in Amos i–ii: "For
three . . . for four . . ." (cf. Hos vi 2 and Prov xxx 15, 18, 29);
the question-and-answer form (Amos vii 1–6, viii 2; Hos ii 21–23
EV), and the common use of proverbs, proverbial phrases, and
rhetorical questions.

Even more specific evidence for the well-established activity of
Wisdom teachers among the people is the making of a collection of
proverbs by "the men of Hezekiah," noted above. The pedagogic
purpose of most of the contents of this collection is manifest—its
rhythmic parallelism of lines suggesting the cue-and-response of
teacher and pupils, and its emphasis on the character and training

[21] Isa xix 1–15, xx 1–6, xxx 1–7, xxxi 1–3, xxxvi 4–10.
[22] Isa xxxi 1–3; cf. v 21, xxix 13–16, xxx 1–7.

which would lead to a sound understanding and satisfying experience in life. These "Solomonic" proverbs, moreover, are preceded in the present form of the Book of Proverbs by two selections of "Sayings of the Sages," xxii 17–xxiv 22, and xxiv 23–34, the first of which is modeled on an Egyptian Wisdom work, *The Instruction of Amen-em-ope.*[23] This may have been composed as early as the thirteenth century B.C., but it was still being copied centuries later and may well have been studied during his training by an Israelite scribe of the prophetic period.

The larger collection of "Solomonic" proverbs in Prov x 1–xxii 16 would also have been assembled by royal scribes like "the men of Hezekiah," but perhaps a century later. The monarchy was still in existence (cf. xvi 10–15), and the positively religious element is more marked than in chapters xxv–xxix. As in the earlier time, Josiah's reign was the occasion of a reform of temple worship and of renewed activity by priests, prophets, and wise men (cf. Jer ix 23 EV; xviii 18). Like Isaiah, the prophet Jeremiah opposed the political policy of dependence upon Egypt for help (ii 18, 36, xxxvii 7), and challenged the validity of the sages' claims (ix 12, 23–24 EV). It is Yahweh who is truly wise (xxxii 18–19), Jeremiah says, as Isaiah did. He too reflects the thought and terminology of Wisdom (iv 22, xv 12, xvii 11), especially in the comparison of Yahweh's discipline of Israel with the teacher's discipline of his pupils (ii 30, vii 28, xvii 23). There can be no question but that the Wisdom movement was flourishing in Jeremiah's time.

THE PERIOD OF THE JUDEAN EXILE in Babylonia in the sixth century B.C., especially the latter part of that period when the Jews began to hope for the restoration of their kingdom, appears to have been of unusual importance in the development of their religious thought and its literature. In the main, however, this development probably did not include the didactic, proverbial type of Wisdom writings. The situation of the deported Jews was at first too agonizing, and later, with the hope of restoration, too temporary, for the further development of a literature displaying the unquestioning traditional ethos of didactic wisdom. It is otherwise with the subject matter of the radical wing of the Wisdom movement. Probably the profound questioning of traditional beliefs in the Book of Job

[23] See further pp. XLIV–XLV below, and the Introduction to Proverbs, pp. 20–21.

had its setting in the last years of the Judean kingdom, or in the early years of the Exilic period, whether in Babylonia or Palestine. Early in the sixth century the prophet Jeremiah spoke much as Job does (cf. Jer xx 14–18 and Job iii; Jer xii 1–2 and Job xxi 7 ff.; Jer xx 7–8 and Job xix 1–12, etc.) though he did not share Job's searing doubt of God's essential justice or find that the heavens sent back only the empty echo of his cry. Moreover, the portrait of the Suffering Servant incorporated in the Exilic prophecy of Second Isaiah seems to be drawn in part from the figure of the suffering Job (cf. Isa lii 14, liii 3, 4b). In the body of Second Isaiah also are many parallels in thought and verbal similarities with Job, which may indicate that the prophet was familiar with that book and drew upon it in presenting his own quite different message.[24] The almighty power of the Creator, his mysterious wisdom, and the impotence and frailty of man are basic doctrines in Job with which Second Isaiah combines his wide-ranging thought of Yahweh's saving power in Israel's history now about to be displayed anew.

THE PERSIAN PERIOD OF JEWISH HISTORY began when Cyrus conquered Babylon, and in 538 B.C. issued the famous decree permitting the captive peoples to return to their homelands and restore the temples of their gods. During the following two centuries until Persia in turn was overthrown by Alexander, the Jewish community in Palestine struggled to re-establish its distinctive identity against many difficulties—poverty, external pressures, and internal divisions. More than twenty years elapsed before the temple was restored and rededicated. At first Judah was a kind of temple state headed by its high priest within the political jurisdiction of the Persian governor of the province of Samaria. Later it became a separate province of the satrapy "Beyond the River," under Jewish governors. The first of these, Nehemiah, rebuilt the city wall of Jerusalem and reorganized the administration. The priest and scribe Ezra arrived from Babylonia bringing with him the "Law of Moses" and bearing royal authority to promulgate it as the basic law of the community in religious matters. From the time of these two men in the second half of the fifth century B.C. the Jews regained their status as a people and an organized religious community, though no longer as an independent state.

With this change it became possible for intellectual and literary

[24] On this see S. Terrien, *The Interpreter's Bible*, III, 1954, p. 889.

activities to develop in Palestine for the first time since Nebuchad-
nezzar's overthrow of the Judean kingdom in 586 B.C. That Ezra
bore the official title of "Scribe" or "Secretary" is significant. He
was a royal official, holding an administrative post which called for
a high degree of literacy. At the same time he was a Jewish priest,
learned in the sacred law he was called upon to establish in Judah.
On the occasion when the law was formally read at a general assembly of the people Ezra was assisted by certain Levites who
"helped the people to understand the law" and "who taught the people" (Neh viii 7–9). Ezra was thus chief of a group of scribes,
professional students of and authorities on the law of Moses. Hence-
forward such scribes were to play a dominant role in the religion
of Judaism. They were in fact an outgrowth of the Wisdom movement in its religious aspect, incorporating the view of Israel's distinctive Wisdom as stated in Deuteronomy: "Behold, I have taught
you statutes and ordinances. . . . Keep them and do them, for that
will be your wisdom and your understanding in the sight of the peoples" (iv 5–6).

The renewed cultural life of Judah after Ezra's time showed itself also in the production of Wisdom works of a more characteristic
type, independent of a concern with the cultic elements of the Mosaic Law. It is difficult to date with any precision such of these as
have been preserved in the Bible, partly because our historical
knowledge of the period is far from complete, and partly because
the indications of date in the works themselves are slight. Consequently we must be content to place them somewhere in the later
Persian period, following the revival of the national religious culture
on Palestinian soil which began with Ezra, or in the earlier part of
the Hellenistic age prior to our next fixed point, the publication of
Sirach-Ecclesiasticus early in the second century B.C.

The latter work, together with Ecclesiastes-Qoheleth and the pedagogical discourses in Prov i–ix, points to the re-emergence and
new importance of the private academies in which professional
wise men gave instruction to the sons of the well-to-do. That something of the sort existed before the Exile seems highly probable
from the making of the collections of instructional materials now
incorporated in the Book of Proverbs (x 1–xxii 16, xxii 17–xxiv
34, and xxv–xxix) and the preservation of at least some of the
material now found in chapters xxx–xxxi. The acceptance of prac-

tical responsibility for the instruction of youth had indeed been a feature of the Wisdom movement ever since Sumerian times. Now in the Persian period the older collections of such material were assembled and edited, apparently by the teacher who composed the long prefatory section in chapters i–ix as a guide to the interpretation and understanding of the remainder. A new note is struck. Whereas in the older collections—and notably in x 1–xxii 16— the sanctions of ethical behavior were reinforced by religion, and wisdom taught how to win the favor both of God and of man, in the prefatory section the religious standpoint is not only dominant but determinative. "The first principle of knowledge is to hold the Lord in awe." "Fools" are defined as those who "despise" *religious* "wisdom and instruction" (i 7). At the same time a theological cosmology and anthropology is enunciated in the two poems, i 20–33 and viii 1–36, in which a poetically personified Wisdom affirms her nature as a creative power coming from God as the living link between God and man. It is not of course possible to say with certainty whether this final editing of the Book of Proverbs took place in the later Persian period or in the early Greek period. It is noteworthy, however, that its standpoint (though not necessarily its chronological date) is midway between that of the Book of Job, where the ultimate Wisdom is a divine secret,[25] and that of Sirach xxiv,[26] where it is said to be revealed in the law of Moses.

The latter theme, as already noted, underlies the "Torah Psalms" i, xix 7–14, and cxix. These cannot be later than the third century; with others of the Wisdom Psalms such as xxxiv, xxxvii and xlix they may be of the Persian age.

In the Introduction to Ecclesiastes-Qoheleth below,[27] reasons are given for dating that work toward the end of the Persian period, or soon after that. It is evident from the nom de plume of the author (Qoheleth=Academician, Teacher), from the philosophical nature of the work and its didactic elements, and also from the specific statement of xii 9, that the author was a Wisdom teacher. Though evidently a Jew, his philosophy diverges so radically from the theology

---

[25] Cf. Job xi 5–9, xii 13, xxviii 12, 20, 23, xxxviii 36. The clearly supplementary verse xxviii 28 is an editorial annotation subsequent to the publication of Prov i 7. Cf. Ps cxi 10.

[26] Cf. Sirach xxiv 1–12, 23–27, and the dependent Baruch iv 1. See also Pss i, xix 7 ff., and cxix.

[27] See pp. 19 ff.

of the national tradition, and even from all other Hebrew Wisdom works,[28] that he and his school are the antithesis of those represented by Prov i–ix and Sirach. The old distinction between the secular and the religious orientation of Wisdom, which showed itself in the conflict between prophecy and politics in the persons of Isaiah and the royal counselors, appears here as a battle between revelational theology and rationalism within the Wisdom movement itself. That Qoheleth's radicalism won a following in the Judaism of the time is evident from the biographical notes appended to his book in xii 9–12, and also from the very fact that such a work, even with the cautionary appendix in xii 13–14, could eventually be accepted into the Hebrew canon of Scripture.

THE HELLENISTIC AGE may be said to have begun in 332 B.C. when Alexander gained control of Palestine on his way to the conquest of Egypt. Yet the inception of political control by Hellenistic rulers did not mark the beginning of Greek cultural influence; this had already been widespread for two centuries, particularly through the coastal cities of Phoenicia and Egypt. But this influence greatly increased when two of the dynasties founded by Alexander's generals successively ruled Palestine: the Ptolemies of Egypt during the third century B.C., and the Seleucid kings of Syria from 198 B.C. to the outbreak of the Maccabean rebellion in 166. New Greek cities and temples were built in the land, and ancient cities were Hellenized. Greek officials, soldiers, merchants, and travelers were everywhere to be seen. Many Jews migrated to neighboring lands, particularly to Egypt where the new port city of Alexandria soon had so large a population of Greek-speaking Jews that a translation, the Septuagint, first of the Law and then of the other scriptures, was made for them.

To these scriptures were added certain works which had not been accepted as authoritative by the Jews of Palestine, even though some of them, such as Sirach, had been composed there in Hebrew or Aramaic before being translated into Greek. In other cases supplements were added, as in I Esdras, Esther, and Daniel; a process facilitated by the fact that different versions of the Hebrew text of some books (other than the Law) were in circulation. Wisdom teachers had a hand in composing some of these additional works

---

[28] Except the skepticism of Agur ben Yakeh in Prov xxx 1–4, which is part of a dialogue and is answered by a representative of piety.

and some of the supplementary material.[29] In the book which comes to us from the hand of Jesus ben Sira' (in Greek, "Sirach") such a teacher describes his own training in religious wisdom through self-dedication in prayer, the discipline of study, of "the law of the Most High" and of "the wisdom of all the ancients," together with the experience of life gained through foreign travel and frequent debate concerning "the good and evil among men" (xxxiv 9–12, xxxix 1–5, li 13–21). What he has learned he would now pass on to his pupils, whom he invites to his "school"[30] to "put [their] neck under the yoke" (li 23–30).[31] Some teachers published collections of their discourses in writing, as ben Sira' does, following the precedent of the author of Prov i–ix and Qoheleth (cf. xii 9–10). Others, like the author of the Wisdom of Solomon, published literary works in the form of public addresses. Still other works—romantic fiction in Tobit and Judith, supplementary reading related to the Scriptures in Baruch, the Letter of Jeremiah, the Prayer of Manasseh, and the additions to Esther and Daniel—were addressed to a wider public. They, too, were a form of religious instruction, even though it was not directed specifically to pupils in the Wisdom academies.

INTERNATIONAL WISDOM AND ITS LITERATURE

In an earlier part of this essay it was noted that the Hebrew Wisdom movement had its antecedents in more ancient cultures and its counterparts among neighboring peoples. These relationships are recognized in the Old Testament itself. Solomon's wisdom is said to have "surpassed the wisdom of all the people of the east and all the wisdom of Egypt" (I Kings iv 30 EV). From the context it seems clear that by "the people of the east" was meant the peoples of the desert and the desert fringe to the east and northeast of Palestine. Job is pictured as one of their great sheikhs.[32] The Edomites on the southeastern frontier were famous for wisdom:

[29] See what is said above on pp. XXII ff. about Sirach, Wisdom of Solomon, Tobit, I Esdras, and Baruch.

[30] Heb. bēt midrāšī, Gr. oikos paideias, "[my] house of instruction," later more specifically a school for instruction in Torah.

[31] Evidently it was customary for teachers to receive a fee, vs. 28; cf. Prov xvii 16.

[32] Job i 3; cf. Gen xxix 1; Judg vi 3; Isa xi 14.

Concerning Edom. Thus says Yahweh of hosts:
"Is wisdom no more in Teman?
Has counsel perished from the prudent?
Has their wisdom vanished?" (Jer xlix 7).

Unfortunately, the Phoenician or Canaanite Wisdom literature, which must have been extensive and influential, has not been preserved[33] except in fragments and possibly in echoes in the biblical Book of Proverbs. Two Canaanite proverbs of the fourteenth century B.C. are quoted in the Tell el-Amarna correspondence. Wisdom in the sense of skill in the arts is attributed to the Tyrian metalworker Hiram who was brought to Jerusalem to direct the manufacture of the bronze fittings for Solomon's temple. A claim of the rulers of Tyre to possess a wisdom greater than Daniel's, and a reference to a Phoenician myth of a first man "full of wisdom . . . in Eden, the garden of God" appear in Ezek xxviii. Sanchuniathon of Tyre and Mochos of Sidon are quoted by later Greek writers as famous Phoenician sages.[34]

The most extensive non-Israelite Wisdom literatures have come down to us from Mesopotamia and Egypt. It is curious that Mesopotamian Wisdom is not mentioned as one of the standards for comparison with Solomon's; possibly this is because of its later identification with illicit practices like astrology and divination.[35] The wise men of Egypt appear again in the Joseph story (Gen xli 8), in the Exodus story (Exod vii 11, 22; Acts vii 22), and in Isaiah's denunciations (Isa xix 11–12). More important is the fact, noted above, that a section of Proverbs is based on the Egyptian work *Amen-em-ope*. The international context of Hebrew Wisdom is seen also in the Book of Esther (i 13) where the wise men of the Persian court are consulted by King Ahasuerus, and in the Book of Tobit (i 21–22) where the Assyrian sage Ahiqar is represented as the nephew of the Jewish narrator.

[33] It is to be hoped that some of it will come to light among the tablets from late bronze age Ugarit (Ras Shamra) that are still unpublished.

[34] Cf. ANET, pp. 426a, 486a; I Kings vii 13, 14; Ezek xxviii 2–5, 12–17; Philo Byblius in Eusebius *Praeparatio evangelica;* Damascius *De primis principiis.*

[35] Cf. Isa xliv 25, xlvii 9–10; Jer l 35; Dan i 20, v 11–12. W. G. Lambert, *Babylonian Wisdom Literature* (abbr. BWL), Oxford, 1960, p. 1, points out that the term "Wisdom" in Babylonia "generally refers to skill in cult and magic lore, and the wise man is the initiate." There was thus some reason for the Hebrew idea of Babylonian Wisdom.

Three roots of this international Wisdom movement can be distinguished: (a) the universal practice of instruction by parents and teachers in the knowledge and skills as well as in the moral standards that have proved advantageous for success in living; (b) the giving of counsel by those men (or women) who have gained a reputation for unusual intelligence, knowledge, and good judgment; and (c) the special skills and intellectual powers associated with literacy in a generally illiterate society. The key figures were thus the parent or teacher, the counselor, and the scribe. The first of these is as old as the family, the second as old as the larger society. Both are logically and chronologically prior to the third; and they retained their importance after the invention of writing had created the scribal profession and eventually produced the thinker and literary artist.

It will be obvious that only through the work of the scribe can we have direct access to the wisdom of the ancient world. The relationship of Hebrew Wisdom to that of the Edomites or any other "people of the east" must remain a hypothetical question, since these have left no literary records.[36] Our principal sources are the literatures of Egypt and of the Mesopotamian peoples.

One of the striking features of these "Wisdom" writings is that, as in the Bible, the concern with Wisdom is of two kinds or on two levels: the first, conservative, practical, and didactic, the second, critical and speculative. The former transmits a view of life and a code of behavior based on experience and accepted beliefs. The latter is skeptical of traditional values, and raises more abstract questions of ethics and religion.

In Egyptian Wisdom writings the conservative and didactic type predominates. The most characteristic form it takes is that of the "instructions" of a king or important official to his son and potential successor. This form appears as early as the Pyramid Age (c. 2600–2175 B.C.), and persists for more than two millennia. About a dozen such texts have come to light. One of the earliest is the *Instruction of Ptah-hotep,* the principal minister of a king of the Fifth Dynasty. Here he instructs his son how to "set an example for the

[36] Except for what may have been incorporated in the Hebrew Bible in brief excerpts of unknown origin such as Prov xxx 1–4, xxxi 1–8, and in the traditional story of Job.

children of officials"[37] by acquiring the skill and poise proper to a responsible position, in accordance with ancestral tradition. He is to learn "the rules for good speech," which refers not to eloquence or to the correct use of language but to the manner of dealing with persons with whom the official's duties bring him into contact. He must be teachable, modest, self-controlled, reliable, honest, respectful to superiors, and of good moral behavior. Above all, he must order his life according to justice and truth: "the strength of justice is that it lasts." This is the wisdom that will ensure success. "To hear is of advantage to a son who hearkens." "If a son accepts what his father says, no project of his miscarries." "When he becomes old . . . he converses in the same way to his children, by renewing the instruction of his father."

A second example of this genre is the *Instruction for King Merika-re* which comes from c. 2100 B.C., at a time when political instability had shaken confidence in the old order. The king's counsel is given to his son in the light of difficulties which he himself has experienced, and is concerned with practical measures for the defense of the state as well as with the qualities of character needed by the holder of "a goodly office, the kingship." Once more, emphasis is laid on being a "craftsman in speech" as evidence of intelligence, firmness of grasp, and possession of ancestral wisdom. "The tongue is a sword . . . and speech is more valorous than any fighting." The king's strength is derived from the prosperity and love of his people and from the quality of his nobles, and even more from his own adherence to justice and integrity. "Be not evil: patience is good. . . . Do justice whilst thou endurest upon earth. . . . Do not oppress the widow; supplant no man in the property of his father. . . . Do not slaughter. . . . Thou shouldst punish with beatings and with arrests." Even a king's behavior has eternal consequences, for the gods will judge him when "after death . . . his deeds are placed beside him in heaps."[38] "Existence yonder is for eternity. . . . As for him who reaches it without wrongdoing, he shall exist yonder like a god." The king must revere the god, be faithful in worship, "act for the god, that he may act similarly

---

[37] Quotations from the "Instructions" (except 'Onchsheshonqy) are from the translations by J. M. Wilson in ANET, pp. 412–24. For 'Onchsheshonqy, see fn. 42.

[38] Cf. Rev xiv 13, "that they may rest from their labors, for their deeds follow them."

for thee," remembering that "more acceptable is the character of
one upright of heart than the [sacrificed] ox of the evildoer."[39]
The king's "place of the necropolis" is to be prepared and embellished, as a token of his constant awareness of death and the coming
judgment. The expectation of the hereafter is thus a decisive
motivation with Meri-ka-re, as it was not with Ptah-hotep.

Three others of these "Instructions" may be mentioned. One from
the end of the Egyptian empire bears the name of a temple scribe
Ani. It enjoins the fulfillment of religious and filial obligations, good
manners, generosity, and reserve in speech, and warns against
adultery, clamor, and presumption before "thy god [who] shows
[his] power in a million forms." A second, the *Instruction of Amen-
em-ope* from about the same period, is particularly important because of its close relationship with Prov xxii 17–xxiii 11.[40] It comprises thirty "houses" or sections, addressed by an official to his
youngest son. The writer declares that his moral precepts point the
way to life and prosperity. Many of them resemble both the form
and the spirit of Hebrew laws and proverbs, quite apart from the
probable literary connection with Prov xxii 17 ff.

> "Do not carry off the landmark . . . nor encroach upon
> the boundaries of a widow";
> "Better is poverty in the hand of the god than riches in a
> storehouse";
> "Better is bread, when the heart is happy, than riches with
> sorrow";
> "Preserve thy tongue from answering thy superior";
> "Do not bear witness with false words";
> "Do not [lean on] the scales nor falsify the weights";
> "Do not laugh at a blind man nor tease a dwarf, nor injure
> the affairs of the lame. Do not tease a man who is [in-
> sane]";
> "Do not find [i.e., "notice"] a widow if thou catchest her
> [gleaning] in the fields."[41]

---

[39] For this prophetic note in the Bible, cf. Isa i 12–17; Mic vi 6–8; Prov
xxi 3.

[40] This section of Proverbs seems to have been composed by a Hebrew
scribe in imitation of the Egyptian work; see p. XLVII, Introduction to Proverbs,
pp. 20–21, and Secs. 24 and 25 and NOTES thereon.

[41] Cf. Deut xix 14; Prov xv 16, 17, xxii 28; Exod xx 16, xxii 28 EV;
Lev xix 9–10, 14, 36.

Even more striking is the way in which morality is defined in terms of what pleases "the god" and carries religious sanctions in the present, rather than in expectation of reward and punishment in the hereafter. Falsehood is "the abomination of the god" (cf. Prov vi 16–19). The idea of God seems for all practical purposes to be monotheistic. The counsel against anxiety recalls the Sermon on the Mount (Matt vi 25–34): "Do not spend the night fearful of the morrow. At daybreak, what is the morrow like? Man knows not what the morrow is like. God is in his success, whereas man is in his failure."

A work more closely resembling the biblical Book of Proverbs is the *Instructions of 'Onchsheshonqy* of about the fifth century B.C.[42] The resemblance lies in the bringing together of a very large number (about 550) of short sayings, precepts, and adages like those of Proverbs—practical, moral, and to some extent religious, in a rather haphazardly arranged collection. The forms of the individual sayings, however, do not display the synonymous or antithetic parallelism characteristic of the biblical proverbs. A further difference is that this work is prefaced by the story of how the priest 'Onchsheshonqy came to compose these "instructions" for his son, when facing long imprisonment. Examples of sayings which recall the content if not the form of biblical proverbs are:

"If a woman is at peace with her husband, it is the will of God" (cf. Prov xix 14);
"Better [to have] a statue for a son than a fool" (cf. Prov xvii 21);
"Do not go to your brother if you are in trouble; go to your friend" (cf. Prov xxvii 10);
"There is no wise man who comes to grief; there is no fool who finds reward" (cf. Prov xii 21);
"He who shakes the stone—it will fall upon his foot" (cf. Prov xxvi 27).

It seems clear that this collection of late Egyptian precepts and proverbs embodies the practical and moral wisdom of the wider community, rather than being directed simply to training for high official position. Only the title and preamble relate it to the disintegrating ancient form.

[42] Edited by S. R. K. Glanville, *Catalogue of Demotic Papyri in the British Museum*, vol. II, 1955.

Related to but different from the "instruction" form is a composition of the Middle Kingdom, the so-called *Satire on the Trades*,[43] in which a sailor, Khety, encourages and advises his son who is on his way to a scribal school. Sundry other occupations are compared unfavorably with the scribe's profession. A poem from the Twelfth Dynasty on the *Divine Attributes of Pharaoh*[44] is addressed to a man's children that they might know "a manner of living aright" and "be unblemished." *The Song of the Harper*,[45] as would be appropriate for a festive occasion, utters the philosophy of *carpe diem:* "Follow thy desire, as long as thou shalt live. Put myrrh upon thy head and clothing of fine linen upon thee. . . . Make holiday, and weary not therein. Behold, it is not given to a man to take his property with him. Behold, there is not one who departs who comes back again."

The tale of *The Eloquent Peasant*[46] who appeals for justice against a man who has wronged him is interesting as a story, and also as a Wisdom document. The peasant's trenchant and epigrammatic speeches of protest are recorded for the entertainment of the king; this is an example of the Egyptians' high regard for sagacious speech as a prime mark of wisdom. The peasant's speeches incorporate not only many figurative sayings but also a series of precepts and proverbs that seem to be derived from, or to reflect, folk wisdom:

"Behold, thou art a town which has no mayor, like a company which has no chief, like a ship in which there is no pilot." "The measurer of piles [of grain] cheats for himself." "Prepare not for the morrow before it arrives; one knows not what mischance may be in it." "The balance of men is their tongue." "That great one who is covetous is not really great." Finally, the ethical demand is grounded in religion: "Do justice for the sake of the Lord of Justice. . . . Justice lasts unto eternity." This work is the nearest approach in Egypt to the theme of the suffering just man.

A work which has some similarities to the Book of Job in its questioning of traditional beliefs and also in its dialogue form is the *Dispute over Suicide*,[47] a composition of the Middle Kingdom or

[43] ANET, pp. 432–34.
[44] ANET, p. 431.
[45] ANET, p. 467. Cf. Eccles v 18–20 EV, ix 7–10.
[46] ANET, pp. 407–10.
[47] ANET, pp. 405–7.

a little earlier. In this document a man who finds life unbearable debates with his soul the desirability of seeking death. "To whom can I speak today?" he cries. "[One's] fellows are evil . . . the gentle man has perished . . . goodness is rejected everywhere." "[But] yonder is a place for settling down . . . the West [i.e., the hereafter] is home." "Death is in my sight today like the odor of myrrh, like sitting under an awning on a breezy day . . . like the clearing of the sky . . . like the longing of a man to see his house [again], after he has spent many years held in captivity." This pessimistic questioning of life's value and yearning for death vividly recalls the anguished outcry with which the dialogue begins in Job, chapter iii: "Why did I not die at birth? For then I should have lain down and been quiet . . . [where] the wicked cease from troubling, and the weary are at rest; . . . the small and the great are there, and the slave is free from his master. . . . Why is light given to him that is in misery, and life to the bitter in soul?" But in the Egyptian work there is no outcry against divine injustice.

The surviving literature of Egyptian Wisdom thus has certain similarities and points of contact with Hebrew Wisdom as represented in the Old Testament. The father-to-son form of moral instruction, the high value placed on the profession of the scribe as a learned man, the idea of wisdom as recognition of a divinely established cosmic order, the grounding of ethics in religion, and—in more radical terms—the exploring of problems of the value of life and the meaning of justice show a common concern. More direct contact at certain points is implied by verbal echoes[48] and by the literary relationship of Prov xxii 17 ff. to the *Instruction of Amen-em-ope*. Many of the same virtues and vices are dealt with in both literatures, and are judged by much the same moral standards. The differences are chiefly theological, and are particularly obvious in Hebrew ideas of reward and punishment in this life, in contrast to the Egyptian orientation toward judgment in the hereafter. Furthermore, there is no real counterpart in Egyptian Wisdom to the profound probing of the problems of justice and religion in

[48] A striking example is the saying about the Lord "weighing the heart" (Prov xvi 2; cf. I Sam ii 3), which seems to be derived ultimately from the Egyptian belief that after death a man's heart will be weighed against truth in the balances of the god. The Hebrews, of course, did not share the Egyptians' view of the afterlife, so that for them the phrase was simply figurative (cf. Ps cxv 17).

the Book of Job, or to the rationalism and agnosticism of Ecclesiastes-Qoheleth.

The Wisdom movement in Mesopotamia[49] had its origins in the oldest culture of that region, that of the Sumerians, who bequeathed much of it to their successors the Babylonians and Assyrians. Although writing was invented early in the third millennium B.C., the oldest extensive literary remains come from the Sumerian renascence a thousand years later, and are known largely from copies and translations made in the Old Babylonian and Cassite periods (c. 1700–1200 B.C.).

Large numbers of Sumerian proverbs and popular sayings, many arranged in standard collections, have come to light. The collections were made, and in part composed, at the scribal academies, and were used for instruction in the art of writing as well as in teaching cultural values. They include adages and maxims and, in addition, thumbnail fables and illustrative anecdotes. Some have the complaining or sarcastic note of popular sayings; others express a more mature wisdom about life. Examples are: "Wealth is distant, poverty is always at hand" (Gordon, p. 49). "In marrying an unseemly wife, in begetting an unseemly child, I satisfied and [then immediately re-]established for myself a discontented heart" (Jacobsen, in Gordon, p. 468; cf. "Marry in haste, repent at leisure"). "Tell a lie [and then] tell the truth: it will be considered a lie" (Gordon, p. 229). "Hand added to hand—the house of a man is built up" (Gordon, p. 271; cf. "Many hands make light labor").

The fable is a widespread Wisdom form of which the oldest literary examples are from the Sumerians. It is an entertaining way of commenting on persons and situations as well as of displaying the characteristics of the natural substances—animals or plants—which it endows with speech. One type is the contest fable, in which the respective virtues or values are recounted, and the superiority of one is decided.[50] Another kind introduces a creature as a speaking participant in an episode involving gods or men, as with the eagle in the

---

[49] In this section the author is deeply indebted to BWL and to E. I. Gordon, *Sumerian Proverbs* (abbr. Gordon), Philadelphia, 1959.

[50] Cf. Cattle and Grain, Bird and Fish, Silver and Bronze, in "The Fable in the Ancient Near East" by R. J. Williams, in *A Stubborn Faith*, ed. E. C. Hobbs, Dallas, 1956, pp. 3–26.

Etana myth,[51] Balaam's ass (Num xxii 21–35), or the serpent in Gen
iii. In still a third type (also represented in the Bible in Judg ix 8–15
and II Kings xiv 9) the speeches and actions of natural creatures
are figurative for those of men. This type was popular in Assyrian
and late Babylonian times, which provide the stories of the mouse
who took refuge in a snake's hole, of the fox who wanted to be a
lion or a wolf, and of the mosquito who took a ride on an elephant.[52]

Sumerian literature also explored profounder problems. The epic
myth *Gilgamesh and the Land of the Living* tells how the hero
sought to become immortal through some outstanding achievement,
but learned that "when the gods created mankind they assigned
death to men," and man must accept the prospect and be happy
while he can.[53] This recalls Ecclesiastes-Qoheleth. In one form
of the Sumerian story of the Deluge, the Sumerian Noah, Ziusudra,
after his survival, is instructed in the right conduct which will guard
against a new destruction. Unfortunately, only a fragment of the
Instructions of Šuruppak has been published,[54] but its intent is
clear. The problem of the suffering just man, which was to receive
its most famous treatment in the Book of Job, was raised also among
the Sumerians. Lambert (BWL, p. 11) refers to an unpublished
bilingual Sumero-Babylonian text in which the speaker says, "I have
been treated as one who has committed a sin against his god."
Kramer has translated a Sumerian poem with the Joban motif
under the title "Man and his God."[55] In this, the sages, like Job's
friends, seek to explain his suffering by saying, "Never has a sinless
child been born to its mother." The nameless victim declares that
his god has "doled out suffering" to him, and for him "the day is
black." He does not defy his god or impugn his righteousness; he
simply asks *Why?* In the end his prayers are heard and he is
delivered, and the inference is that this is the only possible solution
to an innocent sufferer's problem.

[51] *Ibid.*, p. 13; ANET, pp. 114–18.
[52] Cf. Lambert, BWL, pp. 217, 219. Lambert, p. 213, points out that the
last reappears in Aesop. Other examples are found in the *Words of Ahiqar*,
ANET, pp. 429–30.
[53] The Sumerian myth is fragmentary and has been supplemented in the
Old Babylonian version. Cf. BWL, pp. 11–12; ANET, p. 90.
[54] Cf. BWL, pp. 92–95.
[55] S. N. Kramer, in *Wisdom in Israel and the Ancient Near East* (abbr.
WIANE), eds. M. Noth and D. W. Thomas, Leiden, 1955, pp. 170–82.

Two more extensive and better preserved treatments of the same theme come from the Cassite period (1500–1200 B.C.) in Babylonia. The first, entitled *I will Praise the Lord of Wisdom*, from its first line, has been called "the Babylonian Job," though Lambert thinks "the Babylonian Pilgrim's Progress" might be more apt.[56] A good man feels himself forsaken by the gods when everyone turns against him and he is smitten by disease. Like Job, he feels that he is being treated as a sinner, in spite of his piety. He wonders if gods and men can have different ideas of righteousness: Is "what is proper to oneself . . . an offense to one's god? Who knows the will of the gods in heaven?" He cannot understand what life means. "He who was alive yesterday is dead today. . . . One moment people are singing . . . another they groan." Yet he is confident that his day of deliverance will come. Then, while still Marduk's hand is heavy upon him, messengers from the god appear in his dreams to promise cleansing, deliverance, and forgiveness of the fault of whose nature he is still unaware.

The other treatment of the theme has been called alternatively *A Dialogue about Human Misery* or *The Babylonian Theodicy*.[57] Here two sages discuss the dilemma that confronts one of them who has been left an orphan and now suffers from ill-health and poverty, in spite of his religious devotion. It is the wicked, he says, who prosper. To this his friend, like Job's comforters, replies dogmatically that virtue is blessed with wealth, and evil always brings ruin in the end: the sufferer's denial of this is blasphemy. "The plan of the gods is remote." But when the first man instances the oppression of the innocent by the powerful, the second asserts that lies and injustice belong to the nature of man as the gods made him, and thus are only to be expected in this life.

A curious, semi-humorous treatment of the ambiguities of life is the dialogue of a master with his slave, known (inappropriately) as the *Dialogue of Pessimism*.[58] The master proposes a certain series of actions, then changes his mind and proposes to do the opposite. With each suggestion the slave expresses agreement, giving what apparently are equally good but contradictory reasons. For example:

[56] Cf. BWL, pp. 21–62; ANET, pp. 434–37.
[57] Cf. BWL, pp. 63–91; ANET, pp. 438–40.
[58] BWL, pp. 139–49; ANET, pp. 437–38.

"Slave, listen to me."

"Here I am, sir, here I am."

"I am going to love a woman."

"So love, sir, love. The man who loves a woman forgets sorrow and fear."

"No, slave, I will by no means love a woman."

"[Do not] love, sir, do not love. Woman is a pitfall—a pitfall, a hole, a ditch. Woman is a sharp iron dagger that cuts a man's throat." When the master asks finally what [then] is good, the slave replies,

"To have my neck broken and your neck broken and to be thrown into the river." The master demurs and says he will kill the slave first, but the latter retorts that the master would not outlive him by three days. This curious piece of philosophy affirms the ambiguity of morals and sees death as the only real value.

Unquestioning belief in divine justice, on the other hand, is affirmed in such documents as the *Hymn to Shamash*.[59] The beneficent sun-god covers the world with light and shows his care for the people of all lands. He punishes evildoers, protects travelers and fugitives, condemns venial judges, and favors the honest merchant and the doer of kind deeds. Morality is thus undergirded by religious belief.

A series of precepts recalling the Egyptian Instructions and many biblical proverbs and laws is contained in the *Counsels of Wisdom* from the early Babylonian period.[60] "Let your mouth be controlled and your speech guarded. . . . Speak nothing profane nor any untrue report. A talebearer is accursed. . . . Every day worship your god . . . in your wisdom study the tablet. . . . Reverence begets favor, sacrifice prolongs life, and prayer atones for guilt. . . . Do not covet any of [what is entrusted to you]. If you have promised, give. . . . Do not return evil to the man who disputes with you; requite with kindness your evil-doer, maintain justice to your enemy." Such counsels remind one of both the Old Testament and the New.

One more document of Mesopotamian Wisdom remains to be mentioned, the *Words of Ahiqar*,[61] an Assyrian sage mentioned also in the Book of Tobit (i 22, xiv 10, etc.). The oldest extant copy of

[59] Cf. BWL, pp. 121–38; ANET, pp. 387–89.

[60] Cf. BWL, pp. 96–107; ANET, pp. 426–27.

[61] Cf. ANET, pp. 427–30.

this work is in Aramaic of the fifth century B.C., but the setting of
the story which provides the framework for the collection of Ahiqar's
wise sayings is Assyrian. Many of these recall biblical proverbs:

> "Withhold not thy son from the rod" (cf. Prov xiii 24);
> "If I smite thee, my son, thou wilt not die" (cf. Prov
> xxiii 13);
> "Treat not lightly the word of a king" (cf. Eccles viii 2–
> 3);
> "I have lifted sand, and I have carried salt; but there is
> naught which is heavier than [rage]" (cf. Prov xxvii 3);
> "From thee is the arrow, but from God the [guidance]"
> (cf. Prov xvi 1);
> "Hunger makes bitterness sweet" (cf. Prov xxvii 7).

From what has been said above and from the quotations given,
it will be evident that the Wisdom movement in Israel was indeed
part of a much wider and older context in neighboring cultures. The
resemblances are in both form and substance. At the same time
it seems clear that the Wisdom of ancient Israel, as represented in
Proverbs, Job, and Ecclesiastes, compares most favorably as literature with the Wisdom writings of other ancient peoples. Morever,
it strikes its own distinctive note. In intellectual penetration, ethical
awareness, and religious spirit it is approached by these other literatures only here and there. Taken as a whole, it is unmatched in
the surviving records of the wisdom of any other ancient people.

RECOMMENDED READING

W. O. E. Oesterley, *The Wisdom of Egypt and the Old Testament*,
    1927.
H. Ranston, *The Old Testament Wisdom Books and Their Teach-
    ing*, 1930.
L. Dürr, *Das Erziehungswesen im Alten Testament und im Antiken
    Orient*, 1932.
W. Baumgartner, *Israelitische und altorientalische Weisheit*, 1933.
J. Fichtner, *Die altorientalische Weisheit in ihrer israelitisch-jüd-
    ischen Ausprägung*, 1933.
H. Duesberg, *Les scribes inspirées*, 1939.

J. C. Rylaarsdam, *Revelation in Jewish Wisdom Literature,* 1946.

K. Ringgren, *Word and Wisdom,* 1947.

W. A. Irwin, "The Wisdom Literature," *The Interpreter's Bible,* I, 1952, pp. 212–19.

O. S. Rankin, *Israel's Wisdom Literature,* 2d ed., 1954.

M. Noth, and D. W. Thomas, eds., *Wisdom in Israel and in the Ancient Near East,* 1955.

J. B. Pritchard, ed., *Ancient Near Eastern Texts,* 2d ed., 1955, "Didactic and Wisdom Literature," pp. 405–52.

H. Gese, *Lehre und Wirklichkeit in der alten Weisheit,* 1958.

E. I. Gordon, *Sumerian Proverbs,* 1959.

W. G. Lambert, *Babylonian Wisdom Literature,* 1960.

R. E. Murphy, *Seven Books of Wisdom,* 1960.

S. H. Blank, "Wisdom," *The Interpreter's Dictionary of the Bible,* 1962, IV, pp. 852–61.

H. Gese, "Weisheit," "Weisheitsdichtung," *Die Religion in Geschichte und Gegenwart,* 3d ed., Band VI, 1962.

J. Leclant et al., *Les Sagesses du Proche-Orient ancien,* 1963.

PROVERBS

INTRODUCTION

THE PROVERBS OF ANCIENT ISRAEL

If Francis Bacon was right, that "the genius, the wit and the spirit of a nation are discovered in its proverbs," the Book of Proverbs should be one of the most interesting parts of the Bible. It is not, of course, simply an anthology of wise sayings commonly heard in ancient Israel, though many of these are included in it, especially in the two collections entitled "Proverbs of Solomon" which begin at chapters x and xxv. Rather, it is a source book of instructional materials for use in a school or in private study, for the cultivation of personal morality and practical wisdom. It opens with a series of ten admonitory discourses, interspersed with some poetry and some proverbs. It includes in xxii 17–xxiv 22 a distinct work, "Thirty Precepts of the Sages," modeled on an Egyptian composition; and in chapters xxx–xxxi four distinctive appendixes. Yet the two collections of sentence-proverbs under Solomon's name comprise the major part of the book, and give it its distinctive tone.

What, then, is a proverb? The Oxford English Dictionary defines it as "a short, pithy saying in common use." Archer Taylor[1] says that the typical proverb is anonymous, traditional, and epigrammatic, and quotes the observation that it is characterized by "shortness, sense and salt." In Lord John Russell's oft-quoted epigram, a proverb contains "the wisdom of many and the wit of one." It sums up in compact and easily remembered form an observation or judgment which is widely held to be true. Hence the frequent use of proverbs by a speaker to illustrate a statement, to clinch an argument, or to lend authority to an admonition. The teaching function is especially evident in the biblical Book of Proverbs.

Strictly speaking, an epigram, an aphorism, or a maxim does not

[1] *The Proverb*, 1931, pp. 7–8, 95.

qualify as proverbial unless it has passed into common use. An epigram like Lord John Russell's is a perceptive observation wittily expressed, but no one would quote it unless he were discussing the present subject. An aphorism like "Beauty is truth, truth beauty" is philosophical in tone and lacks the common touch. A maxim is an axiom or rule of conduct which may or may not gain widespread acceptance, such as "Knowledge is power." The homeliness of the truth expressed and the simplicity, conciseness, and picturesqueness of its expression characterize the anonymous familiar popular saying. "Dead men tell no tales." A new broom sweeps clean." "Chickens come home to roost."

A good many biblical proverbs have passed into current use in Europe and America, and more might have done so had the terms in which they are put been less strange to our ears. We say, "Hope deferred makes the heart sick" (Prov xiii 12); "The way of transgressors is hard" (Prov xiii 15); "A soft answer turns away wrath" (Prov xv 1); "Pride goes before destruction" (Prov xvi 18). We are less likely to quote: "Better is a dinner of herbs where love is, than a stalled ox and hatred therewith" (Prov xv 17); "The beginning of strife is as when one lets out water" (Prov xvii 14); "Seest thou a man diligent in his business? He shall stand before kings" (Prov xxii 29).

Folk sayings gleaned from the pages of the Old Testament are illustrated above in the essay, "The Wisdom Movement and Its Literature" (pp. xv–lii). They are concise, picturesque, thought-provoking, and sometimes witty and amusing comments on men and their behavior, and on common experience. Not infrequently their tone is scornful or sarcastic, as in I Kings xx 11, "One who is girding himself [for battle] should not boast like one who is ungirding himself [afterwards]." Some sound a warning based on unfortunate experience, for example, Prov xiii 20, "The fellow of fools will fare ill." They carry their own note of authority, that of the obvious truism, or the social authority of general consent; cf. "In all toil there is profit" (Prov xiv 23), and "Without [his] people, a prince is nothing" (Prov xiv 28).

Deep in this folk wisdom may be discerned something that becomes more explicit in the words of the later teachers of practical and speculative wisdom: *the idea of order,* of norms, rules, right values, and due proportions. This is expressed in proverbs which bring to light the identity or equivalence of some things and the non-identity of others, the distinction of the appearance from the reality, common factors and characteristics, cause and consequence; and also what is *contrary to right order:* the irregular, absurd, paradoxical, and impossible. This underlying idea and the proverbial patterns which it creates may be observed in the folk wisdom of many peoples, ancient and modern.

The first of these patterns points to *identity, equivalence,* or *invariable association:* "This is really [or, always] that"; "Where [or, when] this is, that is"; "Without this, there is no that." Familiar examples in English are: "Business is business" (in which the tautology is apparent only); "A friend in need is a friend indeed" (which exhibits the fondness of the proverb maker for alliteration and rhyme); "Easy come, easy go"; "A penny saved is a penny earned"; and (from Aesop's fables), "One man's meat is another man's poison." Among biblical proverbs of this type may be cited: "As the man, so his strength" (Judg viii 21); "The man who cajoles his companion is spreading a net for his feet" (Prov xxix 5); "Without [the labor of] oxen, the manger is bare" (Prov xiv 4); "What a man sows is what he will reap" (Gal vi 7).

The second proverb pattern is that of *non-identity, contrast,* or *paradox:* "This is not really that"; "Not every this is that"; "This, yet paradoxically that." Examples are: "All that glisters is not gold"; "Not all are hunters, who blow horns"; "Much noise, few eggs"; "A cobbler's wife is always ill-shod"; "Good fences make good neighbors." Examples from the Bible are: "What has straw in common with wheat?" (Jer xxiii 28); "A soft tongue can break a bone" (Prov xxv 15); "To the hungry man even the bitter tastes sweet" (Prov xxvii 7); "He who loves money never has enough money" (Eccles v 10 EV); "Can anything good come from Nazareth?" (John i 46).

The third proverb pattern is that of *similarity, analogy,* or *type:* "This is [or, "acts like"] that"; "As this, so that"; "This is [metaphorically] that"; "Like so-and-so, who . . .". Here we have: "A chip off the old block"; "Time and tide wait for no man"; "He who keeps company with a wolf learns to howl"; "Like master, like man." The last corresponds exactly with the biblical "Like people, like priest" (Hos iv 9); "Like mother, like daughter" (Ezek xvi 44). Striking similes are frequent: "Like arrows in the hands

of a warrior are the sons of one's youth" (Ps cxxvii 4); "Like the
coolness of snow in the heat of harvest time is a reliable messenger
to him who sends him" (Prov xxv 13); "It is like having a loose
tooth or a palsied foot to rely on a deceiver in time of trouble"
(Prov xxv 19); "Singing gay songs to a heavy heart is like disrobing
a man on a cold day, or adding sour wine to soda" (Prov xxv 20);
"Good news from a distant land is like a drink of cold water to a
weary man" (Prov xxv 25). Persons who have become types or
standards for comparison are illustrated in: "Like Nimrod, a
mighty hunter before the Lord" (Gen x 9); "Like Rachel and
Leah, who built up the family of Israel" (Ruth iv 11); "No
prophet like Moses" (Deut xxxiv 10).

The fourth proverb idiom focuses on what is *contrary to right
order*, and so is *futile* or *absurd*. It employs the mocking comparison, for example, "A whistling woman and a crowing hen are liked
neither by God nor men"; the rhetorical question: "What's the use
of running when you are on the wrong road?"; and the maxim,
as in "Don't count your chickens before they are hatched."

The Hebrews were especially fond of the taunt or mocking question. When Jeremiah said "Every wine jar shall be filled with wine"
(Jer xiii 12), he was mocking drinkers, not talking about wine
jars. "As a door turns on its pivot, so a lazy man turns on his
bed" (Prov xxvi 14) sounds like a favorite sarcasm of the early
risers. "Do horses run on a cliff [i.e., like insects]? Do you plow
the sea with an ox?" cried the prophet Amos in derision (Amos
vi 12). Jeremiah's challenge is perhaps more familiar: "Can an
Ethiopian change his [black] skin, or a leopard his spots?" (Jer
xiii 23). In Prov xvii 16 a teacher of privileged youth reflects
ruefully, "What good does it do a fool to come fee in hand to buy
wisdom, when he has no mind?" In Prov i 17 another instructor
clinches his warning of the dire results of associating with thieves,
by quoting the proverb, "It's no use setting a net so the birds can
see it."

A fifth type of proverb *classifies* and *characterizes* persons, actions, or situations: "Children and fools speak the truth"; "A rolling
stone gathers no moss"; "He that steals an egg will steal an ox";
"There are three things which drive a man out of the house—
smoke, rain [which gets in], and a scolding wife." The Book of
Proverbs has many examples of such characterizations of the fool,

the scoffer, the sluggard, and the shrewish wife; for instance, "The simpleton believes everything he hears" (xiv 15); "The insolent will not listen to rebuke" (xiii 1); "The lazy man puts his hand into the dish, but he is too weary to raise it to his mouth" (xxvi 15); "A wife's grumbling is a continual dripping [of water]" (xix 13). The most famous of several examples in Prov xxx 15–31 of the numerical proverb of classification is: "Three things astonish me, there are four I cannot fathom—how an eagle soars in the sky, how a snake glides across a rock, how a ship moves over the sea, and how a man wins his way with a girl." What might be called a "progressive classification" appears in Prov xxvii 3: "A stone may be heavy, or a load of sand, but a provoking fool is harder to bear than both together."

The sixth identifiable idiom or pattern is that of *value, relative value or priority, proportion or degree:* "This is worth that"; "The more [or less] this, the more [or less] that"; "Better this than that"; "First this, then that"; "If this, how much more that!" Familiar examples come to mind: "A bird in the hand is worth two in the bush"; "Better late than never"; "The nearer the bone, the sweeter the meat"; "Out of the frying pan into the fire"; "Cut your coat according to the cloth." This is a common biblical type: "A good name is more to be desired than great riches" (Prov xxii 1); "Better to be poor than a liar" (Prov xix 22); "Better the end of something than its beginning" (Eccles vii 8); "The more he talks, the more meaningless it becomes" (Eccles vi 11); "To obey [God] is better than [to offer] sacrifice" (I Sam xv 22). "A sacrifice offered by wicked men is an abomination, all the more so if one bring it with a shameful purpose" (Prov xxi 27).

A seventh proverb pattern in folk wisdom turns on the *consequences of human character and behavior:* "Nothing venture, nothing win"; "Give him an inch and he'll take an ell"; "Don't bite off more than you can chew!" The most famous biblical example of this is quoted by both Jeremiah and Ezekiel: "[When] the fathers have eaten unripe grapes, the children's teeth are set on edge [or "blunted"]" (Jer xxxi 29; Ezek xviii 2). Others are: "They are sowing the wind, they shall reap the whirlwind" (Hos viii 7); "A happy heart lights up the face" (Prov xv 13); "He who digs a pit [for another] will fall into it [himself]" (Prov xxvi 27); "At the onset of winter the idler does not plow, so at harvest time he looks for [a crop] and finds none" (Prov xx 4).

These are by no means all the proverbs patterns which can be traced in the Bible and in the sayings of other peoples, ancient and modern. To be on the lookout for them will add interest to the reading of the Book of Proverbs, where the long sequences of un-connected sayings and precepts all too easily fail to hold the atten-tion. As W. A. L. Elmslie remarks truly in his delightful *Studies in Life from Jewish Proverbs,*[2] "Proverbs cannot be absorbed in quantity," and "Many proverbs speak truth, but a true word can be spoken too often." We must remember, in any case, that the Book of Proverbs is not intended to be an anthology of folk sayings, but a source book of materials for instruction in religious morality. It is deliberately didactic, and its air of somewhat ponderous au-thority and complacent moralizing reflects the schoolmaster, not the village wit. Even the literary form of these proverbs is changed in the interests of instructional method. In place of short, pointed, and picturesque sayings, often characterized by alliteration, we find for-mal couplets in poetic parallelism. The second line may point a contrast,

> A wise son makes a happy father,
> But a foolish son is a grief to his mother (x 1).

Or it may say the same thing in different words, as in

> Vile men will be made to bow before the righteous,
> And the wicked at the gates of the just (xiv 19).

Sometimes the second line simply carries forward what is said in the first:

> Religious belief is a well of life
> By which one avoids deadly snares (xiv 27).

At some points it seems very evident that a banal second line has been added to a picturesque folk saying, as in

> "The toiler's appetite toils for him,"
> For his hunger drives him (xvi 26).

---

[2] London, 1917, pp. 15–16.

What explains this form is almost certainly an instructional method in which a teacher spoke the first line and was answered in chorus by the class (or an individual pupil) responding with the appropriate second line. We have a glimpse of such a method in operation in Isa xxviii 9–10: "Whom will he teach knowledge? . . . precept upon precept, line upon line," and again in Isa xxix 13: "Their fear of me is a human commandment learned by rote." Since the two collections of such two-line parallel in didactic sayings are designated "Proverbs of Solomon" in the titles at Prov x 1 and xxv 1, it is a reasonable inference that *this literary form* is primarily what is meant by the designation, rather than an affirmation of Solomon's authorship.

KING SOLOMON AND HIS PROVERBS

The traditional ascription of the Book of Proverbs to the authorship of Solomon is based on the story in I Kings (iv 29–34 EV) of his superlative wisdom and his composition of three thousand proverbs, and on the present title of the book and the subtitles which have just been mentioned. The full title is "The Proverbs of Solomon ben David, king of Israel." Four questions must be raised in connection with this title. (a) What is its relation to the subtitles at x 1 and xxv 1, since these would surely have been unnecessary if the preceding material in each case, and indeed the whole book, were Solomon's? (b) How is it that the book includes sections ascribed to other authors, to "the sages" in xxii 17 and xxiv 23, to Agur in xxx 1, and to "Lemuel" [?, see NOTE on xxxi 1]? (c) What is the connection of the book with the King Solomon of history? (d) How can the same term "proverb" [Heb *māšāl*] be applied to such heterogeneous materials as the admonitory discourses of chapters i–vii, the theological poem of chapter viii, the moralizing couplets of x 1–xxii 16 and chapters xxv–xxix, the dialogue with a skeptic in chapter xxx, and the acrostic verses about the Capable Housewife in chapter xxxi?

The answer to the first question becomes clear when it is recognized that the first division of the present book, chapters i–ix, was composed (apart from certain interpolations) to serve as an introduction to a previously existing collection entitled in x 1

"Proverbs of Solomon." The preamble in i 2–6 sets forth clearly the objectives of the author as a sage and an instructor of youth, and it is followed by ten admonitory discourses, two poems and some proverbs, in none of which is there the slightest suggestion that the author is anything but a teacher among his pupils. The title to the book then, has been carried forward from the previously existing collection of "Proverbs of Solomon" beginning at chapter x when chapters i–ix were composed to serve as its introduction. Quite likely the material of chapters x–xxxi had already been brought together in substantially its present form, headed by the first of the two sections entitled "Proverbs of Solomon," and hence as a whole designated by that title. The ascription to other authors of parts of what followed raised no difficulty, because the title in x 1 was not understood as a claim of Solomon's authorship of everything that followed.

The question remains as to why Solomon's name was associated in the first place with the two collections beginning at x 1 and xxv 1. Here it must be observed that Solomon had become in tradition the patron saint of the Wisdom movement, and works of various kinds and of different periods were brought under his aegis. In the fourth or early third century B.C. the writer of Ecclesiastes (Qoheleth) assumes in his opening chapters the role of the famous king, only to discard the role later in his argument. Yet tradition ascribes the book to Solomon. In "the Song of Songs which is Solomon's" the bridegroom is called "Solomon" (iii 11), and the name has been appended to the book's title. As late as the first century B.C. an anonymous author gave to *a work written in Greek* the title "The Wisdom of Solomon," and from the same century come the so-called "Psalms of Solomon." The headings of the Book of Proverbs and of two of its subdivisions are not, to say the least, conclusive evidence of authorship by the famous king. It is more than questionable that they were intended to make that claim, though later generations took this for granted.

Nevertheless the question must be faced as to how Solomon's name came to be attached to various writings in the general category of Wisdom literature. What credence is to be placed in the statement that he was "wiser than all other men," and "uttered three thousand proverbs, and his songs were a thousand and five" (I Kings iv 31–32 EV)? If this tradition is to any degree authentic, what connection, apart from the titles, can be established between the historical Solomon and the existing Book of Proverbs?

The account of Solomon's reign in I Kings i–xi is not a consecutive narrative by a single author, but is composed of blocks of different kinds of material in one way or another connected with him. Early records such as the story of his accession to the throne, the organization of his kingdom, and the architectural specifications of the temple which he built are combined with accounts of his prayer for wisdom, of his clever decision between the two mothers, a long liturgical prayer, and finally with highly embellished descriptions of his magnificence and worldwide reputation as a sage. These last are so superlative in their language that they must be recognized as legendary by any sober historian. The multitude and bliss of his subjects (I Kings iv 20, 25 EV), the vast extent of his dominions (iv 21, 24 EV), the power of his chariot force (iv 26 EV; x 26), the wealth which poured in from tribute and foreign trading ventures so that he "made silver as common in Jerusalem as stone" (x 14–29), the incomparable splendor of his court (x 4–6, 16–21), the size of his harem (xi 3)—all this is of a piece with the claim that "his wisdom surpassed the wisdom of all the people of the east, and all the wisdom of Egypt," and that "he uttered three thousand proverbs." The tradition of Solomon's authorship of proverbs rests solely (apart from the titles in the Book of Proverbs) on this statement, included in an account of Solomon's glory which is in extravagant terms throughout.

There is something to be said, however, on the other side of this question. The glory and achievements of King Solomon cannot be dismissed as wholly legendary, simply because one writer's imagination has run riot in describing them. The temple, palaces, and chariot cities which he built had left a visible memorial of his power and wealth. Similarly with the tradition of the king's wisdom, there are indications of historical substance beneath the legendary accretions. The older layers of material dealing with Solomon's reign also refer to the king's wisdom, though in a different sense than that of the intellectual brilliance of the composer of the three thousand proverbs. The wisdom asked for in the famous dream at Gibeon (I Kings iii 5–15) was the power to rule wisely and to judge justly, which is a very different quality from ability to compose proverbs and to solve riddles propounded by the Queen of Sheba. This competence of the successful ruler is evidently the original sense in which Solomon was considered wise (cf. ii 9, v 7, 12 EV).

One aspect of the rapid development of the Israelite kingdom at that time was cultural. Among the high officers of state were "secretaries" and a "recorder" (I Kings iv 3), each of whom undoubtedly stood at the head of numbers of lesser officials. The scribal art and the literature associated with training in it were thus established at the royal court. We know that *material* assistance to Solomon was rendered by the older monarchies of Egypt and Tyre (ix 16, v 1–12 EV), and it seems probable that there was a great inflow of cultural influence at the same time. Both these lands had been the homes of developed Wisdom movements (cf. Isa xix 11–12); in Ezek xxviii 3–5 the prince of Tyre is addressed in terms reminiscent of those claiming pre-eminence for Solomon. One element in Egyptian Wisdom is illustrated in the *onomastika* or classification lists which attempted to introduce a principle of order into the observation of natural phenomena. Albrecht Alt has drawn attention to the remarkable fact that the subject matter of the proverbs credited to Solomon in I Kings iv 32–33 EV is this non-human natural world, in contrast to the "Proverbs of Solomon" in Prov x 1 ff. and xxv 1 ff. where it is the affairs and experience of men. So unexpected a contrast can be explained only on the basis of an authentic tradition underlying the extravagant legendary statement in I Kings. Curiously enough, the examples of this classification of observed natural phenomena are found in Proverbs chiefly in an appendix not attributed to Solomon (xxx 18–19, 24–28, 29–31).

Another piece of supporting evidence for the development of Wisdom literature in Israel in Solomon's reign has been pointed out by G. von Rad. The story of Joseph in Egypt in Gen xxxix–xlvii is part of a national religious history which for various reasons can be assigned to about that time, and it portrays its hero as exhibiting the prudence, practical intelligence, moral integrity, and generosity which were the particular emphases in the training provided by later Wisdom teachers. It thus indicates that moral instruction of a similar kind had already been undertaken in Solomon's day or soon after it, and that Wisdom literature was cultivated at the royal court. The degree to which the king himself participated in such activities must remain problematical. It would be natural for the work of his scholars to be attributed in tradition to their patron.

The connection of King Solomon with the present Book of Proverbs is thus a tenuous one. The phrase "Proverbs of Solomon" in i 1, x 1 and xxv 1 is as ambiguous in Hebrew as in English. Since the king was famed as a poet and a sage, it is reasonable to conclude that the poetic couplets with their parallel lines came to be designated in this way, in order to distinguish them from popular sayings which seldom have a similar poetic form in the Old Testament. It is quite possible that this form originated among the Wisdom teachers of Solomon's court, and that many of the examples we have were composed by them, or even by the king himself under their instruction. But there is no proof of either. When "the king" is mentioned in the Book of Proverbs (cf. xiv 28, 35, xvi 10–15, xx 2, 8, 26, etc.) it does not sound as if the monarch himself is speaking. The most probable conclusion is that, for genuine historical reasons, Solomon's name had come to be associated with Wisdom writing by literary convention, and that the material included came from many unidentifiable sources.

How it came about that such various materials were subsumed under the term "proverbs" also requires explanation. The Hebrew word *māšāl* means primarily "a likeness," in which the real nature of something is exhibited by comparing it with something else. It can also mean a "rule" or standard of behavior, or a saying or poem setting forth the mysterious unseen order with which all things must conform because God wills it so. Thus the word *māšāl* has a much wider range of meanings than the English word "proverb." It is used not only of short and pithy popular sayings and of didactic poetic couplets, but also of prophetic oracles, as in Isa xiv 4; Mic ii 4. The *māšāl* is an utterance of truth, hidden meaning, and right order. It embodies mysterious and powerful *wisdom* as related to a particular matter, as this has been formulated by an authoritative speaker or in accepted tradition. Hence the longer discourses and poems in the Book of Proverbs, as well as the two-line couplets, can be called *mᵉšālīm*, although in English we would not call them "proverbs." The preamble in i 2–6 makes clear that what follows are *mᵉšālīm* of various kinds.

CONTENTS AND COMPOSITION OF THE BOOK OF PROVERBS

PART I. Chapters i–ix: *The Teacher's Introduction*

Section No.	Title, Preamble, and Motto	Ten Discourses	Poems	Maxims and Proverbs
1	i 1–7	(*1*) i 8–19	i 20–33	
2		(*2*) ii 1–22		
3		(*3*) iii 1–12	iii 13–18	iii 27–30
		(*4*) iii 21–26 ⎫ iii 31–35 ⎭	iii 19–20	
4		(*5*) iv 1–9		
		(*6*) iv 10–19		
		(*7*) iv 20–27 ⎫ v 21–23 ⎭		
5		(*8*) v 1–14		
6				v 15–19 vi 22 v 20 vi 1–19
7		(*9*) vi 20–21 ⎫ vi 23–35 ⎭		
8		(*10*) vii 1–27		
9			viii 1–36	
10			ix 1–6 ⎫ ix 10–12 ⎭ ix 7–9 ix 13–18	

PART II. Chapters x–xxii 16: *First Collection of Solomonic Proverbs*

PART III (A). Chapters xxii 17–xxiv 22: *The Thirty Precepts of the Sages*

Parallel with *Amen-em-ope*	Not parallel with *Amen-em-ope*
Preamble: xxii 17–21	
Precepts *one* to *ten:* xxii 22–xxiii 11	Precepts *eleven* to *thirty:* xxiii 12–xxiv 22

PART III (B). Chapter xxiv 23–34: *Appendix to the Thirty Precepts*

PART IV. Chapters xxv–xxix: *Second Collection of "Solomonic Proverbs"*

PART V. *Appendixes to the Book:*

(i) Chapter xxx 1–9: Dialogue with a Skeptic
(ii) Chapter xxx 10–33: Warnings and Numerical Proverbs
(iii) Chapter xxxi 1–9: A Queen Mother's Admonition
(iv) Chapter xxxi 10–31: The Ideal Housewife, an Acrostic Poem

It is evident from the marked differences between the main divisions of the book that it has been composed by the bringing together of various collections and independent pieces, each with its own history. The differences are in literary form, style, ethical emphasis, and religious orientation—in the broad area of concern for the apprehension and inculcation of wisdom for living. The distinction of the parts is indicated also, in most cases, by the clearly marked transitions from one to the other, as well as by the individual headings at x 1, xxii 17, xxiv 23, xxv 1, xxx 1, and xxxi 1.

PART I, chapters i–ix, is the teacher's introduction to the anthology of Wisdom writings which he has brought together for the instruction of his pupils (cf. i 2–6). Its formal structure and some of its subject matter point to its being the latest element in the Book of Proverbs. In contrast to the great array of miscellaneous and unconnected couplets in Part II, and to the sometimes longer but still discontinuous units of Parts III and IV and the Appendixes, Part I, following the preamble, consists principally of ten discourses admonishing young men to live by the standards of religious morals. The section begins and concludes with a motto which serves as a summarizing maxim: *The first principle of knowledge is to hold the Lord in awe* (i 7; cf. ix 10).

The author of the Book of Ecclesiastes similarly begins and ends his work with a summarizing motto: "Vanity of vanities, all is vanity," or *A vapor of vapors, all is vapor.*

The ten discourses in Proverbs i–vii vary in length but have a common structure—a summons to attention, a statement of motive, an

exhortation to embrace wisdom and/or to avoid folly, and a prediction of the consequences of doing one or the other. The note of moral
admonition is stern and constant, and the wisdom urged upon the
hearers is ethical obedience rather than intellectual development.
The knowledge which matters is knowledge of the way to live well,
springing from deep and genuine religious feeling; it is not, as in
the following collections of "Solomonic" proverbs, knowledge of the
ways of the world and of men, and the ability to master them.

The sequence of the ten discourses has been disturbed by the
insertion of three longer and three shorter poems and of some brief
admonitions on particular themes. In the two striking poetic compositions now found in i 20–33 and viii 1–36, a philosophical
poet (probably identical with the author of the discourses but
possibly from an earlier day) personifies in vivid fashion the Wisdom of God which was active in creation and which seeks en-
trance to men's minds. The "Invitation to Wisdom's Banquet" (ix
1–6, 10–12) serves as a peroration to the discourses, and appears
to have been composed in imitation of the older poems. The two
short poems in praise of wisdom in iii 13–18 and 19–20 look like
an earlier draft of chapter viii. At the end of chapter ix a short
supplementary poem has been added in vss. 13–18. In iii 27–30, v
15–20 (with vi 22), vi 1–5, 6–11, and 12–15 are found admonitions
on the themes of marital fidelity, rash pledges, sloth, and rascality.
Together with the numerical proverb in vi 16–19 and the piece on
the scoffer and the wise man in ix 7–9, these disturb the order of
Part I and may have been inserted later from other sources.

The basic literary structure of Part I has suffered some disturbance, possibly in the production of later editions by the original author, and doubtless also from the vicissitudes of subsequent
manuscript transmission. Chapter ii rather than i 8–19 seems more
suitable as the opening discourse because of its more general and
programmatic character. Its thought, too, is more fundamental than
the admonitions and warnings about particular kinds of behavior in
the other discourses. Wisdom here is not simply the characteristic
quality of wise men; it is a function of the religious consciousness.
As in chapter viii, wisdom is God's gift to those who dedicate themselves to moral discipline, a concept which is then personified as
the living link between God and mankind. This is what suggests
that the author of the discourses is identical with the poet; even

though the poems of the personified Wisdom may once have existed separately, since they have a distinctiveness and completeness of their own. Again, the peroration to chapter viii in vss. 32–36 is in the style and corresponds to the substance of the discourses (cf. iii 4, 13, 16, iv 13, vi 32, vii 24).

PART II, the first of the two collections of "Solomonic" proverbs, is so amorphous as to indicate that it is the end result of a long process of accumulating such couplets, composed for use in schools of moral instruction. Occasionally there is a semblance of order in the occurrence of small groups of sayings on one subject, such as xvi 1–7 on God's oversight of man's life, and xvi 10, 12–15 on kings. These, however, mean no more than a grouping through association of ideas or a temporary preoccupation with the theme, since other sayings of the same sort are scattered through the collection. Successive verses may be connected by the use of identical or rhyming words (e.g., x 11–12), possibly a mnemonic device. The repetition in different contexts of almost identical sayings (e.g., x 1 and xv 20, x 2 and xi 4, xiii 14 and xiv 27) points to a process of gradual accumulation of the material. The same may be given as the reason for the fact that in chapters x–xv the second line of the couplets usually states a contrast to the first line, whereas after that point more of the couplets express the same idea, or an extension of it, in both lines.

The fairly frequent references to Yahweh's pleasure and wrath, and to his overruling of men's thoughts and acts, give to this first "Solomonic" collection a positive religious note which may have some bearing on its date. This note is in marked contrast to the secular and prudential counsels, for example, of the opening chapters of Part IV (chs. xxv–xxvii). If—as there seems no reason to doubt—the latter were assembled by the schoolmen of King Hezekiah (c. 715–687 B.C.), we may trace a connection between this humanistic self-reliant type of wisdom and the political effects of it which were denounced by the prophet Isaiah (cf. Isa xix 11–15, xxviii 14–29, xxix 13–16, xxx 1–2, xxxi 1–3). In Part II [and also in the two final chapters of Part IV] the invocation of Yahweh's name and the acknowledgment of his moral government of the world and men, point to a growing influence of prophecy and to the assimilation of Wisdom teaching to piety. This is a step toward the viewpoint and objectives of the teacher who composed the introduction in chapters i–ix. Much, perhaps most, of the material in both "Solomonic" collections is traditional and pre-Exilic in origin. Some of it belongs to the ageless popular wisdom which Israel shared with surrounding peoples. The most that we can say with confidence about the date of Part II is that it was the fruit of a long process, and reached its present form probably in the fifth or fourth century B.C.

The most obvious difference of the "Solomonic" proverbs from the adages of folk wisdom is their formal regularity of parallelism and meter. This, coupled with the lack of continuity, is what makes the reading of Parts II and IV so monotonous. Parallelism is, of course, not peculiar to them; what is peculiar is that it is so constant, as is the persistent monotone of the rhythm. This supports the assumption that the first line was intended to be spoken by the teacher, calling forth the second line as an antiphonal response from the pupils. When, as sometimes happens, a third line is added (as in xix 7) it seems to be an alternative to the second line. That such alternative forms of the same proverb were in circulation is shown by their appearance in different contexts (cf. x 15 and xviii 11, xi 13 and xx 19, xii 14 and xiii 2). Where there are four lines (in Part IV, e.g., xxv 4–5, 6–7, 9–10), it seems evident in each case that the first pair is the cue and the second pair the response.

The way in which the form of the parallel is varied shows that such responses were intended to be more than mechanical echoes. Sometimes the mind is stimulated to discover a parallel not expressly stated. In xviii 17, for instance, the second line must be recast in order to provide the antithesis:

> He seems right who states his case first,
>   Until his opponent comes and cross-examines him

(i.e., but under cross-examination he can be proved wrong). In xx 14 we have:

> "It is no good, no good!" says the buyer,
>   But as he goes away he congratulates himself,

which is another way of saying:

> When a man is bargaining he depreciates his purchase,
>   But when he has bought it, he boasts about it.

In xx 12 we have a variant of synonymous parallelism:

> The ear that hears, the eye that sees—
> The Lord is the maker of them both.

Proverbs of comparative degree are another type of synonymous parallelism:

If a good man gets his deserts on earth,
  How much more [certainly] will the wicked and the transgressor!

Cf. xii 9:

> Better to be a common man who has employment,
> Than to give oneself airs, and be starving.

In another type of parallelism, the second line is a completion or development of the thought of the first line; for example, xix 24:

> The lazy man puts his hand into the dish,
> He will not even raise it to his mouth.

Variants of this synthetic or projecting type of parallelism are (a) where the first line provides the subject and the second line the predicate, as in xv 31:

> He whose ear listens to correction will find life,
> And will be at home among the wise;

(b) where the first line forms the protasis and the second line the apodosis of a conditional sentence, as in xvi 7:

> When the Lord is pleased with a man's conduct
> He makes even his enemies to be at peace with him;

(c) where the second line states the result of what is said in the first line, as in xx 17:

> A man may delight in making his living dishonestly,
> But after a time his mouth will be filled with gravel;

(d) where the second line gives the reason for what is said in the first, as in xvi 12:

> Wrongdoing is hateful to kings,
> For through the right the throne stands secure.

These variants of the "Solomonic" couplet are too elaborate and contrived to have arisen spontaneously. They reflect the literary skill, and sometimes the pedantry, of the professional wise man. Further, although the seven patterns of folk proverbs already discussed appear also in these more formal couplets, they are not nearly so prominent and characteristic. The tone of the "Solomonic" proverbs is predominantly didactic, sententious, and moralizing, rather than picturesque, pointed, witty, and sarcastic, as so many folk proverbs are. It is curious, however, that the admonitions are mostly indirect, instead of consisting of formal precepts and maxims with imperative verbs. Nearly half the proverbs in Part II are declarations of the personal and social consequences of particular acts and qualities of character. A smaller number describe what is to be emulated or avoided. More general observations on conduct and circumstances, virtue and vice, make up the remainder.

Part III, chapters xxii 17–xxiv 22, with its appendix in xxiv 23–34, presents the sayings of anonymous contributors to the tradition, "the wise men." Here a remarkable and interesting fact emerges from study of the international context of Hebrew Wisdom writings. In the discussion of this in the General Introduction (see above, pp. XL–XLII) attention was drawn to that typical form of Egyptian Wisdom literature, the "Instructions" of a king or important official to his son or successor. One of these "Instructions," that of *Amen-em-ope,* displays striking similarities to Part III of Proverbs, especially to xxii 17–xxiii 11, as is shown in detail in the commentary on this passage. There is similarity in structure, and also in subject matter. Like the *Instruction of Amen-em-ope,* Prov xxii 17–xxiv 22 appears to consist of thirty precepts or exhortations of which the first ten (two are variants) correspond to nine of the thirty in the Egyptian work, though not in the same order. In addition, the preamble in xxii 17–21 appears in somewhat different form as the conclusion of *Amen-em-ope.* The clinching proof of the relationship of the two works was Erman's recognition that the puzzling Hebrew word *šālīšīm* in xxii 20 is a corruption of the word *šᵉlōšīm,* meaning "thirty" (see NOTE on this verse).

How is such a relationship to be explained, since it is too close to be a coincidence, but not close enough or complete enough to indicate direct literary dependence in either direction? The profession of scribe was international, and the schools where scribes were trained undoubtedly provided opportunity for the study of a wide range of Wisdom writings. What is more likely than that a Hebrew scribe has modeled his work on *Amen-em-ope,* reproducing with modifications those sections of which he had a copy or which he remembered, and then filling out their number to thirty? Some of his precepts are counsels on behavior in the Egyptian fashion, while the rest more closely resemble the admonitions of the Hebrew Wisdom teachers. In each work the sections vary considerably in length, but exhibit the same predominance of quatrains. It is perhaps some confirmation of the suggestion that the Hebrew scribe had before him, or remembered, only the first nine or ten of the Egyptian sections, that where the close parallels end at xxiii 11, a hortatory subheading is provided to introduce the remainder.

PART IV, chapters xxv–xxix, is distinguished by its opening: "These are further wise sayings of Solomon transmitted by the men of Hezekiah, king of Judah." Evidently these "men" were members of a scribal establishment under royal patronage, to whom the king assigned the task of assembling the traditional Wisdom literature of Judah. Within chapters xxv–xxix there is a distinction between the first three chapters, and the last two. Chapter xxv opens with a series of four-line precepts resembling those of Part III, and in the rest of chapter xxv through chapter xxvii precepts and similes predominate over the declaratory form common in the first collection of "Solomonic" proverbs. The tone also is more secular and less moralizing; the name of Yahweh is mentioned only once (xxv 22), and the familiar contrast of the "righteous" and the "wicked" also occurs only once (xxv 26). In chapters xxviii–xxix, on the other hand, the resemblance to the larger collection in x 1–xxii 16 is much greater both in form and content. Six identical proverbs occur in both (e.g., xviii 8 and xxvi 22), seven others are nearly identical, and in four other cases there are identical single lines. This is a much greater proportion of similarity than between any other two divisions of Proverbs. Much the same virtues are extolled, and much the same vices are held up to scorn. In chapter xxvi the fool, the sluggard, and the quarrelsome man are stereotyped in sarcastic terms. On the other hand, not so much stress is laid as in Part II (especially in chs. x and xvi) on Yahweh's pleasure and anger, his rewards and punishments, and his overruling of the thoughts and actions of men.

PART V, chapters xxx–xxxi, contains the four appendixes to the book. The first, xxx 1–9, looks like a miniature Book of Job in which a skeptic is answered by an orthodox believer, who then addresses a prayer to God. Agur ben Yakeh is presumably the name of the skeptic. His skepticism, however, resembles that of Ecclesiastes-Qoheleth more than that of Job, in that he appears to deny the possibility of the knowledge of God. Like the Job of the Prologue he is apparently not a Hebrew. The reply and accompanying prayer are in the language of Jewish piety.

Chapter xxx 10–33 is a collection of warnings and numerical proverbs of classification, most of them beginning with the "x, x+1" formula found also in vi 16–19. Unlike the latter passage which lists seven kinds of behavior "hateful to Yahweh," the numerical sayings of chapter xxx list phenomena mostly in fours, and several of these are observations on the behavior of creatures other than man.

In xxxi 1–9 a queen mother, apparently not an Israelite, vigorously admonishes her royal son with regard to the conduct to be expected of kings. This is followed in vss. 10–31 by an acrostic poem describing the virtues and accomplishments of an ideal wife and mother, mistress of the household of a prominent man. The acrostic form is found in the later strands of Old Testament poetry, but there is no reason in principle why it could not have been developed once the order of letters in the Hebrew alphabet had been firmly established, as it certainly was long before the sixth-century Exile.

RELIGIOUS AND ETHICAL TEACHING OF THE BOOK OF PROVERBS

Although the ethical and religious content of the several parts of Proverbs is not uniform, the whole—with the possible exception of the appendixes—was intended by the Hebrew editor to be understood in the light of his introduction in chapters i–ix. Suitable sayings of secular origin and tone could lend additional support to the positive religious morality he was seeking to inculcate. We may suspect that it was part of the teacher's pedagogical technique to include sayings of a type with which his pupils would be familiar, in order to maintain their interest. His was a course in applied religion. It was essential to establish contact with the traditional mores of the community and the proverbial lore of the common life.

The primary meaning of *ḥokmāh,* "wisdom," is skill, the ability to excel in a particular activity. As is evident from what is said in Exod xxxv 30–35 of the master craftsman Bezalel, this was compounded of intelligence, special aptitude, knowledge gained by experience, and above all, of "divine spirit." We read of God's special endowment with wisdom of judges and kings (cf. I Kings iii 11–12, v 7, 12 EV; Isa xi 1–5, xxviii 5–6; Prov viii 15–16). The intellectual element in Hebrew Wisdom usually is secondary to the religious and ethical element. Wisdom manifests itself in demonstrated ability, in wise choices, in living according to the moral norms of the covenant community. It is not primarily a human achievement—yet through instruction and self-discipline a young man might prepare himself to receive it as God's gift (Prov ii 1–8). To those who do receive it, this wisdom becomes a moral guide and mentor.

The editor of Proverbs defines the relationship of wisdom to religion in his famous aphorism, "The fear of the Lord is the beginning of knowledge," or, inverting subject and predicate, "The first principle of knowledge [in the sense of wisdom] is to hold the Lord in awe" (Prov i 7; cf. i 29, ix 10). In the programmatic Second Discourse in chapter ii, the teacher shows how the sincere desire for wisdom leads first to the knowledge of God (vss. 1–5), who is the source and guarantor of moral understanding (vss. 6–8). This in turn gives ethical perception and the power to live by it (vss. 9–22). Wholehearted trust in God rather than one's own conceit of wisdom (iii 5–7) is to be shown by acknowledging that God is the giver of material possessions (iii 9–10), and by submission to the discipline of moral obedience (iii 11–12). Thus wisdom grows through experience, and at the same time serves as an inward monitor (ii 10–11). Wisdom means understanding of the way of the good life for man, and of its dynamic relationship to the right order established by God the Creator (ch. viii). The religious wisdom concerning life is not, however, alien to the common sense gained by intelligent and perceptive men from the long experience of community living. Folk wisdom expresses the norms of behavior which produce social approval and personal satisfaction. The religious teacher sets these in a more ultimate context, and relates them to first principles of religious obligation. He would have his pupils desire the approval of God and of good men, and find a satisfaction "more precious than jewels."

When we pass from the moral admonitions of Part I to the first collection of "Solomonic" proverbs, the miscellaneous character and disjointed arrangement of these make it more difficult to discern the nature of the thought. The parallelism of Semitic verse, which in prophetic oracles and longer poems can be a device of great beauty and effectiveness, produces in these lists of proverbs a tone of monotonous iteration. With rare exceptions, the proverbs affirm and declare, rather than persuade and exhort. They are dicta carrying the authority of the acknowledged teacher of wisdom, and often the compulsion of obvious truth as well. But there are other cases where the truth of the assertion made is far from obvious, as when we are told that "Wealth gained through wickedness will prove of no advantage" (x 2), or that "The consequence of humility and reverence for the Lord is wealth and honor and life" (xxii 4). Positive religious belief has produced logically a dogmatic morality. This is the way things must be because it is the way they *ought* to be, since the Creator is the moral governor of the life of man!

We would think that such declarations might provoke objections; no doubt they did so among the more mature. But inexperienced youths were in no position to dispute the assertions of their venerable instructors. In any case, each distinct bilinear couplet may have served as a sort of thesis for discussion among the sages, in the presence of their juniors (cf. i 4–6; Luke ii 46–47).

One of the remarkable features of the religious teaching of Proverbs is that it completely ignores the obligations of temple worship and cultic festivals, which the rest of the Old Testament would lead us to believe occupied so large a place in the religious consciousness of Israel. The only references to them in the Book of Proverbs are oblique ones, such as the summons in iii 9–10 to "honor the Lord from your possessions, and from the first returns of all your revenue." In fact, what is said in xvi 6 seems to dispense altogether with the need for cultic sacrifice to atone for sin:

> By loyalty and integrity guilt is atoned for,
> By reverence for the Lord and turning from wrong.

God is to be acknowledged as man's "Maker" (xiv 31, xvii 5, xx 12), the sovereign overseer of all life (x 3, xx 24), and the

guarantor of the moral order (x 27, 29, xii 2). His pleasure or
displeasure with the thoughts and actions of men (xv 9, xvi 2) is
the basis in belief from which, together with broad generalizations
from social experience, the doctrine of earthly reward and punishment is derived. Health, wealth, honor, and long life are to be seen
as visible evidences of divine approval (xxii 4). An untimely death,
on the other hand, is the reward of wickedness; it is Yahweh's "Day
of wrath" (xi 4). Men's character and conduct are patently of a
piece with what happens to them: "The man who tills his land will
have plenty to eat" (xii 11); "In all toil there is profit, but mere
talk leads only to want" (xiv 23); "If one returns evil for good,
trouble will never depart from his home" (xvii 13).

The view that the ethics of Part II of Proverbs are simply utili-
tarian and external is a superficial one. The primary importance of
human character and motivation is emphasized in the repeated
statement that God examines and weighs and tests men's thoughts
(xv 11, xvi 2, xvii 3, xx 27). The religious man finds his security
in committing his way to God (xvi 3), accepting God's discipline,
and looking for his guidance (xvi 9, xx 22). Uprightness is the
evidence of piety (xiv 2), and the necessary condition of acceptable
worship (xv 8).

Particular virtues and vices, good deeds and bad, together with
their specified rewards and punishments, are not so isolated from
basic principles as their discontinuous topical treatment at first suggests. They are to be seen as manifestations of personal righteousness and true wisdom on the one hand, and of ingrained wickedness,
impiety, stupidity, and folly on the other. Their consequences are
not only outwardly visible good fortune or misfortune, but also the
inner effects on men themselves (x 23, xi 17, xiv 30, xxii 9). The
motivations of conduct, moreover, are by no means confined to the
sanctions of material rewards and punishments. The pleasure or
displeasure of God (xii 22), the honor or shame brought to parents
(x 1), the effect upon other members of the community (x 12,
21, xi 10), the inner satisfaction of a clear conscience and a
happy heart (x 28, xii 5, xiii 5), and, above all, the desire for the
divine gift of wisdom (xii 1, xiii 14)—all play a significant part.

The virtues and vices specifically named in Part II define the
sense in which the general terms "righteousness" and "wickedness"
are used. The standard set is not conformity to cultic obligations, to

positive law, or to social custom. It is the pattern, strength, and
quality of life exhibited by the truly religious and truly wise man.
His typical virtues are diligence, prudence, integrity, forthrightness,
calm restraint in speech, trustworthiness, steadfastness, patience,
generosity, modesty, peaceableness, self-discipline, kindness to the
weak and the unfortunate. Such qualities of life seem to imply an
established and stable society as their background, free from severe
social upheaval and religious tensions. "The wicked" are those who
fail to measure up to these moral standards of the community with
which Yahweh has established his covenant.

In Part III, the "Thirty Precepts of the Sages" with its appendix,
the ethics, though basically similar, have a different thrust. They
take the form of admonitions addressed to youth who will face the
responsibilities and temptations of life as members of the urban
upper classes (xxii 22–23, xxiii 1–8, 20–21, 26–35). Warnings
against sexual immorality and drunkenness are here joined with
advice on polite and discreet behavior at the table of a prominent
man.

Part IV, the second collection of "Solomonic" proverbs, is more
secular in tone than the first collection, especially in chapters xxv–
xxvii. Many of its sayings are simply observations on life and experience, without much positive moral content. Their sanctions tend
to be self-regarding, and to consider social approval rather than
ethical and religious principle. Yet it is in Part IV that we come
across the remarkable injunction to do good to one's enemy (xxv
21–22 [see NOTES there]). In the two final chapters, xxviii and
xxix, the theme of positive religious faith as the door to wisdom is
again asserted (xxviii 5, xxix 26).

The four short appendixes in Part V, chapters xxx–xxxi, are
disparate in content as well as in form. In the "Dialogue with a
Skeptic" (xxx 1–9), the issue is primarily theological rather than
ethical, but in the appended prayer it is noteworthy that the temptation to impious pride is associated with wealth, and the temptation
to steal, with poverty. In the numerical proverbs which follow in
xxx 10–33, only one has special ethical reference: vss. 11–14 list
four types of despicable behavior—impiety toward parents, self-
righteous hypocrisy, arrogance, and cruelty to the poor. Three single
proverbs in this section touch on talebearing, contempt of parents,
and adultery. In xxxi 1–9 a queen mother cautions her royal son

against dissipation that will divert him from his duty to see justice done to the poor and needy. Finally, the acrostic poem on the "Ideal Housewife" sets her up as an example of the "Wisdom" virtues of diligence, perspicacity, kindness, and dignity.

The most important and subsequently most influential theological contribution of the Book of Proverbs is found in chapter viii, where the writer explores the nature and origin of Wisdom as a cosmic principle and power, linking man to God. (On this subject see the introductory and other NOTES on Sec. 10.)

A NOTE ON THE PROBLEM OF TRANSLATING THE BIBLE

If a reader compares the following translation of the Book of Proverbs with that of the King James Version (KJ) of 1611 (the so-called "Authorized Version"), with the Revised Standard Version (RSV) of 1952, or with any other of the many official, semi-official, or privately undertaken versions, Jewish, Protestant, or Roman Catholic, he may wonder how they can differ as much as they do, since all (presumably) are translations of the same original text.

The first thing to be recognized is that not all are in fact direct translations from the Hebrew. The best known Roman Catholic versions, the standard Douay-Challoner translation (1609–10, revised 1750), and the private (but authorized) translation by Fr. Ronald Knox (1949), were made from the Latin Vulgate (Vulg.). This is the translation made by Jerome about the end of the fourth century A.D., which passed into common use (hence "Vulgate") and became the authorized Roman Catholic version. The Confraternity Version in the United States and the Westminster Version in England are Roman Catholic translations from the original Hebrew of the Old Testament, which is the basis also of the Jewish and Protestant renderings. The standard form of the Hebrew Bible is the "Masoretic Text" (MT), which is the result of several centuries of editorial work on manuscripts by the Jewish scholars of the *Masorah* ["tradition"], culminating in the *ben Asher* text of the tenth century A.D.

The Masoretic Text, however, is not a perfect copy of the original writings. For many centuries these had been handed down in handwritten copies, and in the process suffered some modification and developed some defects which the best efforts of the final editors could not correct. There are a few gaps where words are missing (e.g., Gen iv 8; I Sam xiii 1). In a few cases words are accidentally repeated (e.g., Lev xx 10), run together (Amos vi 12) or wrongly divided (Isa ii 20), and errors involving single letters are quite numerous. To correct these we have first of all the aid of the traditional interpretation and marginal notes of the Masoretic scholars; second, the evidence of the principal translations made in ancient times into Greek, Latin, and Syriac; of the Aramaic paraphrases known as "the Targums," and (for the Pentateuch) of the Samaritan form of the Hebrew. Thirdly, there are the recently discovered manuscripts, and fragments of manuscripts, of Hebrew biblical books found in caves in the Judean wilderness in the vicinity of Qumran. The last-named range in date of writing from the third century B.C. to the second century A.D., and are thus many centuries closer to the time of the original compositions than the medieval manuscripts of the standard Masoretic Text. The Qumran scrolls show, however, that the medieval manuscripts represent with remarkable accuracy the form of the Hebrew text which became the official Bible of Judaism about the end of the first century A.D., though prior to that time somewhat differing forms had been in use as well. The most important of these was the Hebrew from which the Septuagint (LXX), or ancient Greek version, was made. This was translated for Greek-speaking Jews between the fourth and second centuries B.C., but was abandoned by them when the Christian Church took it over as its Old Testament.

All this must be taken into account by the modern translator. Where he finds that the Masoretic Text apparently is defective, he may leave the passage blank in his rendering, or try to restore the original wording with the aid of the ancient versions, the notations of the Masoretic scholars, linguistic research, and sometimes, of external archaeological evidence. Wherever this is attempted in the following translation, the Masoretic Text as well as the emendation is cited for purposes of comparison.

A second difficulty is one common to all efforts to convey the meaning in one language of a literary text composed in another. Rarely, if ever, do words in the two tongues correspond in their use and range of meaning. A literal translation of idiomatic constructions may suggest a wrong meaning, or no meaning at all. Equivalent words and phrases sometimes are unavailable in English, because the physical environment, the social structure, and the way of life with which we are familiar are so different from those taken for granted by the ancient authors. Hence a translation which seeks to bring out the full meaning of the original will be to some degree, and of necessity, a paraphrase. Here the explanatory notes should be of assistance.

In the third place, the nature of any translation is largely determined by the purpose for which it is made. A rendering into somewhat colloquial modern English may be quite unsuitable for use in a dignified service of worship. For a student engaged in literary comparisons and analysis on the basis of the English Bible, a quite literal translation is to be preferred. The present translator is well aware of these considerations, but he has attempted to convey to the reader the sense and feeling and movement of the original in a way that more formal and more literal renderings often fail to do.

SELECTED BIBLIOGRAPHY OF WORKS
ON THE BOOK OF PROVERBS

C. H. Toy, *Proverbs* (International Critical Commentary), Edinburgh, 1899 (still useful).

W. A. L. Elmslie, *Studies in Life from Jewish Proverbs,* London, 1917.

W. O. E. Oesterley, *The Book of Proverbs* (Westminster Commentaries), London, 1929.

G. Boström, *Proverbiastudien,* Lund, 1935.

J. H. Greenstone, *The Book of Proverbs,* Philadelphia, 1950.

C. T. Fritsch, *Proverbs* (The Interpreter's Bible, IV), New York, 1955.

W. G. Plaut, *Book of Proverbs* (Jewish Commentary for Bible Readers), New York, 1961.

Edgar Jones, *Proverbs and Ecclesiastes* (Torch Bible Commentaries), New York, 1961.

S. H. Blank, "Proverb," "Proverbs, Book of" (*The Interpreter's Dictionary of the Bible,* III, New York, 1962.

H. Ringgren, *Sprüche,* 1962.

M. Dahood, *Proverbs and North West Semitic Philology,* 1963.

B. Gemser, *Sprüche Salomos,* 2d ed., 1963.

A. Barucq, *Le Livre des Proverbes,* 1964.

For a fascinating comparative study of the folk proverbs of many peoples, see Archer Taylor, *The Proverb,* Cambridge, Massachusetts, 1931.

I. The Teacher's Introduction

1. TITLE, PREFACE, AND MOTTO;
THE FIRST DISCOURSE; A POEM
(i 1–33)

Title, Preface, and Motto

I 1 The wise sayings of Solomon, son of David, king of Israel—
2 for education in wisdom and moral discipline, for the understanding of thoughtful speech, 3 for training in discernment of
what is right and proper and equitable; 4 to sharpen the wits of
the ignorant, to give to youth knowledge and foresight 5 (the
scholar too may give heed and add to his store of knowledge,
and the discerning man may find guidance); 6 for the compre-
hension of proverb and metaphor, the words of the wise and
their riddles.

7 The first principle of knowledge is to hold the Lord in
       awe;
    They are fools who despise wisdom and instruction.

*First Discourse: The Ornament of Virtue, and the Dangerous
Seductions of Crime*

8 My son, follow your father's instructions
    And do not abandon your mother's teaching;
9 They will be your graceful headdress
    And an ornamental necklace for your throat.
10 My son, if vicious men entice you,
     Do not consent when they say,
11 "Come with us! Let us make a bloody ambush!
     Let us for sport waylay some innocent!

12   Let us swallow them up alive, like Sheol,
         As they tumble whole into the Pit!
13   We shall lay hands on all manner of wealth,
         We shall fill our houses with plunder.
14   Throw in your lot with us! We shall have a common
           purse!"
15   My son, do not go their way, nor take the step they
           propose,
16   (for they are rushing toward trouble in their eagerness
           for crime^*).
17   "It's no use setting a net so the birds can see it,"
18   Yet these men are setting a bloody ambush—for them-
           selves!
         They are lurking against their own lives.^b
19   Such is the end^c of all who commit crime;
         It takes the lives of those who give themselves to it.

*Poem: Wisdom Personified Confronts Men in Admonition and
Warning*

20   Wisdom shouts aloud in the street,
         She makes her voice heard in the open squares,
21   From the top of the walls^d she cries out,
         Where the gates open into the city^e:
22   How long, you simpletons, will you prefer ignorance?
         The^f insolent ones delight in their insolence?
         The^f brazen hate knowledge?
23   If you would heed my warning I would pour out my
           thought to you,
         I would make you understand my words.

---

^a Mss. B, S of LXX omit; possibly a gloss from Isa lix 7.
^b Or, when they lurk for the life of the innocent; cf. xxix 10.
^c *'aḥᵃrīt*, for MT *'orḥōt*, "paths."
^d LXX; Heb. "noisy places."
^e Hebrew adds "she utters her words."
^f Hebrew inserts "and."

24 But, since I have called and you have refused [to listen],
    I have beckoned but no one has paid attention,
25 Since you spurn all my advice and will not accept my
    warning—
26 I in turn will laugh when sudden calamity strikes you,
    I will mock when terror overtakes you,
27 When panic strikes you like a squall wind,
    And disaster falls on you like a gale,
    When distress and anguish come on you.
28 Then men will cry out for me, but I will not answer.
    They will seek for me but will not find me.
29 Because they showed no love for knowledge
    Nor any wish to reverence the Lord,
30 Because they would have none of my counsel, derided
    my reproof—
31 Now they shall eat the fruit of their behavior
    And be gorged on their own devices.
32 Thus the waywardness of the witless will be the death
    of them,
    And the carelessness of fools will destroy them:
33 But he who listens to me will dwell assured [in mind],
    Untroubled by fear of calamity.

NOTES

i 1–6. The title of the Book of Proverbs is adapted from the titles
of two older collections of proverbs which were incorporated in it (x 1,
xxv 1) in line with the tradition which glorified Solomon as the wisest of
all men and the author of three thousand proverbs (I Kings iv 29–34
EVV, x 1–8). (On the authorship and dates of the several parts of the
book and the connection of these and other Wisdom writings with the
historical Solomon, see General Introduction.)

The Preface in vss. 2–6 states the purpose of the editor to provide
a textbook which would serve for the intellectual awakening and moral
training of youth, and which at the same time the educated man might
study with profit. The series of clauses is syntactically dependent on the
title and with it forms a single unbroken sentence. This recalls the form

of the prefatory paragraph of the Egyptian Wisdom work, *The Instruction of Amen-em-ope:*

> The beginning of the teaching of life, the testimony for prosperity, all precepts for intercourse with elders, . . . to know how to return an answer, . . . to make him prosper upon earth, . . . to steer him away from evil . . . (ANET, p. 421b).

This work served also as a model for the writer of xxii 17–xxiv 22 (see below). It is an example of a distinctive type of didactic treatises in which an Egyptian ruler or high official is represented as instructing his son in the conduct requisite for success as a ruler or administrator. The editor of Proverbs has the broader objective of the intellectual and moral training of youth for life in the Jewish community, although presumably only members of well-to-do families would have the leisure and resources to avail themselves of opportunities for education (xvii 16). The Preface includes much of the favorite terminology of the Wisdom teachers.

1. *wise sayings.* The Hebrew word *māšāl* has a wider connotation than the English word "proverb"—a short, pithy, and often figurative saying in common use—though it includes such sayings (I Sam xxiv 13 EVV). Its root meaning is "likeness, pattern, rule," and often it has the added sense of a profound or mysterious utterance which has in it effective power (Num xxiii 7; Jer xxiv 9). Hence it may be used of a prophetic oracle (Isa xiv 4), of an allegory or riddle (Ezek xvii 2), of a taunt (Deut xxviii 37), of a solemn declaration (Job xxvii 1), a didactic poem (Ps lxxviii 2), or an admonitory discourse (Prov 2). The proverbs in poetic couplets which make up most of chs. x–xxii 16 and xxv–xxix are distinctive but not unique (see General Introduction).

2. *wisdom (ḥokmāh)* is the subject and goal of education in the Wisdom school, *moral discipline* is its method and process.

5. *find guidance.* Literally "steering." The word is related to that for "rope"; in Job xxxvii 12 God "steers" the clouds across the sky.

6. *metaphor.* Parable, allusion requiring interpretation, e.g., vs. 17; LXX "dark saying."

riddles. Originally puzzles propounded in a contest of wits (Judg xiv 12–18; II Kings x 1; I Esdras iii 4–41); here probably a teacher's elicitation of the right response to a statement or question, cf. xxvi 20a, 20b, xxx 24–28.

7. The motto stands by itself between the Preface and the first of the admonitory discourses which make up most of chs. i–ix. In a slightly different form it stands also (ix 10) at their conclusion, just as the motto of Ecclesiastes, "A vapor of vapors, All is vapor," marks the beginning and end of that book. (See also Ps cxi 10; Job xxviii 28.) The translation given inverts the subject and predicate of the first sentence (RSV:

"The fear of the Lord is the beginning of knowledge") because the second line and the general context show that this is intended as a statement about knowledge rather than about religion.

first principle. Literally "beginning," either "first in order" as in Gen i 1, or "first in importance" as in Amos vi 1: this translation preserves the ambiguity, as does the quotation and paraphrase of this verse in Sirach i 14–15.

to hold the Lord in awe. Literally "the fear of Yahweh." "Yahweh," wrongly vocalized as "Jehovah," was the personal name of the God of Israel; for reasons of reverence the honorific title "the Lord" was substituted for it some centuries before the Christian era, in reading from the Hebrew Bible; to indicate this the vowels of the word for "Lord" were combined with the consonants of "Yahweh." This practice of substituting "the Lord" for the proper name was followed in the ancient Greek and Latin versions and is adopted here with most modern translations, since the use of a proper name for God belongs to a world of thought where Yahweh was thus distinguished from other gods. *To hold . . . in awe* or "fear" is used in different contexts in OT with varying intensity of meaning: numinous awe (Job xxxvii 23–24), healthy respect (Exod ix 30), humble obedience (Jer xxvi 19), deep and genuine piety (Gen xxii 12). In I Kings viii 43 and II Kings xvii 27–28 it refers to the worship of Yahweh adopted by non-Israelites. In Prov xxiv 21 a man is enjoined "to fear the Lord and the king." Here in i 7 the reference is clearly to belief in God as the necessary premise to the understanding of truth and the acquisition of learning. The author further develops his meaning in iii 5–12; to fear God is to rely on him rather than on one's own unaided intelligence, to avoid wrongdoing, and to accept misfortune as a God-sent discipline. In Isa xi 2–3 the wisdom of the ideal king is similarly associated with knowledge of God which is the fruit of belief, trust, and humble submission to him.

8–19. The first of the series of admonitory discourses in chs. i–ix calls on the youth, when tempted by the plausible suggestion of bad companions that violent crime is a safe and easy way to wealth, to be faithful to the moral training received from his parents. The warning is conveyed through a starkly realistic portrayal of scheming bandits and the retribution which inevitably overtakes them. Doubtless the illustration is intended to have a wider application, since, as the prophets declared, all commercial dishonesty and greed is in principle a crime of violence against one's own people (Amos iii 9–10; Mic iii 1–3). This discourse is probably out of place in ch. i; like chs. iii–vii it develops part of what is said in the programmatic ch. ii. See General Introduction.

8. *My son.* The customary form of address in Egyptian, Babylonian,

Assyrian, and Jewish Wisdom books (ANET, pp. 412–21, 427–28; cf. Eccles xii 12; Tobit iv 5 ff.; Sirach ii 1, iii 1). The convention was derived from the fact that the primary responsibility for moral instruction of sons lay with the father (Deut vi 7; Prov iv 3–4); a father's final admonitions, like David's last words to Solomon (I Kings ii 1–9), of Tobit to Tobias (Tobit iv), and of the vizier Ptah-hotep (ANET, p. 412) were particularly significant. A prophet similarly stood in a paternal relationship to his disciples (II Kings ii 12).

mother's teaching. For an illustration see xxxi 1–9.

9. *headdress.* A rare word, from a root "to wind, twist," hence presumably a turban of some sort. Authority and honor were marked by a special headdress (Ps viii 5 EV; II Sam i 10; Job xix 9).

necklace. A masculine adornment, probably of wrought silver or beads. The lesson has in view young men whose home training lies behind them and who are now going out into the world; in their new-found freedom the moral principles learned from their parents will be their safeguard.

10. *entice.* Literally "make a fool of."

12. *Sheol* and *the Pit.* Name and byname of the underworld, a place of dust and worms, darkness and silence, where the shades persist as pale and feeble reflections of the men they have been (Isa xiv 9–11, xxvi 14, 19; Ps cxv 17; Eccles ix 10). Sheol is often pictured as a hungry monster, opening wide its mouth and never satisfied (Isa v 14; Prov xxx 15–16; cf. Num xvi 32–33). The verse perpetuates ideas and language which can be traced back to the ancient Canaanite myth of Baal and Anath, where the god Mot (death) reigns over the Pit, a land of filth beneath the earth, and *swallows up* Baal and all who "go down into the earth" (ANET, pp. 135, 139–40). The figure survives *in reverse* in late eschatological prophecy; the Lord in turn "will swallow up death for ever" (Isa xxv 8).

14. *Throw in your lot . . . common purse.* Literally "Cast your lot among us," i.e., either "be one of us when we cast lots to divide the proceeds," or figuratively, "join us, associate your fate with ours." Lots, small objects of stone or ivory possibly resembling dice, were used to discover what was fated or what was God's will—in the division of land (Num xxxiii 54), selection of persons (Judg xx 9), detection of the guilty (Jon i 7). Hence a lot could mean also "an allotment" (Josh xvii 1) or "fate" (Isa xvii 14). The *purse* or "pouch" may have been that in which the lots were kept; or the sentence may mean simply "we shall share and share alike."

17. A popular proverb of the type of our "It's too late to lock the stable door when the horse is stolen"; such sayings often are used as

maxims to clinch an argument. The snaring of wild birds for food or for sacrifice was the occupation of the fowler, who sold them from cages in the market (Jer v 26–27). The Mosaic Law listed birds which might be eaten (Deut xiv 11–20). The practice indicates the relative poverty of the country. Domestic poultry were possessed only by the wealthy; cf. the cock pictured on the seventh-century seal of "Jaazaniah, officer of the king" (G. E. Wright, *Biblical Archaeology*, Philadelphia, 1957, p. 177).

18. Criminals are less intelligent than birds, for they fail to see that they will be caught in the trap of their own violence (cf. xxvi 27).

20–33. Here and in ch. viii the sage personifies the Wisdom he is commending to his pupils in two remarkable poems in which Wisdom addresses men on her own behalf. It is clear from the concluding verses of the second poem (viii 32–36) that the teacher himself is speaking in figurative language. But the vivid personification reflects the imagery of older mythological material. Such personification contributes to the imaginative power and vigor of much OT poetry. It is applied to inanimate nature (Pss xcvi 11–12, cxiv 3–7; Isa i 2; Job xxviii 14), to cities and peoples (Isa xl 2, 9; Amos v 2), to concepts like love, jealousy, and death (Song of Sol viii 6; Hos xiii 14), and to marks or attributes of the divine presence (Ps lxxxv 9–13 EV). In addition to the longer poems in chs. i and viii, the Wisdom which is God's gift (ii 6) is personified as a woman in iv 5–9, vii 4; and in the parable in ix 1–6. The resemblance to prophetic oracles of what Wisdom says to men here and in ch. viii, in appeal, denunciation, threat and promise, suggests at first that Wisdom is being personified as a prophetess. Yet she is not pictured as a messenger conveying to man an oracle beginning "Thus saith the Lord. . . ." Rather she speaks for herself, and with her own authority, like a goddess. This does not suggest that the sage had any place in his theology for divine beings in addition to Yahweh, even though subordinate. Nevertheless he personifies Yahweh's attribute of wisdom in terms which seem to be derived ultimately from ancient representations of a goddess of wisdom. In particular, the mocking laugh at man's deserved calamities has a mythological rather than a prophetic sound, recalling the laughter of the goddess Anath when she does battle with her enemies, in the Ugaritic myth of Baal and Anath (ANET, p. 136a), cf. Ps ii 4. See further comments on ch. viii below.

20. *Wisdom*. Here the word is an unusual and probably an archaic Canaanite form (*ḥokmōt*). This does not necessarily mean that the poem itself is derived from an ancient source, since the same form is found in an adage in xxiv 7 and in a Wisdom psalm (Ps xlix 3 EV).

21. Where traffic converged at the fortified gateways of a walled city

was a usual place for public assembly (Ruth iv 11), for a market (II Kings vii 1), and for the adjudication of disputes (Amos v 15).

22. *simpletons* and *brazen*. Two grades of fool.

insolent ones. Usually translated "scoffers," these are the reckless and derisive, the very antithesis of the prudent and reserved wise man (x 19).

23. *thought*. Literally "spirit."

24. *Beckoned*. As in the gesture of a public speaker (Acts xxi 40).

2. THE SECOND DISCOURSE
(ii 1–22)

The Benefits of an Earnest Search for Wisdom

II

1   My son, if you will accept what I tell you
      And will treasure my injunctions,
2   With your ears attuned to wisdom,
      Setting your mind on understanding,
3   If you will even cry aloud for insight
      And raise your voice for understanding,
4   If you will search for it as men search for silver
      And hunt it like hidden treasure—
5   Then you will perceive what "reverence for the Lord" is,
      And discover what it means to know God.
6   For it is the Lord who gives wisdom,
      It is he who teaches knowledge and discernment,
7   He is the secret of upright men's good judgment,
      The shield of virtuous lives,
8   Guarding the paths of the just,
      And vigilant for those devoted to him;
9   Thus[a] you will come to discern what is right and just,
      And the way you go will be good.[b]
10 For wisdom will enter your mind
      And knowledge will be a joy to your spirit,
11 Discretion will become your mentor
      And understanding your protector,

[a] Heb. "then."
[b] Literally "you will step forward on every good path," reading *te'ešar* for MT *ūmēšārīm* "and uprightness."

12   Saving you from the way of the wicked,
         And from the man whose speech is perverse,
13   From those who forsake paths of honesty,
         Walking in ways of darkness,
14   Who find their pleasure in wrongdoing
         And delight in the perversity of evil,
15   Men whose paths are crooked, and their ways devious—
16   Saving you also from "the adulteress*,"
         From "the stranger woman" with her seductive words,
17   Who forsakes the companion of her youth,
         Forgetting her pledge before God—
18   Indeed, her house is the slope down to death
         And her tracks lead to where the shades are;
19   None who visit her ever come back
         Nor set foot on the paths of the living.
20   But you will have good men for companions
         If you keep to the paths of the just,
21   For the upright shall live on in the world,
         And the blameless shall survive in it;
22   But the wicked's life on earth will be cut short,
         And lawless men will be torn up by the roots*.

*Literally "an alien woman."
*Reading *yusshū,* for MT *yisshū,* "they will uproot."

NOTES

ii 1–22. This chaper is a kind of prospectus of the "course" in wisdom which the teacher offers, and probably it originally preceded the discourse in i 8–19 in the original sequence of chs. i–ix. This is the only one of the ten discourses to begin with a protasis, stating the prerequisites for the successful pursuit of wisdom (vss. 1–4); the others begin with authoritative admonitions. Chapter ii forms a single periodic sentence in the original, and it is not accidental that it consists of twenty-two verses, the number of letters in the Hebrew alphabet. The apodosis is in five parts: vss. 5–8, on the knowledge of God which comes with growth in wisdom and without which wisdom cannot be obtained (cf. i 7); vss. 9–11, on growth in moral understanding; vss. 12–15, on the resulting deliverance from the ways of wicked men; vss. 16–19, on escaping the clutches of "the adulteress"; and vss. 20–22, on the meaning and rewards of an upright life. Evidently the purpose of this chapter is programmatic, since its several parts are later resumed as the subjects of separate discourses.

4. The same figure of the arduous search for precious metals appears in the striking poem on the inscrutable source of wisdom, in Job xxxviii.

5. Wisdom starts from and ends with religion.

16. *"the adulteress"* and *"the stranger woman."* In quotation marks because the words here have a double meaning, a literal and a symbolic. When this subject is resumed in later discourses (v 1–14, 15–23, vi 24–35, vii 5–27) the ideas and phraseology are markedly similar. Since "Wisdom" is correlated throughout with "reverence for the Lord," by inference "the adulteress" represents both folly and the seductive way of life associated with pagan religion. The figure of marital unfaithfulness for the lapse of Israel into idolatry is familiar from the writings of the prophets (Hos i–iii; Jer ii–iii). The figure was particularly appropriate because of the practice of cultic prostitution associated with Canaanite religion. Here in Proverbs also the stern warning against adultery has in view not only the looser morals of the "foreign" or non-Jewish members of the community, but specifically the offering of themselves by female devotees of the Astarte or a similar cult. It seems clear from ii 17, vi 26, vii 19 that these were chiefly married women, so that the teacher is renewing also the traditional condemnation of sexual aberration and marital infidelity (Exod xx 14; Lev xx 10; Deut xxvii 20–23). The similarity of the language of the *Instruction of Ani,* from the end of the Egyptian empire is striking: "Be on thy guard against a woman from abroad. . . . Do not know her carnally: a deep water . . . (is) a woman who is far away from her husband. . . . She has no witnesses when she waits to ensnare thee" (ANET, p. 420).

17. *the companion of her youth.* Her husband.

her pledge before God. Her marriage covenant; cf. Mal ii 14.

18–19. For the figure, cf. v 5, vii 27, ix 18; the language is an echo from the Akkadian "Descent of Ishtar to the Nether World," "to the dark house . . . , to the house which none leave who enter it, to the road from which there is no way back" (ANET, p. 107a).

18. *death* in Proverbs means untimely death, the penalty of folly. Ptah-hotep also speaks of death as the consequence of adultery (ANET, p. 413a).

21. The promise of "possessing the land" to those who obey Yahweh's commandments is traditional (Gen xvii 8; Deut iv 1); it recurs in Messianic prophecy (Jer xxiii 5–6) and in the Beatitudes of Jesus (Matt v 5).

3. THE THIRD DISCOURSE; TWO POEMS; THE FOURTH DISCOURSE
(iii 1–35)

The Rewards of the Religious and Disciplined Life (Third Discourse)

III

1 My son, forget not my teachings
   And take my instructions to heart,

2 For in a long life and a full one
   They will ensure felicity.

3 Let kindness and fidelity be with you always[a],
   Fasten them round your throat,
   Write them on the tablet of your mind;[b]

4 So you will find favor and approval in the sight of God
     and man.

5 Trust in the Lord wholeheartedly
   And do not rely solely on your own intelligence;

6 Recognize him in whatever you do
   For it is he who will keep your paths straight.

7 Do not pride yourself on your wisdom,
   Revere the Lord and avoid what is wrong;

8 This will bring health to your body[c]
   And give fresh life to your bones.

9 Honor the Lord from your possessions
   And from the first returns of all your revenue;

[a] Literally "not leave you."
[b] The third line may have been added from vii 3; it is omitted here in Mss. B and S of LXX.
[c] Reading *bāśār*, "flesh, body," for MT *šōr*, "navel."

10   Then your bins will be filled with grain
         And your vats will overflow with new wine.
11   Disdain not the Lord's discipline, my son,
         Nor resent it when he corrects you,
12   For the one whom the Lord loves he corrects,
         As a father the son he delights in.

The Precious Gifts (A Poem)

13   How blest is the man who finds wisdom!
         The one who has gained understanding!
14   For her profit is more than profit of silver,
         And her reward greater than payment in fine gold.
15   She is more precious than jewels,
         And nothing you desire can compare with her.
16   Long life she proffers with her right hand,
         With her left hand riches and honor.
17   Her ways are ways to delight,
         And all her paths lead to felicity.
18   She is a "tree of life" to those who take hold of her;
         Fortunate are they who [can] hold her fast.

Divine Origin of Wisdom (A Poem)

19   The Lord by wisdom founded the world,
         By reason he established the heavens,
20   Through his knowledge the watery deeps burst forth
         And the skies drip dew.

The Security and Obligations of the Wise (Fourth Discourse)

21   My son, cherish sound judgment and foresight,
         Never lose sight of them,

22 They will be the life of your spirit,
      [Like] a graceful ornament at your throat;
23 Then you will go safely on your way
      And your foot will not stumble;
24 When you lie down you need have no fear,
      When you take your rest you will sleep well.
25 Have no dread of sudden alarms
      Or that wicked men will come storming against you,
26 For the Lord will be at your side
      And will keep you from stepping into a trap.

27 [Do not refuse help to one who has need of it
      When you have from God the power to give it;
28 Do not say to your neighbor, "Come back later,"
      Or "Tomorrow I will give it," when you have it with
        you.
29 Do not plot harm to your neighbor
      While he sits unsuspecting in your company.
30 Do not dispute with a man without cause,
      When he has done you no injury.]

31 Do not envy a ruffian nor imitate any of his ways,
32 For a perverse man is an abomination to the Lord,
      Whereas the upright are in his confidence.
33 The Lord's curse rests on the house of a wicked man,
      But his blessing is on the abode of the just.
34 He will defy the defiant, but show kindness to the
        humble.
35 Wise men will inherit honor,
      Fools will but heighten [their] shame.

NOTES

iii 1–12. This discourse resumes the theme of the motto of the book
(i 7) and of vss. 5–8 in the programmatic ch. ii. It consists of six
quatrains, each beginning with an exhortation which is then followed by
the promise of a special reward for obedience to it. This structure, to-

gether with the common subject, distinguishes the third discourse from the fourth which begins with vs. 13; the recurrence in vs. 11 of the words "my son" has misled some commentators into thinking that the fourth discourse begins at that point.

2. *a long life and a full one.* A traditional mark of divine favor (Exod xx 12). "Abundant life" (John x 10) was also seen as the fruit of the higher wisdom (cf. viii 18, 35, and the concluding words of Ptah-hotep's *Instruction,* ANET, p. 414b).

felicity. Heb. *šālōm,* "wholeness, harmonious well-being."

3. *kindness and fidelity.* The quality of the relationship of the true son to his father (Gen xlvii 29), of Yahweh to his people (Exod xxxiv 6), and of a covenant of friendship (Josh ii 14).

4. Cf. "in favor with God and man," Luke ii 52.

8. *fresh life.* Literally "refreshment."

11–12. A necessary corrective of the idea which might be derived mistakenly from the previous verses that prosperity will always accompany piety. The good man's suffering remained a problem to the prophets (Jer xx 7–8; Hab i 3), the psalmists (Pss xxxvii 1 ff., lxxiii 12–14) and the Wisdom writers (Job ix 22–24, x 1–3; Eccles ix 2). The explanation of such suffering as a beneficent divine discipline is found also in Hos vi 1; Ps xciv 12–13; Job v 17.

13–18, 19–20. Two short poems in praise of wisdom here interrupt the series of didactic addresses. Although independent, they appear to have been joined before the composition of ch. viii which seems to be based on them. The first poem, vss. 13–18, is a beautifully finished expansion of the exclamatory blessing with which it opens. The second poem, vss. 19–20, is a single quatrain which may once have formed part of a longer composition (cf. Pss civ 24, cxxxvi 5 ff.).

13. *How blest.* Literally "the blessedness of . . . !" an idiom characteristic of Wisdom poetry (cf. Ps i 1; Prov viii 34; Matt v 3–11).

15. *jewels.* Necklaces of pearls or coral.

17. It seems literary sacrilege to substitute this modern rendering for two of the loveliest lines in KJ: "Her ways are ways of pleasantness, and all her paths are peace." The translator may be forgiven if his rendering makes the meaning a little clearer.

18. *"tree of life."* Put in quotation marks to indicate that it is a traditional figure for "health, long life," derived from Gen ii 9, iii 22 and ultimately from Mesopotamian mythology and glyptic art (cf. *Epic of Gilgamesh,* ANET, p. 96b). It recurs as a feature of prophetic and apocalyptic eschatological imagery (Ezek xlvii 12; Rev ii 7, xxii 2). Sirach xxiv 12–17 pictures wisdom as a rich and beautiful fruit tree.

See also W. F. Albright, "The Goddess of Life and Wisdom," AJSL 36
(1919–20), 258–94.

19. *wisdom.* The attribute of God displayed especially in his works of
creation (Isa xl 12–14, 28; Jer x 12; Pss civ 24, cxxxvi 5; Job ix 10,
xxxviii–xxxix). The personification of wisdom in chs. i and viii must
be viewed in the light of these passages.

20. *watery deeps burst forth.* An echo of Gen vii 11 where the water
which submerged the world in the days of Noah is said to have surged
up like a tide from the subterranean ocean and fallen from sluices in
the sky.

dew. Believed to fall from the night sky; it was a precious gift of
Providence (Mic v 7 EV).

21–35. Some discontinuity in this discourse results from the insertion
in vss. 27–30 of four negative admonitions which have only a slight
relationship with their context. These verses can be distinguished also
by their form, which omits the religious reason given for observing the
injunctions preceding and following them.

22. *life of your spirit.* Fullness of life, as in vs. 2.

27. *who has need of it.* Literally "to whom it belongs"; cf. xi 24.

have from God the power. A traditional expression recognizing the
conditional nature of human powers.

28. LXX here inserts an extra line from xxvii 1b as a reason for the
command.

29. Cf. xxiii 7, xxvi 24–26.

31. *imitate.* Literally "choose."

32. *are in his confidence.* Or "he takes counsel"; cf. Amos iii 7.

4. THE FIFTH DISCOURSE; THE SIXTH DISCOURSE; THE SEVENTH DISCOURSE
(iv 1–27, v 21–23)

Fifth Discourse: Wisdom as an Inheritance

IV

1 Hear, my sons*, a father's admonition,
   Pay attention, that you may grow in understanding,
2 For it is good advice that I give you,
   [So] do not treat my teaching with indifference.
3 When I myself was a son with my father,
   At a tender age my mother's darling*,
4 His words as my teacher were these—
   "Let your mind grasp firmly what I tell you,
   Keep my instructions if you would find life.
5 Get wisdom! Get understanding!
   Neither forget nor stray from what I tell you.
6 Forsake not Wisdom and she will protect you,
   Love her, and she will preserve you.
7 [As the first of your wealth* acquire wisdom,
   And whatever you get, get understanding.]
8 Embrace her and she will exalt you,
   She will bring you honor if you hold her fast,
9 She will provide for your head a graceful garland,
   And will bestow on you a crown of beauty."

a Heb. "O sons."
b Reading *yādīd*, "beloved," with LXX, for *yāhīd*, "only."
c Reading *hōnkā*, "your wealth," for *hokmāh*, "wisdom."

Sixth Discourse: The Two Ways of Life

10 Hear, my son, and accept my advice,
That many years of life may be yours.
11 I am directing you to wisdom's way,
And setting your feet on the right paths.
12 Where your pace will not be retarded,
Where when you run you will not stumble.
13 Keep up your training without weakening;
Guard it as you would guard your life!
14 Do not venture on the path of evil men,
Nor put your foot on the same road as the wicked;
15 Avoid it! Do not cross it! Make a detour and keep on
your way.
16 For the wicked cannot rest until they have done harm,
They are robbed of sleep unless they have tripped
someone up;
17 For wickedness is the bread that nourishes them
And they drink violence like wine.
18 The ongoing life of good men is like the light of dawn
That grows ever brighter until full day;
19 The wicked walk in a deep darkness
Where they cannot perceive what it is that trips them
up.

Seventh Discourse: On Self-Discipline

20 My son, attend to my words
And listen carefully to my injunctions,
21 Keep them constantly in view,
Cherish them in your heart of hearts;
22 For they mean life to him who possesses them
And health to his whole body.
23 With utmost vigilance watch your thoughts
For from them flow the springs of life.

24   Avoid deceitfulness in speech,
         Let there be no trace of dishonesty in what you say.
25   Keep your eyes on the road ahead; look straight forward;
26   Watch where you are going, so as to step only on firm
            ground.
27   Turn neither to right nor to left;
         Walk away from evil.

V

21   For where a man goes is plainly visible to the Lord,
         And all his paths are under observation.
22   The wicked man's guilty acts will catch up with him,
         He will be entangled in the ropes of his own sin;
23   He will die, because he is undisciplined
         And in his great folly he has gone astray.

NOTES

iv 1–9. The usual structure of these discourses—summons to listen,
motivation, admonitions, consequences—is here varied by the quotation
of a discourse within the discourse.
   5. *Get*. In the sense "obtain at a cost."
   6. *Wisdom*. A feminine noun, here capitalized because of the quasi-
personification in vss. 6, 8–9.
   7. This verse seems intrusive, and is omitted in LXX. For *hōn*,
"wealth," cf. iii 9, vi 31, viii 18, etc.
   9. *garland*. Or "headdress"; see NOTE on i 9.

10–18. The pointed contrast of two paths of life, as in Ps i 6 and
elsewhere, marks the application to individual conduct of Deuteronomic
teaching about the choice lying before Israel as the People of God.
In Deut viii, e.g., "the way" is (i) the way in which God has led his
people (vss. 2–5); (ii) the way of obedience to God's commands (vs. 6);
and (iii) the forked road into the future, where obedience will lead to
blessing, and disobedience, to curse (vss. 7–20; cf. ch. xxviii, xxx 15–20;
Jer xxi 8). In Proverbs "the way" refers to the ongoing experience of
life (xx 24), to conduct (i 15, ii 12–13, iii 31, etc.), and to the consequences of conduct (iii 17, iv 26, etc.).

10. *advice*. Literally "words."

17. *drink violence like wine*. Literally "drink the wine of violent deeds."

18. *until full day*. Or "until high noon," literally "until day is established." The felicitous rendering of KJ is justly famous: "But the path of the just is as the shining light, that shineth more and more unto the perfect day."

iv 20–27, v 21–23. The discourse beginning in iv 20–27 lacks the usual concluding statement of consequences, whereas in v 21–23 there is such a statement which is more suitable following iv 27 than in its present location. Hence the two passages are here combined. LXX in fact supplies two extra verses as a conclusion to iv 20–27, but they do not appear to be original.

iv 23. *thoughts*. Heb. "heart," the seat and symbol of intelligence and will rather than of emotion.

24. Falsehood and dissimulation are repeatedly condemned by Wisdom teachers; cf. x 18, xii 17–20, xxi 6; so in Egyptian and Akkadian Wisdom, cf. *Amen-em-ope,* ch. 10; *Ahiqar,* ix (ANET, pp. 422a, 429b).

25. *on the road ahead*. Literally "straight ahead."

26. *step only on firm ground*. Literally "that all your ways may be established."

v 21. This thought of the all-seeing eye of God is adduced again in xv 3, 11, and xxiv 12 as a reason for doing what is right.

5. THE EIGHTH DISCOURSE
(v 1–14)

The Misery to which Adultery Leads

V
1 My son, attend to my wisdom,
    And lend your ear to my insight,
2 That you may come to treasure discretion,
    And the knowledge I speak may protect you,
    (May preserve you from the adulteress,
    From the "stranger woman" with her smooth talk)[a].
3 For the "stranger woman's" lips drip with honey
    And her mouth is smoother than oil;
4 But in the end she will turn bitter as wormwood
    And will cut like a two-edged sword.
5 Her feet lead the way down to death,
    Her steps come surely to Sheol,
6 She gives no heed to life's path,
    Her tracks stray whither she knows not.
7 So now, my son[b], listen to me,
    Depart not from my instructions:
8 Keep far away from her,
    Approach not the door of her house,
9 Lest you give up your honor to others
    And your worth to one without mercy,

[a] The second couplet is copied from vii 5; see introductory NOTE to this section.
[b] *My son*, singular as in LXX, Vulg., and vss. 8–12. The final consonant of *bnym* apparently is an enclitic *m* mistaken for a plural ending, which led to the corresponding change in the number of the verbs.

10   Lest strangers devour your strength
         And you must toil in an alien's household,
11   Until at last you bemoan your fate,
         When flesh and body are wasted—
12   Saying, "Why did I resist discipline?
         O why did I resent reproof?
13   I did not heed the voice of my teachers,
         Nor pay attention to my instructors;
14   Now I am facing final ruin
         In the [judicial] assembly and the community.

NOTES

v 1–14. For a reason which is not altogether clear, the four warnings against "the adulteress," ii 16–19, v 1–14, vi 24–35, and vii 5–27 (see NOTE on ii 16) begin abruptly in each of these contexts without a clear connection with what precedes (except possibly at vi 24). Three of these passages begin with almost identical words (ii 16, vi 24, and vii 5), and part of this opening also appears here in v 3. It seems that a couplet corresponding to vi 24 and vii 5 has dropped out after v 2 owing to the fact that vs. 2 and the missing lines began with the same word; this has been restored in the translation.

2. *the adulteress . . . the "stranger woman."* See NOTE on ii 16.

3. *drip with honey.* May refer to kisses rather than to words; cf. Song of Sol iv 11, vii 9.

4. *will cut.* Literally "will be sharp."

5. *come surely to.* Literally "grasp."

Sheol. See NOTE on i 12.

9. *worth.* Or "dignity," from a root *s-n-y*, "to be exalted"; cf. D. W. Thomas, WIANE, p. 286, fn. 8.

one without mercy. I.e., death (cf. vs. 5). Others interpret of the vengeful husband (cf. vi 34–35).

10. *you must toil.* Or, "the fruits of your toil will be."

6. FOUR EXPANDED PROVERBS
AND A NUMERICAL SAYING
(v 15–19, vi 22, v 20, vi 1–19)

On Marital Fidelity

V

15 [As the saying is], "Drink water from your own cistern,"
    And fresh water from your own well,
16 Lest your springs overflow in public
    Like rivulets in the open streets—
17 Springs which should be yours only,
    Not to be shared with strangers.
18 Be grateful for your own fountain,
    And have your pleasure with the wife of your youth;
19 A lovable doe! A sweet little mountain goat!
    May her breasts always intoxicate you!
    May you ever find rapture in loving her!

VI

22 Whatever you do, she will help you;
    When you lie down to rest she will cherish you,
    And when you awake she will talk with you.

V

20 Why should you swoon over the fruit of a "stranger
    woman"*a*,
    And clutch the bosom of a foreigner?

a b*e*nīb zārāḥ, for MT b*e*nī b*e*zārāh.

On Rash Pledges

VI

1 My son, if you have mortgaged yourself for your
      neighbor,
    Or have struck a bargain with a foreigner,

2 You have been ensnared by the words of your mouth,
    And are caught by what you have promised;

3 Do this at once, my son, to save yourself—
    For you are now in your neighbor's power—
    Go about looking disconsolate; pester your friend;

4 Give yourself no sleep; do not close your eyes,

5 [Until you] escape like a gazelle from a hunter's hand,[b]
    Like a bird from a fowler's snare[c].

On Sloth

6 Go watch an ant, you loafer!
    Observe her behavior and become wise!

7 Though she has no chieftain, overseer, or ruler,

8 She makes sure of her [year's] food in the summer,
    She gathers her provisions at harvest time.

9 How long, you loafer, will you lie there?
    How long until you rise from your sleep?

10 "A little more sleep, a little more slumber,
    a little longer with hands folded in repose"—

11 And poverty will overtake you like a vagabond,
    And destitution like a beggar man.

[b] *miyyad ṣayyād*, the second word having been omitted through homoio-
teleuton.
[c] *mippaḥ*, for MT *miyyad*; cf. Ps. xci 3.

On Rascality

12   A knave or a villain is never straightforward;
13   He winks his eyes, makes signs with his feet, points with
         his fingers;
14   His malicious mind is always thinking of some evil
         scheme,
      Or stirring up discord;
15   Therefore disaster will overtake him suddenly,
      And the moment will come when he is ruined beyond
         recovery.

Seven Vices Hateful to the Lord (A Numerical Saying)

16   There are six things the Lord hates,
      And seven that he abominates,
17   Proud eyes, a lying tongue,
      Hands that shed the blood of the innocent,
18   A mind full of evil schemes,
      Feet running toward wrong;
19   A false witness breathing out lies,
      And one who stirs up quarrels between brothers.

NOTES

v 15–19, vi 22, v 20, vi 1–19. The series of didactic discourses with
a common structure is interrupted at this point by the insertion of these
five short independent admonitions. The first four, dealing respectively
with marital infidelity (v 15–19, vi 22, v 20), rash pledges (vi 1–5), sloth
(vi 6–11) and rascality (vi 12–15), resemble some of the more dis-
cursive treatments of proverbial themes in the later collections (e.g., xxiii
1–8, 29–35, xxiv 30–34, xxvii 23–27), rather than the couplet form
which predominates in chs. x–xxii 16 and xxv–xxix. The fifth, vi 16–19,
is a statement which resembles in form the numerical proverbs or riddles
found in xxx 15–31, but in substance it is a cultic declaration like Ps xv.

There is evidence of disarrangement at this point in chs. i–ix: in the separation of the two parts of the Seventh Discourse (iv 20–27 and v 21–23), and in the displacement of vi 22, which appears to belong between v 19 and v 20. The warning against marital infidelity has been inserted here by the editor as appropriately following the Eighth Discourse, and indeed some scholars have taken it to be a continuation of the latter. But in structure and language it differs from the discourses which warn against adultery; indeed, it is primarily a positive commendation of faithfulness in marriage, and a little homily on the text of the figurative maxim which serves as its opening line. Apparently when it was attached as appropriate to the end of the Eighth Discourse it brought with it the succeeding independent admonitions in vi 1–19 which have been generally recognized as intrusive here.

v 15. A metaphorical maxim like xxv 16a is here quoted and expanded upon, as another popular adage in xxvi 27a is variously developed in xxvi 27b, xxviii 10; Eccles x 8–9; Ps vii 15 EV. For the figure of a woman as a spring satisfying sexual thirst, cf. Song of Sol iv 12, 15. A cistern usually was privately owned (II Kings xviii 31; Jer xxxviii 6), which gives point to the metaphor.

16. The husband's unfaithfulness may lead to the promiscuity of his wife.

18. *Be grateful for.* Literally "let it be blessed" (i.e., by you).

19. *breasts.* Or, "love"; cf. vii 18.

vi 22. Apparently belongs after vs. 19.

v 20. For the eating of fruit as another metaphor for sexual intercourse, cf. Song of Sol iv 13–16; *Epic of Gilgamesh* vi, 8 (ANET, p. 83b).

vi 1. The urgency of this warning and its parallels in xi 15, xvii 18, xx 16=xxvii 13, xxii 26–27, together with its listing here along with cautions against vices like adultery, sloth, and villainy, indicates that what is intended is more than a simple counsel of prudence in financial transactions. The pledge involves the risk of being reduced to abject poverty or even to slavery (xx 16, xxii 26–27; Gen xliv 32–33; II Kings iv 1), especially if it is a bargain with a foreigner (cf. xi 15, xx 16). Deut xv 2–3 shows that business transactions between Israelites and non-Israelites were conducted more ruthlessly than within the community itself. The warning, then, is against lightly risking irreparable harm. If through careless words or vanity one has done so, no time is to be lost in obtaining release from the arrangement, which apparently has been agreed to but not yet carried into effect.

6. *ant.* Mentioned in the OT only here and in xxx 24–28, where again it is an example of the wisdom of small creatures. Albright points

to a Canaanite aphorism in the Amarna letters: "When [even] ants are smitten, they do not accept it [passively], but they bite the hand of the man who smites them" (ANET, p. 486a).

loafer. The *'āṣēl* is the object of much scorn and ridicule in Proverbs (x 26, xiii 4, xv 19, xix 24, xxii 13, xxvi 13–16). Chapter xxiv 30–34 is an expanded comment resembling the present one, and concludes with the same words.

11. *beggar man. mōgēn* or *maggān*, as suggested by Ugaritic (W. F. Albright, "Some Canaanite-Phoenician Sources of Hebrew Wisdom," WIANE, pp. 9–10).

12. *never straightforward.* Or, "always dishonest [crafty] in speech." A similar description of a corrupt person, with a prediction of his coming to a bad end, occurs in xxvi 23–26. This "prophetic" form is unusual in Proverbs.

13. By such gestures the rogue makes evil suggestions, but will not speak out.

winks. Cf. x 10, xvi 30.

makes signs. Literally "talks," by shuffling or tapping.

15. Cf. xxiv 22; xxix 1.

16. *six* and *seven.* The use of numerals in succession or in multiples is a characteristic feature of Semitic poetic parallelism, probably originating with the Sumerians. Familiar occurrences in the Bible are Amos i 3–ii 8; Prov xxx 15–33; Gen iv 24; cf. Matt xviii 22. In this form the first two lines display in synonymous parallelism the common quality or feature shared by the examples that follow. The larger figure corresponds with the total number of these, the smaller figure being its closest parallel term. When used, as here, to list things pleasing or displeasing to a god, the "counting" feature may have originally been intended to assist in remembering what the religious teacher or priest has declared. That the cultic form is very old is evident from its occurrence in the Ugaritic myth of *Baal and Anath* (II AB, iii 17–21, ANET, p. 132b):

> "Two [kinds of] banquets Baal hates,
> Three, the Rider of the Clouds,
> A banquet of shamefulness,
> A banquet of baseness,
> A banquet of handmaids' [lewdness]."

Adaptation of the cultic form to Wisdom teaching appears also in the proverbs of *Ahiqar* (Akkadian, but preserved in Aramaic, ANET, p. 428b):

"Two things are meet, and the third pleasing to Shamash:
One who drinks wine and gives it to drink,
One who guards wisdom, and one who hears a word and does not tell."

17. In the *Instruction of Amen-em-ope,* as here, moral offenses like lying are said to be "the abomination of the god" (cf. ANET, p. 423a). The term seems to have meant originally what was ritually forbidden (cf. Deut xii 31, xxiii 18). In Jer vii 9–10 the breaking of the Ten Commandments is described as "doing all these abominations." The vices condemned here form a list specially characteristic of Proverbs—proud eyes (iii 34, xxi 24, xxx 13), lying (xii 19, xvii 7, xxi 6), criminal violence (i 10–19, iv 14–17, xii 6).

18. Cf. i 16, vi 14, xix 2, xxiv 2, xxviii 22.

19. Cf. x 12, xii 17, xiv 5, xv 18, xxv 18, xxviii 25.

7. THE NINTH DISCOURSE
(vi 20–21, 23–35)

The Self-Destructive Folly of Adultery

VI

20 My son, keep your father's precepts,
      And do not stray from your mother's teaching,
21 Bind them continually to your breast,
      Wind them around your throat;*ᵃ*

23 For a maxim is a lamp, and a precept is a light,
      And rules of discipline point the way of life—
24 Keeping you from another man's wife*ᵇ*,
      And from the smooth tongue of the "stranger woman."
25 Do not in your thoughts lust for her beauty,
      Nor be captivated when she makes eyes at you.
26 A prostitute's price*ᶜ* is a loaf of bread,
      But a married woman hunts with keener appetite.
27 Can a man build a fire in his lap without burning his
      clothes?
28 Can he walk on red-hot coals without scorching his feet?
29 So it is with one who has intercourse with his neighbor's
      wife—
      He cannot be exonerated who touches her.
30 They do not acquit*ᵈ* a thief because he stole only to
      satisfy his hunger;

ᵃ Vs. 22 has been transferred to follow v 19.
ᵇ Reading with LXX *'ēšet rēᵃ'*, for MT *'ēšet rā'*, "bad woman."
ᶜ Taking *bᵉ'ad* as a noun meaning "exchange, price"; so G. R. Driver, VT 4
(1954), 244.
ᵈ Reading *yābērū*, for MT *yābūzū*, "they despise."

31   When he is caught he must pay seven times over,
      He gives up all the goods in his house.
32   One who commits adultery with a woman is senseless,
      And one who violates her destroys himself.
33   He will encounter blows and ignominy,
      And his disgrace will not be blotted out;
34   For jealousy inflames*e* a husband,
      He will show no mercy when he takes revenge,
35   He will not look at any compensation,
      Nor be mollified though you make him many gifts.

e Reading *tāḥēm,* for MT *ḥᵃmat,* "anger of"; cf. G. R. Driver, *Biblica* 32 (1951), 173 ff.

NOTES

vi 20–21, 23–35. After the usual opening commendation of moral education, this passage, like ii 16–19, v 1–14, vii 5–27, ix 13–18, turns to the subject of adultery with a married woman. In this case the penalty is disgrace and the fury of the jealous husband, rather than early descent to Sheol as in the other contexts.

24. The language of ii 16 and vii 5 has been modified to suit this passage.

26. *keener appetite.* Literally "costly desire." For the metaphor of eating for sexual intercourse, cf. xxx 20.

27. *a man . . . fire.* Heb. *'īš 'ēš* provides a wordplay on the preceding *'ēšet 'īš,* "a man's wife."

30. *They do not acquit.* Literally "they do not count pure."

32. *violates.* Literally "presses," a second meaning of the root *'-s-y.*

8. THE TENTH DISCOURSE
(vii 1–27)

The Temptress

VII

1   My son, guard my words and treasure my instructions;

2   Keep my instructions if you would find life,
     And my teaching like the pupil of your eye;

3   Bind them on your fingers,
     Inscribe them on the tablet of your mind—

4   Say to Wisdom, "You are my sister,"
     Call Discernment "Friend"—

5   To guard you from "the adulteress,"
     From the "stranger woman" with her seductive words.

6   For as I have gazed*ᵃ* from the window of my house
     And looked down from my lattice,

7   Watching the fools [below], I have observed among
       them*ᵇ* a silly youth

8   Passing by on the street near her corner,
     Strolling in the direction of her house,

9   In the dusk when evening was coming on,
     When the time for sleep comes with the darkness.

10   See—a woman comes to meet him,
     Dressed up as a prostitute and heavily veiled*ᶜ*,

11   Boisterous and bold, never at home,

12   Now in the street, now in the square,
     Lurking at every corner—

ᵃ The verb *hibbaṭtī* seems to have been omitted accidentally from MT after *bēī*.

ᵇ Reading *bēnēhem*, for MT *babbānīm*, "among the sons."

ᶜ Reading *ūneṣōrat lōṭ*, for MT *ūneṣūrat lēb*, "with secret plans in mind."

13   She catches hold of him and kisses him
      And with brazen face says to him—

14   "I have sacrificial meat on hand,
      For today I discharge my religious vows;

15   That is why I have come out to meet you,
      I was looking for you and I have found you.

16   I have spread coverlets on my couch,
      Of gaily colored linen from Egypt;

17   I have sprinkled my bed with myrrh, aloes, and
      cinnamon.

18   Come, let us drink deep of love,
      Till morning let us revel in love-making.

19   For my husband is not at home,
      He has gone on a distant journey,

20   He has taken the moneybag with him,
      He will not be home until the full moon."

21   She sways him with her many allurements,
      And by her smooth words she persuades him.

22   All at once he is walking with her,
      Like an ox being led to the slaughter,
      Like a stag prancing into captivity,[d]

23   Till an arrow pierces its heart;
      Like a bird darting into a snare,
      Not knowing its life is in danger.

24   So now, my son[e], listen to me,
      And pay attention to what I say.

25   Do not toy with the thought of meeting her,
      Do not stray into her paths;

26   For she has felled many victims,
      And numberless are those she has slain;

27   Her house is the way to Sheol,
      Descending to the chambers of Death.

[d] Reading *ke'akkēs el mōsēr 'ayyāl*, for MT *ūke'ekes el mūsar 'ewīl*, "and like a fetter for the discipline of a fool."

[e] MT "sons"; another example of an enclitic *m* mistaken for the plural ending; cf. iv 1, v 7.

Notes

vii 1–27. The usual introductory commendation of Wisdom as a guide for life (vss. 1–5) is followed by a vivid description of the seduction of a youth by a married woman (vss. 6–23) and a concluding warning in familiar words (vss. 24–27; cf. ii 18–19, v 5–6, ix 18).

3. *Bind them on your fingers.* I.e., as a reminder. The figure is traditional in connection with divine commandments; cf. Deut vi 4–8.

5. See NOTE on ii 16.

9b. Literally "at the sleep of night and darkness"; cf. M. Dahood, *Proverbs and North West Semitic Philology* (abbr. PNWSP), 1963, pp. 14–15.

10. For the heavy veiling of a harlot, cf. Gen xxxviii 14–15.

14. *sacrificial meat.* The portion of a sacrificed animal retained by the one who brings the offering (cf. Lev vii 11–21; I Sam ix 11–13; Jer vii 21; I Cor x 25–28) provides the opportunity for a feast.

vows. May refer to the proceeds of sacred prostitution associated with pagan cults, vowed to a goddess of fertility. Cf. Deut xxiii 17–18; Amos ii 7–8; Hos iv 12–14; and G. Boström, *Proverbiastudien*, 1935, ch. 4.

23. *heart.* Literally "liver," the vital organ.

27. See NOTE on ii 18.

9. A POEM
(viii 1–36)

VIII

1 Do you not hear Wisdom call aloud,
  And reason raise her voice?

2 Ascending the road^a to the acropolis,
  Taking her stand where pathways meet,

3 Beside the city gates, where men enter the portals,
   she cries out—

4 "To you, O men, I call,
  And my appeal is to the human race.

5 You simpletons, learn sense!
  You fools, acquire intelligence!

6 Listen, for I would speak of virtues^b
  And open my lips concerning equity,

7 Indeed it is truth I shall recite,
  To utter wickedness would be abhorrent to me;

8 Whatever I say is said honestly,
  There is nothing devious or distorted in it;

9 All of it is right to the discerning mind
  And straightforward to those apt for knowledge.

10 Accept my discipline in preference to silver,
  And knowledge rather than the choicest gold.

11 For wisdom is better than jewels,
  There is nothing so desirable as it is."

---

^a '*ōlāh baddérek*, for MT '*alē dérek*, "beside the road."
^b *n^ekōḥīm*, for MT *n^egīdīm*, "nobles."

SECOND STROPHE

12 "I am Wisdom. My neighbor*c* is intelligence.
     I am found in [company with] knowledge and
          thought.*d*"
13 [To reverence the Lord is to hate evil.]
     Pride, arrogance, wicked behavior
     And perverse speech I hate.
14 Mine are good counsel and power of achievement,
     I am discernment and the strength that goes with it.
15 By me kings reign,
     And princes make just decrees;
16 By me princes rule, and chieftains,
     And all who bear authority on earth.*e*
17 I love those who love me,
     And those who seek me earnestly find me.
18 Riches and honor accompany me,
     Venerable dignity and approbation.
19 My fruit is more precious than pure, fine gold,
     And my revenue than the choicest silver.
20 I walk firmly the way of right,
     Where the paths of justice meet,
21 Bestowing integrity*f* on those who love me,
     And filling their treasuries."*g*

c šᵉkēnī, for MT *šākantī*, "I dwell."
d bᵉdaʿat ūmᵉzimmōt ʾimmāṣēʾ, for MT *wᵉdaʿat mᵉzimmōt ʾemṣāʾ*, "I find knowledge of thoughts."
e Reading with LXX *bāʾāreṣ*, for MT *ṣédeq*, "righteousness."
f yōšer, for MT *yēš* ("existence," "substance"?), a word which is not used
as a noun elsewhere in OT.
g LXX inserts after vs. 21 an additional (editorial?) couplet which smooths
the transition to the third strophe:
     "If I declare to you what happens daily,
      I shall remember also to recount what happened long ago."

THIRD STROPHE

22 "The Lord possessed me, the first principle of his
      sovereignty,
      Before any of his acts,
23 Ere then, from of old I was poured out,
      From the first, before the beginnings of the world;
24 I was brought forth when there were no watery deeps,
      No primeval sources or springs of the sea[h],
25 Before the mountains were settled on their bases,
      Before the hills, was I born,
26 When he had not yet made the wide world,
      Nor the first morsels of the earth's soil;
27 When he established the heavens, I was there,
      When he inscribed a circle on the face of the deep;
28 When he set the zenith firmly on high,
      And made the mighty fountains of the abyss;
29 When he made his statute for the sea—
      That the waters should not pass the bounds he
         commanded;
      When he laid the strong[i] foundations of the earth—
30 Then I was beside him binding[j] [all] together;
      I was his daily joy[k],
      Constantly making merry in his presence,
31 Rejoicing in the habitable world
      And delighting in the human race."

EPILOGUE

32 "So now, O sons [of men], hear me!
      They will be fortunate who observe my ways.
33 Give heed to instruction and reject not wisdom!

[h] nibᵉkē yām, as in Job xxxviii 16, for MT nikbaddē máyim, "heavy with
water." maʿyānōt, "springs," seems to be a gloss on this rare expression.
[i] bᵉḥazzᵉqō, with LXX, for MT bᵉḥūqō, "when he marked out." Cf. Ps civ 5.
[j] Vocalizing the consonants '-m-n as 'ōmēn rather than as 'āmōn of MT.
[k] šaʿᵃšūʿāw, "his joy," for MT šaʿᵃšūʿīm, "joy."

34   Happy will be the man who listens to me,
        Wakeful daily at my doors,
        Watchful by the posts of my gates!
35   For he who finds me finds life,
        And obtains the Lord's favor;
36   But the man who wrongs me hurts himself,
        And all who hate me love death."

NOTES

viii 1–36. In this important poem, "The Divine Wisdom Manifest in Creation Offers Herself to Mankind," Wisdom is vividly personified, as in i 20–33, and addresses men in the tones of a goddess who has been associated with Yahweh in the creation of the world and its inhabitants. (See NOTES on i 20–33, on the figurative attribution of personality to collective entities and abstract ideas, in OT poetry.) But the monolatry of early Israel had become an unequivocal monotheism (cf. Isa xliv 6) before the poem was composed, and there is no trace of polytheistic beliefs in references to the deity elsewhere in Proverbs (except possibly in the companion piece in ch. i). Indeed, the language of monotheism and the absence of mythological traits may be said to be generally characteristic of Wisdom writings not only in Israel but also in Egypt (cf. the *Instructions of Ani* and *of Amen-em-ope*, ANET, pp. 420–24). Thus the writer of Proverbs viii is not thinking here of Wisdom as a distinct deity like the Egyptian Maat, goddess of truth and order, Ishtar the Babylonian "creatress of wisdom," or her counterpart Siduri Sabitu, the genius of life and wisdom consulted by Gilgamesh (cf. ANET, pp. 213a, 383a b, and Albright, AJSL 36 [1919–20], 258–94). How then are we to explain the fact that Wisdom is here represented *as if* she were a self-conscious divine being, distinct from though subordinate to Yahweh? Scholars differ sharply as to what the poet has in mind. Is Wisdom an hypostasis of Yahweh, that is, an attribute or activity of his which is endowed with a personal identity? Or, is what we have here simply an unusually striking example of personification for poetic effect?

Several facts must be taken into account in the attempt to settle this problem. The problem is important not only for the understanding of the poem itself, but because of the far-reaching influence of the poem's central passage (vss. 22–31) on later theological thought. The Wisdom of Solomon speaks of "Wisdom, the fashioner of all things" (vii 22 EV), as "an associate in His works" (viii 4), and as "fashioner of all that exists" (viii 6). Philo (*de Sacerdot* 5) says that "the universe was fabricated" through the agency of the Logos-Wisdom; the same thought appears in John i 3, "through him all things came to be"; in Col i 15–16, "the first-born of all creation, for in him all things were created"; and in Heb i 3, "through whom also he created the world." The influence of Proverbs viii on these passages, and consequently on later Christological doctrine, is evident.

These later interpretations of the figure of Wisdom seem to assume that the writer of this poem thought of Wisdom as an hypostasis of Yahweh, that is, as having some kind of independent existence. Certainly the notion of the existence of divine beings, "the host of heaven," under the authority of Yahweh—"angels" or messengers, functionaries of his royal court, members of the divine council—was not felt to be incompatible with his unique deity (cf. I Kings xxii 19–22; Isa vi 1–8; Job i 6; Zech vi 5). Some OT poets draw upon imagery surviving from pre-Israelite mythologies (e.g., Isa xiv 12–14, xxvii 1; Pss lxxiv 13–14, lxxxii 1) without any feeling of inconsistency. Consequently it is not surprising that the acts of *Yahweh's* wisdom in creation should take the form of a portrait resembling that of a goddess of wisdom. The association of a god or goddess of wisdom with the creation of the world and man was frequent in the myths of surrounding peoples. In Egypt, Ptah of Memphis was said to have created the world by his thought and his word. At Hermapolis, similarly, the god Thoth was both the personification of divine intelligence and a creator god. In Sumerian mythology Ea or Enki, "the very knowing one," the "master of prudent words," was empowered by Anu, god of the sky, "to guide and form." In the Babylonian creation myth, Ea "set up . . . the configuration of the universe"; Marduk his son, "wisest of gods," overcame in battle Tiamat, the ocean dragon of chaos, and made earth and sky and man. Although no creation myth has been found so far in Ugaritic literature, the supreme god El is addressed as one whose "decree is wise" and whose "wisdom is eternal" (cf. E. O. James, *Myth and Ritual in the Ancient Near East*, 1958, pp. 149–62; ANET, p. 133a).

It has been suggested that here El's wisdom "was becoming a kind of objective entity, the starting point of a hypostatization" (H. Ringgren, *Word and Wisdom*, 1947, p. 80). But in fact there is no semantic difference between saying "El is eternally wise" and saying "El's wisdom is eternal." In the same way, when we read in Prov iii 19 that "Yahweh through wisdom founded the world" (cf. also Ps civ 24), "wisdom" is neither instrument nor agent but the attribute displayed by Yahweh in creating. This is important for the interpretation of Chapter viii, which recapitulates and develops the thought of iii 13–20 and cannot be treated in isolation from the earlier passage. When further we observe that in viii 32–36, the peroration of the poem, the language echoes that of the speaker in the ten discourses (cf. i 8, iii 1–2, iv 1–2, v 1–2), it seems clear that the authorship of the discourses and of the poems in chapters i and viii is the same. The writer may have drawn on and adapted old mythological material for his purpose, but we cannot infer from this that he was making anything more than a figurative poetic use of it (cf. "the tree of life" in iii 18, xi 30, xiii 12, xv 4).

Chaper viii is a unified formal composition comprising three strophes, vss. 1–11, 12–21, 22–31, and a peroration, vss. 32–36. The first and third strophes contain twenty-two lines, as does the second in LXX; the peroration has eleven lines. The author is using twenty-two (the number of letters in the Hebrew alphabet) as a structural form, as he does also in the earlier poem i 8–19, in the programmatic discourse of chapter ii, and elsewhere in chapters i–ix. This additional evidence of common authorship increases the probability that the personification of wisdom in chapter viii is indeed poetic only and not ontological. The *'āmōn* (or rather *'ōmēn;* see below) of viii 30 is a divine attribute displayed in creative action, not an aspect of the divine reality having a quasi-independent identity.

The ambiguity of the two key words *'āmōn* and *qānāh* (vs. 22) has led to various interpretations of them by ancient translators and commentators. It is these ancient *interpretations* which have created the impression that Wisdom in chapter viii is in some sort a hypostasis. The most usual meaning of *qānāh* is "acquire, possess what has been acquired" (e.g., Gen xlvii 22, of the acquisition of real estate; Isa i 3, of the ownership of an animal). This is clearly the meaning intended in the twelve other passages in Proverbs where the word is used, and it is the meaning given it also here by Vulg., Aq., Symm., Theod. and Syro-Hex., among the ancient versions. Three other versions (LXX, Syr., Targ.), however, take *qānāh* here to have its less usual meaning "create," as in Deut xxxii 6; Ps. cxxxix 13; and (probably) Gen xiv 19, 22. A related meaning "engender, give birth to" is found apparently in Gen iv 1; some commentators hold that this is the meaning here also because of the birth metaphor in vss. 24–25. In the Ugaritic Baal epic the goddess Athirat-Asherah is given the epithet *qnyt 'lm,* "progenitress of the gods (cf. ANET, pp. 131–32), and the verb undoubtedly means "create" in the phrase *'l qn 'rṣ,* "El, creator of the earth" (cf. W. F. Albright, "Notes on Psalms 68 and 134," *Interpretationes ad Vet. Test. Pert. S. Mowinckel,* 1955, pp. 7–8).

These last references are pertinent for an explanation of Gen xiv 9, 22, but not necessarily for Prov viii 22. What is here being affirmed is not that Yahweh is creator, but that Yahweh's attribute of wisdom "existed" prior to its expression in his acts of creation. The meaning "possess" for *qānāh* is entirely suitable and is in keeping with the author's usage in i 5, iv 5, 7. Yahweh "possessed" wisdom as an attribute or faculty integral to his being from the very first, and "in [with, or by] his wisdom founded the earth" (iii 19). This seems to be the more probable interpretation, even when full allowance is made for mythological echoes in the poetic imagery of personification.

The second ambiguous key word is *'āmōn* in vs. 30. Two *mutually exclusive* meanings have been given to this word since ancient times, (i) "master workman, craftsman," and (ii) "little child, ward." The former has the support of the principal ancient versions, LXX, Vulg., Syr., and Targ., and also of a strong exegetical tradition (cf. Wisdom of Solomon vii 22 EV, viii 6; *Midrash Bereshith Rabbah* i 1; Philo *de Sacerdot* 5; John i 3; Col i 16). The latter is favored by Aq., *Midrash Mishlē*, and by many commentators, because of the birth metaphor in vss. 24–25 and the references in vss. 30–31 to Wisdom's "playing" like a child in Yahweh's presence. *Both* interpretations require the supplying of vowels different from those of the Masoretic tradition, so as to read *'ommān* and *'āmūn* respectively. Each supports the idea of Wisdom's independent identity by its vocalization of the consonants *'-m-n*. Unquestionably, the view that Wisdom in this passage is an hypostasis has been strongly influenced by these alternative readings of an obscure word, *one of which must be wrong*. In fact, there are three other possible readings with some ancient support: (i) the noun *'ōmēn*, "guardian, teacher"; (ii) the participle *'ōmēn*, "uniting, binding"; (iii) the adjective *'āmēn*, "true, faithful." In the present writer's view the poet intended the vocalization *'ōmēn*, with the meaning "uniting, binding together," as in Sirach xliii 26, "by his word all things hold together" (cf. Wisdom of Solomon i 7; Col i 17; Heb i 3; R. B. Y. Scott, "Wisdom in Creation: the *'āmōn* of Proverbs viii 30," VT 10 [1960], 213–23). One of the main props of the hypostasis theory is thus only a dubious interpretation of an obscure term.

1. Or, "Does not Wisdom cry aloud?" The question form is rhetorical, as if demanding attention from someone present.

4. *the human race*. Literally "the sons of men." Cf. vs. 31.

11. *jewels*. Corals or pearls.

13. The prosaic first line is bracketed, as apparently a marginal note. Cf. i 7, ix 10.

14. Cf. II Sam xvii 23. In Job xii 13 these are attributes of God.

15. Wisdom to maintain social order and to administer justice was the essential endowment of a king, whether as the incarnate deity in Egypt, or as the vicegerent of God in Mesopotamia and Israel. Cf.

Hammurabi of Babylon, "the wise king, obedient to Shamash," "named
. . . to cause justice to prevail in the land"; Amen-hotep IV's hymn to
the Aton, "Thou hast made him well-versed in thy plans and in thy
strength" (ANET, pp. 164a b, 371a); Solomon's famous prayer "for an
understanding mind to govern thy people" (I Kings iii 9); and the promised endowment of the ideal "Messianic" king (Isa xi 2). See N. W.
Porteous, "Royal Wisdom," WIANE, pp. 247–61.

18. *approbation.* Literally "righteousness," i.e., approval as righteous.

22. *possessed me.* I.e., in himself, as a function or attribute. On the
alternative translation "created me," see NOTE on viii 1–36. This verse
had an important place in the fourth century Arian controversy about
the nature of Christ. Arius contended that since Christ was "the Wisdom
of God" (I Cor i 24) he was spoken of here as a created being, subordinate to God. Athanasius, on the other hand, translated the crucial
phrase by, "constituted me as head of creation." The definition in the
Nicene Creed, "begotten not made," may have rested in part on the
birth metaphor in vss. 24–25 and the translation "little child" for *'āmōn*
in vs. 30.

first principle of his sovereignty. Or (less probably, and depending
on the translation of the verb by "created me"), "the beginning of his
work" or, "as his first act." *darkō,* "his sovereignty" has the sense of the
Canaanite word *drkt,* "dominion." Canaanite words and spellings (e.g.,
ḥokmōt for *ḥokmāh,* "wisdom," i 20, ix 1, xxiv 7) persist in the Wisdom
writings, though usually avoided in the remaining more specifically Israelite literature of the OT.

his acts. In creation and history.

23. *Ere then.* Transferred from preceding line, because of the meter
and the sense.

I was poured out. Like the Spirit (Isa xxix 10; Joel ii 28 EV) or
"emanated" (W. F. Albright); LXX "he established me."

24. *brought forth.* Or, "originated." The birth metaphor is used also
of the creation of mountains and sea in Ps xc 2; Job xxxviii 8–9, and so
need not refer to a personal being.

primeval sources. Cf. Job xxxviii 16. The supreme god El in the
Ugaritic Baal epic dwells at "the Sources of the Two Floods . . . the
headwaters of the Two Oceans" (ANET, p. 133a; cf. Gen vii 11).

26. *the wide world.* Literally "the earth and the outside."

first. Or, "sum total of."

28. *made the mighty fountains.* Literally "made powerful the fountains."

30. *binding [all] together.* Or, "in support." See NOTE on viii 1–36. For
the divine *joy* in creation, cf. Job xxxviii 7.

10. TWO POEMS AND AN EXPANDED PROVERB
(ix 1–6, 10–12, 7–9, 13–18)

Poem: Invitation to Wisdom's Banquet

IX

1   Wisdom has built her house,
    She has erected*ᵃ* her seven pillars;

2   She has slaughtered her sacrifice,
    She has poured out her wine,
    She has also prepared her table;

3   Having dismissed her maids, she proclaims
    From the summit of the upper town—

4   "Whoever is untutored, let him come hither!"
    To the ignorant she says,

5   "Come, feast on my food,
    And drink of the wine I have poured out;

6   Forsake your ignorance*ᵇ* and find life,
    And set your feet on the road to understanding:

10   The beginning of wisdom is to hold the Lord in awe,
    And knowledge of the Holy One is understanding.

11   For by it your days will be multiplied,
    And the years of your life will be added to.

12   If you become wise your wisdom will be your own,
    If you scorn it, you alone will be responsible."

ᵃ hiṣṣībāh, for MT *ḥāṣᵉbāh*, "hewed out." Cf. xiv 1, Note.
ᵇ pᵉtīkem, for MT *pᵉtāʾyim*, "the ignorant."

Expanded Proverb: The Scoffer and the Wise Man

7   One who admonishes a scoffer is abused for his pains,
     To complain about a wicked man is to invite insult.
8   Reproach a scoffer and he will hate you,
     Reprove a wise man and he will love you.
9   Give [advice] to a wise man and he will be still wiser,
     Inform a just man and he will add to his knowledge.

Poem: Folly Personified as a Wanton Woman

13   Folly is [like] a woman*ᶜ*,
     Boisterous, ignorant*ᵈ*, and shameless*ᵉ*,
14   Who sits in the doorway of her house,
     [Or] on a seat in the upper town,
15   Calling out to passers-by pursuing their own affairs,
16   ["Whoever is untutored, let him come hither!"
     To the ignorant she says,]
17   "Stolen water tastes sweet,
     Food eaten secretly is delightful";
18   But he does not perceive that ghosts will be there,
     That her guests are in the hollows of Sheol.

ᶜ ʾēšet here is not a construct of *ʾiššāh*, "woman of folly" (since Folly itself is being personified), but the Canaanite absolute form, equivalent of *ʾiššāh*. This is another example of the persistence of Canaanite forms in Hebrew Wisdom writings.
ᵈ pᵉtīyāh, for MT *pᵉtayyūt*, "ignorance."
ᵉ kᵉlimmāh with LXX; MT *māh* has accidentally omitted the first two letters.

NOTES

ix 1–6, 10–12, 7–9, 13–18. This concluding chapter of Part I of the Book of Proverbs gives further evidence of the disarrangement of its materials to which attention has been drawn in the NOTES on i 8–18, ii 1–22, v 15–vi 19. The invitation to Wisdom's banquet in vss. 5–6 is incomplete without some such statement of Wisdom's rewards as is found in vs. 11 (cf. i 33, ii 9–11, iii 2, 4, 6, 8, 10, 13–18, viii 18–19, 34–35, etc.). Instead, what follows in vss. 7–9 is an expanded proverb (cf. xiii 1) like those in vi 1–19; its chiastic structure identifies it as a distinct literary unit, and its abrupt introduction of a totally different theme and audience shows that it has intruded in this context. The picture of Folly as an adulteress in vss. 13–18 is certainly intended as a counterpart to vss. 1–6, with which it has no close connection in the present form of the chapter. Further evidence of the fluid state of the text when the LXX translation of it was made is the expansion in that version of vss. 6 and 10, and the addition of seven lines after vs. 12 and of eight lines after vs. 18.

The view taken here is that vss. 10–12 are the continuation of Wisdom's invitation in vss. 5–6, and mark the original conclusion of chs. i–ix. The motto of this collection, stated at the outset in i 7, is repeated in the slightly different words that follow naturally upon vs. 6. The expanded proverb contrasting the scoffer and the wise man, vss. 7–9, was then brought in by a later copyist because of the language of vs. 12. The portrait of personified Folly in vss. 13–18 is also on this view secondary, rather than an original companion piece of vss. 1–6, 10–12, as is usually assumed. The identification of the adulteress, though she is pictured in language drawn from ii 16 ff., v 1–23, and vii 1–27, is not the same as in those passages. Here she is specifically *Folly* (*kᵉsîlût,* a word not used elsewhere), the opposite of Wisdom as such; there, she is the *fruit* of the lack of wisdom in a particular form of behavior, the sexual immorality associated with pagan religion (cf. NOTE on ii 16). Though admittedly the two ideas are closely related, they are not the same. When in addition we observe that the collection has already been formally concluded with vss. 10–12, it seems at least very probable that vss. 13–18 form a later supplement. Its material is derived from earlier passages, especially ch. vii, and vs. 16 is similarly repeated from vs. 4, where it is clearly more suitable than here.

1. *built her house.* The imagery is doubtless mythological in origin. The house of Wisdom is the "habitable world" (viii 31) of which she is the "uniting force" (viii 30), the constructive power of reason in Yahweh's creation. The world is spoken of elsewhere in OT poetry in the imagery of a house, with foundations (viii 29; Ps civ 5), a cornerstone (Job xxxviii 6), pillars supporting it from below (I Sam ii 8) and above, the dome of the sky or the firmament (Job xxvi 11; Gen i 6–8), and windows in the sky-dome (Gen vii 11).

seven pillars. Like the four "posts" or "pillars" of the Egyptian cosmology, these support the roof of heaven (cf. Judg xvi 29). It is as pointless to look for mythological or architectural precedents for the

number "seven" as it would be to ask why this number is chosen in
xxiv 16, xxvi 16 and many other and various contexts in OT and in
Mesopotamian and Ugaritic literature. The number "seven" had originally
ominous or sacred associations, but its use later became simply a favorite
literary convention for a small number.

2. The animal *slaughtered* for *sacrifice* provided meat for a feast; cf.
Note on vii 14.

3. *Having dismissed.* Literally "sent out," i.e., from the banquet hall,
once preparations have been completed. It is Wisdom herself who *proclaims* the invitation, as in i 20–21. Cf. PNWSP, pp. 16–17.

7. *scoffer. lēṣ,* the arrogant, cynical, worldly, opposite and opponent
of the religious wise man.

16. Repeated from vs. 4 where the words are more suitable.

17. The first line may have been a folk proverb on clandestine behavior. For the metaphor of eating and drinking for sexual indulgence,
cf. v 15, 20; xxx 20; Song of Sol iv 13–15. *Water* might be *stolen* because it was a salable commodity in a land of minimal rainfall (cf. Deut
ii 6).

18. *ghosts.* Or "the dead," who led a shadowy existence in *Sheol* (cf.
Job iii 13–19; Pss lxxxviii 5, 10 EV, cxv 17; Isa xiv 9–11). In earlier
times necromancers claimed to communicate with the dead on behalf of
the living (I Sam xxviii 6–15; Isa viii 19). Ptah-hotep speaks similarly of
the penalty for adultery, "one attains death through knowing her"
(ANET, p. 413b).

II. The First Collection
of Solomonic Proverbs*

* The proverbs found here, x 1–xxii 16, are classified by topic at the end
of Part II.

11. THE WISE SAYINGS OF SOLOMON
(x 1–32)

X

1   The Wise Sayings of Solomon.

    A wise son makes a happy father,
      But a foolish son is a grief to his mother.
2   Wealth gained through wickedness will prove of no
          advantage,
      But honesty will save a man in mortal danger.
3   The Lord will not let a good man starve,
      But he rebuffs the craving of the wicked.
4   Careless work makes a man poor,
      Whereas diligent effort brings wealth.
5   A son who gathers [fruit] in summer shows intelligence,
      But a son who sleeps at harvest time is a disgrace.
6   Men call down blessings on the head of a good man,
      But the mouth of the wicked uncovers violence.
7   The memory of a good man is blessed,
      But the reputation of evil men will rot away.
8   A sensible man will take orders,
      But the fool who talks back will be crushed.
9   "He who lives innocently lives confidently,"
      While a dishonest man will be found out.
10   He who winks his eye makes trouble,
      But one who reproaches frankly makes peace.[a]
11   The speech of a good man is a well of life,
      But the mouth of the wicked uncovers [his] violence.

[a] The second line of the translation follows LXX; MT repeats 8b.

12 Hatred provokes quarrels,
       But love covers over all offenses.
13 A discerning man talks sense,
       But the senseless needs a stick to his back.
14 Wise men keep their knowledge to themselves;
       When a fool talks, trouble is brewing.
15 A rich man's wealth is his fortress;
       Their poverty is what desolates the poor.
16 The good man's reward is life indeed,
       But the wicked man's harvest is death[b].
17 Self-discipline is a path to life,
       And one who ignores correction gets lost.
18 One who reveals hatred with lying words,
       One who spreads slander, is a rogue.
19 In too much talk there is sure to be some error,
       So a shrewd man holds his tongue.
20 What a good man says is pure silver,
       But the views of the wicked are worthless.
21 The words of a good man sustain many,
       But fools perish from their own stupidity.
22 It is the Lord's blessing that makes a man rich,
       And painful toil can add no more.
23 As a vicious fool enjoys lewdness,
       An intelligent man relishes wisdom.
24 What a wicked man dreads is what happens to him,
       But the desire of good men is granted.
25 When the storm has passed the wicked will have
              vanished,
       But the good man has a permanent foundation.
26 Like vinegar on the teeth and smoke in the eyes
       Is a laggard to one who sends him [on an errand].
27 Reverence for the Lord prolongs life,
       But the years of bad men are cut short.
28 The expectation of good men flourishes[c],
       But the hopes of wicked men come to nothing.

---

[b] Reading lᵉmāwet, for MT lᵉḥattā't. Cf. xi 19.
[c] Reading ṣamᵉḥāh, for MT śimḥāh, "[is] joy."

29 The Lord is their stronghold whose way of life is
       blameless,
    But he is the terror of evildoers.
30 A good man can never be shaken,
    But the wicked have no permanence in the land.
31 The speech of a good man flows with wisdom,
    Whereas a malicious tongue will be cut off.
32 The lips of a good man pour out good will;
    The mouth of the wicked drips with malice.

NOTES

x 1–xxii 16. The title, "The Wise Sayings of Solomon," covers the
collection of independent and mostly miscellaneous two-line aphorisms
and precepts which comprise Part II. A second collection, also connected
with the name of Solomon, is found in chs. xxv–xxix (Part IV); it is
broadly similar to the first collection but is more secular and less didactic
in tone. For the possible connection of these two collections of proverbs
with the Solomon of history, see Introduction to Proverbs. The view
taken here is that "proverb of Solomon" had become the conventional
term for the two-line proverb in poetic parallelism which is characteristic of these two collections, rather than an affirmation of authorship.

1. *A wise son makes a happy father.* This looks like a folk saying, to
which a contrasting parallel has been appended. The saying itself recurs
in xv 20, but in that instance the second line is different. The theme is a
favorite one in Proverbs; cf. xvii 21, 25, xxiii 24–25, xxviii 7, xxix 3.
For an Egyptian parallel, see *Ptah-hotep,* ANET, p. 413a.

2. *honesty.* Literally "righteousness"; other possible renderings here
are "virtue," "charity."

in mortal danger. Or "from death." See further x 16, xiii 21, xx 21,
for the thought that divine Providence will support the moral code.

4. *Careless work.* Literally "a slack hand." This is another favorite
theme; cf. xii 11, 24, 27, xviii 9.

6. The second line seems to have been supplied from vs. 11, where it
provides a more suitable parallel. Evidently the second line of vs. 6 was
missing.

7. Cf. *Meri-ka-re* in ANET, p. 415a: "Make thy memorial to last
through love of thee."

8. *talks back.* Or, "talks foolishly."

9. The first line, *hōlēk battōm yēlēk betaḥ,* has the alliterative, epigrammatic form of an adage.

will be found out. Or (reading *yērōᵃ'*), "will suffer for it"; cf. xi 15.

10. *makes trouble.* Because he insinuates what he will not say frankly; cf. vi 12–15; Sirach xxvii 22–23.

11. *uncovers.* Or (conversely), "covers up." The antithetical parallelism supports the former meaning, as does Job xxxvi 30. Cf. PNWSP, pp. 18–19.

12. The second line is quoted in I Pet iv 8.

13. Cf. xxvi 3.

14. This adage commends the circumspect self-possession of the sage rather than simply his modesty, and contrasts it with the thoughtlessness of the impulsive, undisciplined man. The same contrast of human types was made in Egyptian Wisdom between the "heated" man and the "silent" man; cf. *Ptah-hotep,* "If thou art silent, it is better . . . do not answer in a state of turmoil," ANET, pp. 414a, 423a. Cf. vs. 19, xii 23, xiii 16, xv 2; Sirach v 11–12; James iii 13–18.

15. There is no hint here that the writer considers the division of the community into rich and poor to be unjust. Wealth, by which is meant not vast riches but substantial prosperity, is considered the result of diligent work (vs. 4) and of the Lord's blessing on an upright life (vs. 22). Poverty, conversely, is regarded as the fruit of indolence (vs. 4). The Wisdom teachers, unlike the prophets, were socially conservative. As Sirach acknowledges, "The wisdom of the scribe depends on the opportunity of leisure" (Sirach xxxviii 24).

16. Paul seems to be quoting from this verse when he says in Rom vi 23, "The wages of sin is death."

18. *reveals.* Or, "conceals"; see NOTE on vs. 11.

lying. I.e., about persons, whether as slander or as false witness, is a vice much condemned in Wisdom writings; cf. vi 17–19; xii 22; xxvi 28; Job xxxi 5; *Amen-em-ope,* ch. 10 (ANET, p. 423a), *Ahiqar* ix (ANET, p. 429b).

22. Complementary to the view of prosperity in vs. 15 is the counsel against pursuit of wealth for its own sake, and the warning against the uncertainty of its possession; cf. xi 28, xv 27, xxiii 4–5, xxvii 24; Eccles v 10–17.

25. For the figure, cf. Matt vii 26–27.

26. A sarcastic simile on the stereotype of the idler; cf. vi 6–11, xx 4, xxvi 13–16. For the converse, cf. xxv 13. Similes of this kind are frequent in chs. xxv–xxvi, and include double and even triple comparisons; cf. xxv 12, 18, 20, 26.

31 and 32. *flow* and *pour out.* For these renderings, cf. PNWSP, pp. 20–21.

12. THE WISE SAYINGS OF SOLOMON (*continued*)
(xi 1–31)

XI

1   Dishonest scales are abominable to the Lord,
     But a true weight pleases him.

2   "To show disdain is to show you're vain,"
     For wise men are humble.

3   Their innocence guides the upright,
     And the hypocrisy of rogues leads them to destruction.

4   Wealth will be of no avail on the day of wrath,
     But virtue will stand between a man and death.

5   The virtue of good men keeps them on the right road,
     But a wicked man falls by his own wickedness.

6   The virtue of the upright is their salvation,
     And rogues are trapped by their own cupidity.

7   When a man*a* dies it is the end of hope,
     And his expected achievement comes to nothing.

8   When a good man escapes from trouble
     The bad man falls into it instead.

9   When a vile man by his talk would ruin his neighbor,
     The sagacity of good men will save them.

10 When things go well with the just a city is happy,
     When the wicked are overthrown there is jubilation.

11 A town prospers when it has the blessing of upright men,
     But the words of evil men can destroy it.

12 A man who shows contempt for his neighbor is not
       intelligent;
     A far-sighted man keeps his opinions to himself.

---

a MT reads "a wicked man." LXX translates "When a good man dies, hope does not perish."

13   The confirmed gossip betrays a confidence,
> But a trustworthy man can keep a secret.

14   Without skillful leadership a people will perish;
> Security lies in having many counselors.

15   A man who goes bond for a stranger is sure to suffer[b]
> for it;
> To be free from anxiety one should avoid rash bargains.

16   A gracious lady gains respect,
> But aggressive men grasp riches.

17   A kindly man does his own soul good;
> A cruel man makes himself odious.

18   A wicked man's wage turns out to be counterfeit;
> It is the one who sows virtue who has the true reward.

19   He who discerns[c] what is right is headed for life,
> And he who pursues wrong is headed for death.

20   The Lord abominates dissemblers,
> But delights in men of blameless life.

21   Be assured of this—the evil man shall not go free,
> It is the company of good men that will be victorious.

22   "Like a gold nose ring in a wild pig's snout
> Is a pretty woman who lacks good manners."

23   The desire of just men can end only in good,
> Whereas the wicked can hope for nothing but wrath.

24   One man spends freely and yet grows richer,
> Another will not spend what he ought, yet is headed
> for poverty.

25   A generous man grows fat,
> And he who waters [another's garden] will have his
> own [garden] watered.

26   [A dealer] who withholds grain—the people will curse him,
> But they will bless one who offers it for sale.

27   He who is eager to do good wins good will,
> But one who looks for trouble meets it.

---

[b] Infinitive absolute *rōaʻ* for adjective *raʻ*.
[c] *mēbîn*, for MT *kēn*, "so."

28   A man who trusts in his riches withers
      While good men burgeon like green leaves.
29   He who shuns his family becomes heir to the wind,
      To a man of intelligence he is [like] a stupid slave.
30   Right conduct^d is a tree of life,
      But crime^e takes lives away.
31   If a good man gets his deserts on earth,
      How much more will the wicked and the transgressor!

^{d} *ṣedeq*, for MT *ṣaddiq*, "righteous man."
^{e} *ḥāmās*, for MT *ḥākām*, "a wise man."

NOTES

xi 1. Dishonest merchants are the target of Wisdom teachers (xvi 11, xx 10, 23), prophets (Amos viii 5; Ezek xlv 10) and lawmakers (Deut xxv 13–16) in Israel, in Egypt (*Amen-em-ope*, ch. 16, ANET, p. 423b) and among the Babylonians (*Hymn to Shamash*, ANET, p. 388b) and Sumerians (Ur-Nammu law code, twenty-first century B.C.). Payments were made in lump silver weighed in *scales* against a stone *weight*. Actual weights recovered vary considerably from official standards.

2. Literally "comes insolence, comes disgrace." The alliteration and rhyme in the first line, (*ba' zādōn, wayyābō' qālōn*), singles it out as a colloquial saying (cf. "By hook or by crook"). This is a retort to one who expresses contempt, that in so doing he displays his own conceit.

4, 5, 6. The survival value of virtue or "righteousness."

7. Cf. Eccles iii 19–20. But the text is doubtful, and may originally have resembled x 28.

his expected achievement. Literally "the expectation of strength." Cf. Wisdom of Solomon iii 1–4, but the original adage resembles rather Eccles iii 19–20, v 13–16 EV.

9. *vile*. Or, "impious."

11. Cf. *Meri-ka-re* (ANET, p. 415a), "the contentious man is a disturbance to citizens."

13. Cf. xx 19; Sirach xxvii 16–17.

14. The second line recurs in xxiv 6, and in different words in xv 22; it may have been a popular saying.

15. Literally "he who hates bargains is confident." See NOTE on vi 1.

17. Cf. Sirach xxi 27–28.

18. One of the answers to the problem of the prosperity of the wicked is that this prosperity does not last (cf. Ps lxxiii 12, 16–20).

21. Or, "my hand upon it!", as in striking a bargain. Cf. NOTE on vs. 18.

22. The earthy humor, in marked contrast to the moralizing context, suggests that this is a colloquial saying.

25. Or, "who gives a drink of water will in turn be given a drink."

26. In time of scarcity; cf. Gen xli 53–57.

29. *shuns.* Or, "neglects." Cf. xv 27, which suggests that the neglect is due to absorption in the pursuit of wealth.

30. *tree of life.* See NOTE on iii 18.

crime. Or, "violence." Cf. i 19.

31. Quoted in I Pet iv 18, in variant text of LXX.

13. THE WISE SAYINGS OF SOLOMON (*continued*)
(xii 1–28)

XII

1 A lover of learning delights in its discipline;
   He who refuses to be corrected is a boor.

2 The good man basks in the Lord's favor,
   But the schemer he condemns.

3 A man cannot make himself secure by wickedness,
   Nor can the good man's roots be disturbed.

4 A worthy wife is her husband's crown,
   But like rot in his bones is a wife who shames him.

5 The thoughts of worthy men are directed to what
      is right,
   The skills of evil men to deceit.

6 The words of evildoers are bloodthirsty,
   But the speech of the upright delivers them.

7 When evil men are overthrown nothing is left of them,
   But the house of just men stands firm.

8 A man of insight wins praise,
   But the muddleheaded is despised.

9 Better to be a common man who has employment*,
   Than to give oneself airs, and be starving.

10 A good man cares if his beast is hungry,
   But the "mercy" of evil men is cruel.

11 The man who tills his land will have plenty to eat,
   But the stupid spends his time chasing rainbows.

---

*a ʿaḇōḏāh, "work," for MT ʿeḇed, "slave." Cf. Sirach x 27.

12   The stronghold of the wicked will be blotted out,[b]
          But the roots of the just are enduring[c].

13   A bad man is tripped up by a slip of the tongue,
          Whereas a good man comes out unharmed from
              trouble.

14   A man receives the good that his words deserve,
          He will be paid according to what he has done.

15   A fool is cocksure about what he is doing,
          But one who welcomes advice is wise.

16   A fool is quick to show[d] annoyance,
          But a shrewd man restrains his retort.

17   One who brings out the facts makes evident his
              innocence[e],
          But a lying witness shows his deceitfulness.

18   A man's thoughtless talk may cut like a sword,
          But wise men's speech is healing.

19   True words have the quality of permanence,
          Untruths last only for a moment.

20   Those who plot trouble are deceiving themselves,
          But men who counsel peace will be happy.

21   No harm shall befall the just man,
          But the wicked have their hands full of trouble.

22   Falsehood is an abomination to the Lord,
          But honest men win his favor.

23   A shrewd man keeps quiet about what he knows,
          But the stupid have no thought but to proclaim their
              folly.

24   The hand of the assiduous gains control,
          While the lackadaisical must be forced to work.

25   Anxiety in a man's heart weighs him down,
          Yet an encouraging word will make him happier.

[b] *tiššāmēd mᵉṣūdat*, for MT *ḥāmad rāšā' mᵉṣōd*, "the wicked man desires the
net."
[c] *'ētān*, for MT *yittēn*, "he gives."
[d] *yōdī͏a'*, for MT *yiwwāda'*, "is made known."
[e] *ṣidqō*, for MT *ṣedeq*, "innocence," (inserting "his").

26   The good man survives his misfortune[f],
         But the path of the wrongdoer leads him astray.
27   "A careless hunter takes no game,"
         But the keen one gets plenty of it[g].
28   On the road of righteousness there is life,
         And the treading of its[h] path is deathlessness.

[f] *mērā'ātō*, for MT *mērē'ēhū*, "from his friend."
[g] The order of two words has been changed to follow LXX.
[h] *nᵉtībātō*, for MT *nᵉtībāh*, "path" (inserting "its").

NOTES

xii 1. Cf. "There is no royal road to learning."

4. Cf. xviii 22, xix 13, xxxi 10–31.

7. Cf. Matt vii 24–27.

10. *cares if his beast is hungry.* Or, "is sympathetic with his beast"; cf. xxvii 23.

11. *rainbows.* Literally "empty things." This proverb is found also at xxviii 19 with a slightly different ending. LXX here inserts an additional adage, "One who takes his pleasure in banquets of wine will leave dishonor in his strongholds."

13. LXX adds: "A man whose glance is gentle wins kindness, but the contentious causes hurt."

14. Literally "From the fruit of a man's mouth he will be satisfied with good, and the reward of a man's work will be returned to him." Cf. xiii 2.

17. Literally "He who breathes out faithfulness declares righteousness." The setting is a trial scene.

18. Cf. Ps lvii 4 EV, and *Meri-ka-re,* "the tongue is a sword" (ANET, p. 415a).

19. *moment.* Literally "eyewink."

20. Or, "Deceit is in the mind of those . . ."; the contrast with *will be happy* suggests that it is self-deceit. Cf. x 23.

23. See NOTE on x 14. R. Akiba is reported to have said, "Silence is a fence around wisdom."

25. Cf. xv 13, xvii 22.

27. *A careless hunter.* Literally "Slackness [feminine] will not take [?] his prey." The verb is otherwise unknown and its meaning must be inferred from the context and the ancient versions. The first line sounds like a folk proverb.

the keen one gets plenty of it. Literally "the wealth of a keen man is weighty."

28. M. Dahood [in *Biblica* 41 (1960), 176–81] has pointed to the synonymous parallel *hym/blmt,* "life, non-death" in the Ugaritic poem *Aqhat A,* section vi, lines 26–27 (ANET, p. 151b). This view of the relationship of righteousness and immortality is found in the later Greek work The Wisdom of Solomon (i 15, ii 23–24, iii 4–8), but not certainly elsewhere in Proverbs (cf. x 28, xi 4, xiii 14, xiv 12, 27, etc.).

14. THE WISE SAYINGS OF SOLOMON (*continued*)
(xiii 1–25)

XIII

1   A wise son values*ᵃ* correction,
      But the insolent will not listen to rebuke.

2   A man receives the good that his words deserve,
      The appetite of rogues is only for crime.

3   "One who guards his lips protects himself,"
      And a loquacious man invites his own downfall.

4   The indolent craves [food] but has none,
      While the industrious is amply fed.

5   A good man hates an untrue word,
      But an evil man's talk is a shame and a disgrace.

6   Right will protect the blameless life,
      But sin overturns the wicked.

7   One kind of man pretends to be rich when he has
            nothing,
      Another professes poverty though he has great
            possessions.

8   A rich man has the wealth to ransom his life,
      But a poor man hears no threat.*ᵇ*

9   The light of just men shines brightly,
      But the lamp of the wicked will be extinguished.

10 The vain man*ᶜ* generates strife by his arrogance,
      And with the well-advised there is wisdom.

ᵃ ʾōhēb, for MT *ʾāb*, "father."
ᵇ LXX seems to have read *ʿāmad*, for MT *šāmaʿ*. The second line which is
suspiciously like xiii 1b, may originally have read *wᵉrāš lōʾ ʿāmad neged
rāʿāh*, "but a poor man cannot withstand disaster."
ᶜ rēq, for MT *raq*, "only."

11 Wealth gained in haste[d] will dwindle,
   But one who has worked for it keeps it growing.
12 Expectation deferred makes one sick at heart,
   But a desire fulfilled is a tree of life.
13 One who disdains a warning will pay for it,
   But he who respects an order will be rewarded.
14 The sage's teaching is a well of life
   Which diverts him from deadly snares.
15 A fine intelligence is gracious,
   But the manners of rogues are rough.
16 A clever man acts intelligently in everything he does,
   Whereas the stupid spreads folly around.
17 An unprincipled envoy makes trouble[e].
   But a dependable messenger makes things better.
18 Indifference to discipline wins no admiration,
   Whereas he who learns from a rebuke will be respected.
19 When what is desired happens, this is indeed pleasant;
   Hence fools hate to give up their evil plans.
20 If you would become wise, seek the company of wise
      men,
   Just as "the fellow of fools will fare ill."
21 Disaster dogs the steps of sinners,
   But good overtakes the just.
22 The good man passes on a heritage to his grandsons,
   But a sinner's possessions are reserved for the just.
23 Litigation[f] devours the poor man's farm land,
   And his dwelling[g] is swept away by injustice.
24 He who will not punish his son shows no love for him,
   For if he loves him he should be concerned to
      discipline him.

---

[d] Reading with LXX *mᵉbōhāl*, for MT *mēhebel*, "from vanity, emptiness."
LXX adds "by injustice," perhaps correctly; cf. Jer xvii 11; *Amen-em-ope*,
ch. 7 (ANET, p. 422b).
[e] *yappīl*, for MT *yippōl*, "falls into." Cf. xxv 13.
[f] *rīb 'ōkēl*, for MT *rab 'okel*, "much food."
[g] *rā'š ūmōšābō*, for MT *rā'šīm wᵉyēš*.

25   A good man eats only to satisfy his hunger,
     But the belly of base men is never filled.

NOTES

xiii 2. Cf. *Ptah-hotep* (ANET, p. 413a), "The eating of bread is under the planning of God." Cf. xii 14, xviii 20.

3a. The conciseness and internal rhyme of *nōṣēr pīw šōmēr napšō* suggest that this is a popular saying.

8. *threat.* Literally "rebuke." This means, apparently, that the poor man is better off than the rich because he has no wealth for thieves to covet. The sentiment is surprising, since elsewhere in Proverbs the advantages of riches are stressed; cf. x 15, xiv 20.

9. *light.* As symbolic of life, cf. Job iii 20; Ps xxxvi 9 EV.

the lamp. As signifying the continuity of the family, cf. I Kings xi 36.

13a. Literally "will have his pledge seized," a metaphor from the laws of debt. (Exod xxii 26 EV; Deut xxiv 6).

14. *well of life.* Like "tree of life," a stock phrase (cf. x 11, xiv 27, xvi 22), which explains what looks like a mixed metaphor.

15. *rough.* Literally "strong," "enduring," "hard" (KJ). Cf. Gen. xlix 24; Job xii 19.

19b. Literally "It is abomination to fools to turn away from evil." The first line is a variant of vs. 12b, and its connection with the second line is puzzling. "Abomination" means what is sacrilegious, ritually and morally unacceptable to God or the king, rather than to fools. Possibly *tōḥelet,* "expectation" should be read instead of *tō'ēbāh,* "abomination," and the line translated "And the (unfulfilled) expectation of fools is to avoid disaster."

20. Possibly a quoted popular epigram, because of the wordplay *rō'eh yērōa'.*

22. This seems to mean that only the just can leave an inheritance, and they also inherit from the wicked.

23. There is no moral indignation in the observation, which serves only as a warning against involvement in litigation (cf. xv 18, xxv 7–10).

15. THE WISE SAYINGS OF SOLOMON (*continued*)
(xiv 1–35)

XIV

1   Wisdom*ᵃ* builds her house,
    And Folly tears [hers] down with her hands.

2   The right-living man shows his reverence for the Lord,
    And the immoral man displays his contempt for him.

3   When a fool talks they take a stick to his back*ᵇ*,
    Whereas the words of wise men are their protection.

4   "Without [the labor of] oxen, the manger is bare";
    Abundant crops depend on the bullock's strength.

5   A reliable witness will not lie,
    But a false witness pours out falsehoods.

6   A scoffer tries to be sagacious but cannot,
    Whereas knowledge comes easily to the perceptive.

7   Leave the presence of a fool,
    And do not lavish*ᶜ* wise words [on him].

8   A clever man's wisdom makes him behave intelligently,
    And the folly of the stupid misleads them.

9   A fool mocks at*ᵈ* guilt,
    But divine favor is with the upright.

10 The heart knows its own bitterness,
    And no stranger shares its joy.

11 The house of the wicked shall be destroyed,
    But the tent of honest men shall flourish.

12 There is a road which may seem to run straight,
    But finally it becomes the way to death.

ᵃ Omitting *nāšīm*, "women."
ᵇ *gēwōh*, for MT *ga'ᵃwāh*, "pride."
ᶜ *tabbēᵃ'*, for MT *yāda'tā*, "thou knowest."
ᵈ *'ewīl mēlīṣ*, for MT *'ewīlīm yālīṣ*, "fools, it mocks."

13 Even when he laughs, a man's heart may be aching
       And joy gives way to grief.
14 The man of perverted mind will be requited for his
          behavior,
       And the generous man for his [good] deeds^e.
15 The simpleton believes everything he hears,
       But the sharp-witted looks where he is going.
16 A wise man is cautious and avoids trouble,
       But the fool gets angry and overconfident.
17 A short-tempered man commits folly,
       And a schemer makes himself hated.
18 The fatuous deck themselves with folly,
       But the clever crown their heads with knowledge.
19 Vile men will be made to bow before the righteous,
       And the wicked at the gates of the just.
20 A poor man is shunned even by his [former] companion,
       But "a rich man has many dear friends."
21 He who spurns a hungry man^f is committing sin,
       But blessed is one who is good to the poor.
22 Do not wicked schemers go astray,
       While affection and trust are theirs who seek good?
23 In all toil there is profit,
       But mere talk leads only to want.
24 The crown of wise men is their virtue^g,
       The garland^h of fools is folly.
25 A witness who tells the truth saves lives,
       But one who spreads lies is a betrayer^i.
26 In religious belief there is confident strength
       And security for one's children.
27 Religious belief is a well of life
       By which one avoids deadly snares.

---

^e *ūmimma'ᵃlālāw*, for MT *ūmē'ālāw*, "and from upon him."
^f *lᵉrā'ēb*, for MT *lᵉrē'ēhū*, "his neighbor."
^g *yošrām*, for MT *'ošrām*, "their riches."
^h *liwyat*, for MT *'iwwelet*, "folly."
^i *mᵉrammeh*, for MT *mirmāh*, "deceit."

28   A king's majesty is derived from a populous nation,
        Without [his] people, a prince is nothing.
29   A man not easily angered has great perception,
        But the irascible man shows what a fool he is.
30   Bodily health comes with a tranquil mind,
        But passionate feelings are like rot in the bones.
31   The oppressor of the weak insults his Maker,
        And the benefactor of the needy does him honor.
32   A bad man is knocked down by his own wrongdoing,
        While a good man finds shelter in his innocence[j].
33   Wisdom reposes in the mind of the wise,
        It is unknown among fools.
34   Righteousness exalts a nation,
        But sin leads to the impoverishment[k] of peoples.
35   A king's favor is granted to a capable servant,
        But the worthless will feel his anger.

[j] *b^etummō*, with LXX, for MT *b^emōtō*, "in his death."
[k] Reading with LXX *ḥeser*, for MT *ḥesed*, "shame."

NOTES

xiv 1. The word "women" after *Wisdom* is a scribal gloss explaining the archaic Canaanite form *hokmōt* as a feminine plural, when in fact it is equivalent to the normal Hebrew singular *hokmāh*. The former appears also at i 20 and ix 1 where, as here, Wisdom is personified; in a similar context at viii 1 it may have been lost through haplography. Since the personification of wisdom is found outside of chs. i–ix only here at xiv 1, the archaic form may have been chosen in poetic allusion to an ancient goddess of wisdom. The complete verse may originally have followed ix 6 and preceded ix 13, since it certainly is heterogeneous in its present context.

3a. Literally "In the mouth of a fool is a stick for [his] pride."

4. *bare.* Literally "pure." This is an analogical adage on *human* behavior; for the sentiment cf. II Thess iii 10, "If one will not work, he shall not eat."

7. *lavish.* Literally "pour out."

13b. Or, "After rejoicing he may lapse into grief."

17. *schemer*. Or "man of ideas." The word is used in both good and bad senses.

20. The second line has the sarcastic tone of many popular sayings; cf. Sirach 13–21.

21. Cf. vs. 31 and xvii 5, xix 17, xxi 13, xxviii 8. Charity is enjoined, as in the Akkadian *Counsels of Wisdom,* ii, 12–13, "Give food to eat; give date wine to drink; the one begging for alms, honor, clothe" (ANET, p. 426b).

24. Cf. i 9, iv 9; Job xxxi 36.

26. *religious belief*. Or, "the fear of the Lord." Cf. NOTE on i 7.

28b. Or, "When a people comes to nothing, the ruler falls with it."

30. *tranquil*. Or, "benevolent," "tolerant."

33. *unknown*. For MT "known"; the negative particle has been accidentally dropped.

35. Cf. xvi 14, xix 12.

16. THE WISE SAYINGS OF SOLOMON (*continued*)
(xv 1–33)

XV

1 A gentle answer turns aside anger,
   But a cutting retort makes a man angrier still.

2 The tongue of wise men commends knowledge,
   But the mouths of fools spout folly.

3 The eyes of the Lord are everywhere
   Watching bad men and good.

4 Gentle words are a tree of life,
   But falsity betrays a disturbed mind[a].

5 A fool is contemptuous of his father's training,
   But he who will accept reproof shows intelligence.

6 In the house of a good man there is great plenty,
   But the wages of the wicked will fail.

7 The lips of wise men disseminate[b] knowledge,
   But the mind of fools, untruth.

8 A sacrifice offered by wicked men is abominable to the
      Lord,
   But he is pleased with the prayer of the upright.

9 The Lord detests bad men's behavior,
   But he loves one who follows virtue.

10 One who abandons the [right] path will be sternly
      corrected,
   And he who resents rebuke will die.

11 Sheol and Abaddon are wide open to the Lord,
   How much more are the thoughts of men!

---

[a] *bᵉhiśśābēr rūᵃḥ*, for MT *bāh šeber bᵉrūᵃḥ*, "in it a breaking of spirit."
[b] *yōrū*, for MT *yᵉzārū*, "scatter."

12 An arrogant man has no love for his critic,
    [So] he keeps away from the wise.
13 A happy heart lights up the face,
    But the spirit is lamed by an inner hurt.
14 An intelligent mind is avid for knowledge,
    But the mouth of the fool feeds on folly.
15 To the miserable every day is a bad day,
    While for the cheerful, life is a continual feast.
16 Better to possess little and have religious faith,
    Than to be rich and live in turmoil.
17 Better a serving of vegetables where love is,
    Than prime beef [garnished] with hate.
18 A bad-tempered man stirs up strife,
    But patience will silence a dispute.
19 The path of the lazy man, [he says], is blocked with
        thorns,
    Whereas to the upright his road is a highway.
20 A wise son makes his father happy,
    And he is an oaf who shows contempt for his mother.
21 To act the idiot is fun to the empty-headed,
    But the man of intelligence forges straight ahead.
22 Plans miscarry when there is no consultation,
    But in the advice of many lies success.
23 An apt answer gives pleasure,
    And how good it is to hear the fitting word!
24 The path of life leads upward for the enlightened,
    Taking him ever farther from Sheol below.
25 The Lord will tear down the house of the proud,
    But he will preserve the property of the widow.
26 The Lord abhors the thoughts of an evil man,
    But he approves the words of the virtuous.
27 The profiteer will bring trouble on his home,
    Whereas one who refuses bribes will live [in peace].
28 The mind of a just man ponders what to answer,
    While the mouth of the wicked pours out threats.

29 The Lord is far from the wicked,
   But he listens to the prayer of the just.
30 The light in [a friend's] eyes gladdens the heart,
   And good news puts fat on the bones.
31 He whose ear listens to correction will find life,
   And will be at home among the wise.
32 One who neglects education holds himself cheap,
   But he who heeds a reprimand gains understanding.
33 Reverence for the Lord is the foundation*c* of wisdom,
   And humility must precede honors.

c mūsad, for MT *mūsar*, "instruction in."

NOTES

xv 2. *commends*. Or, "pours out."

3. Cf. v 21, xv 11, xxiv 12; Job xxxi 4. So the divine Pharaoh's "eyes search out everybody," says the Treasurer of Amen-em-het III, in instructing his son (ANET, p. 431a).

4. *tree of life*. See NOTE on iii 18. Cf. xiv 30.

5. A favorite theme in Proverbs, cf. i 8, vi 20, x 1, etc., and *Ptah-hotep*, ANET, p. 414b.

6. The bland general assertion of material reward and penalty (cf. x 3, xiii 20–21, xvii 20) raised doubts in ancient times as now (Job ix 24, xxi 7–26; Eccles vii 15). It was an unwarranted generalization from two more defensible claims: (a) that virtues and vices often have visible consequences (cf. x 4, 12, xi 17) and (b), that virtue points men toward life and vice points them toward death (cf. iii 18, vi 23, x 16, xii 28).

7. *untruth*. Literally "what is not so."

8. Cf. vs. 29, xxi 3, 27; Eccles v 1. This teaching echoes the prophets, cf. Isa i 10–17; Amos v 21–24, and *Meri-ka-re*, "More acceptable is the character of one upright of heart than the ox of the evil-doer" (ANET, p. 417b).

11. *Sheol*. Cf. NOTE on i 12.

Abaddon. "Destruction," a synonym for Sheol or the grave (Ps lxxxviii 11 EV; Job xxviii 22, xxxi 12). With 11a cf. Job xxvi 6. In Rev ix 11, *Abaddon* has become the name of the angelic ruler of the underworld.

13. Cf. xii 25, xvii 22, xviii 14; Sirach xiii 26.

16. *have religious faith*. Literally "with fear of the Lord." The wise say that possession of wealth is good (x 4), but not if it has been ob-

tained through injustice (xvi 8), or is accompanied by unhappiness (cf. vs. 17, xx 21). Amen-em-ope says (ch. 6), "Better is poverty in the hand of the god than riches in a storehouse." (ANET, p. 422b).

17a. Literally "Better a portion of greens."

17b. *prime beef*. Literally "a stall-fed bullock." So again *Amen-em-ope*, ch. 6, "Better is bread when the heart is happy, than riches with sorrow" (ANET, p. 422b).

18. Cf. xx 3.

21. Cf. xxvi 18–19.

25. Cf. xxiii 10–11; Luke i 52–53.

17. THE WISE SAYINGS OF SOLOMON (*continued*)
(xvi 1–33)

XVI

1 A man plans what he will say,
   But his tongue utters what the Lord wills.

2 Everything a man does seems right to him,
   But the Lord weighs the heart.

3 Turn over to the Lord what you [plan to] do,
   And your designs will come to fruition.

4 The Lord has made everything with its counterpart,
   So the wicked will have his day of doom.

5 The Lord detests all pride of heart,
   Be assured of this—it will not be condoned.

6 By loyalty and integrity guilt is atoned for,
   By reverence for the Lord and turning from wrong.

7 When the Lord is pleased with a man's conduct
   He makes even his enemies to be at peace with him.

8 Better to have a little that you have come by honestly,
   Than to have great revenues gained through injustice.

9 A man plans in his mind what he will do,
   But it is the Lord who directs his steps.

10 Inspired words are on the lips of a king,
   When he renders judgment he does not err.

11 A true balance and scales are the Lord's [concern],
   He has to do with all the weights in the bag.

12 Wrongdoing is hateful to kings,
   For through the right the throne stands secure.

13 Honest words give pleasure to kings,
   And one who speaks uprightly is favored.

14   A king's wrath heralds death,
       Yet a wise man may appease it.
15   If a king's look is benevolent, this portends life,
       And his favor is like a cloud promising spring rain.
16   To obtain wisdom is better than to obtain gold,
       And to possess insight than to possess silver.
17   The roadway of just men leads away from evil,
       And he who watches his step preserves his life.
18   "Pride precedes overthrow,"
       And arrogance leads to downfall.
19   Better to be of lowly spirit with the humble
       Than to share plunder with the proud.
20   One who understands what he is taught will find success,
       And he will be fortunate who trusts the Lord.
21   The wise-hearted becomes known for his intelligence,
       And persuasive speech is an additional
                   accomplishment.
22   Wisdom is a well of life to its possessor,
       But fools are educated only in folly.
23   The wise mind makes its meaning clear,
       And to be a master*a* of words is a further advantage.
24   Felicitous words are liquid honey,
       Sweet to one's taste and refreshing to one's being.
25   There is a road which seems to run straight ahead,
       But finally it becomes the way to death.
26   "The toiler's appetite toils for him"
       For his hunger drives him.
27   A scoundrel is a furnace*b* of evil,
       From his lips comes scorching fire.
28   A malicious man starts a quarrel,
       And a slanderer breaks up a friendship.
29   A criminal deceives his confederate,
       And leads him into ways that are not good.

a *ūbaʿal,* for MT *weʿal,* "and to."
b *kūr,* for MT *kōreh,* "digs up."

30 One who winks his eye is surely hatching some villainy,
   And he who purses his lips has concocted some evil.
31 Gray hair is a beautiful crown,
   Won by a life of virtue.
32 A patient man is better than a mighty one,
   And to master oneself is better than to take a city.
33 A lot is cast in the lap,
   And the decision comes from the Lord.

NOTES

xvi 1. Literally "The plans are man's, but from the Lord is the tongue's answer." The close parallel in vs. 9 makes the point clear: whatever man may intend, that which actually eventuates is decided by God. "Man proposes, God disposes." Cf. vs. 33, xix 21, xxi 30–31; Matt x 19–20; *Ahiqar* ix, "From thee is the arrow but from God the [guidance]" (ANET, p. 429b).

2. *weighs the heart.* Or, "considers motives." "To weigh the heart" is an idiom derived ultimately from Egyptian religious belief, in which judgment after death followed the weighing of a man's heart against Truth, in the balances of the supreme god Re (cf. J. B. Pritchard, *The Ancient Near East in Pictures*, 1954, p. 210). The phrase is here used of divine judgment in this life.

4. *counterpart.* Or, "purpose." Perhaps an answer to the question why evil men were created.

6. Cf. Hos vi 6; James ii 14–26.

8. Cf. xv 16; Ps xxxvii 16–17.

10. *Inspired words.* Literally "divination, an oracle." Cf. II Sam xxiii 1–2; I Kings iii 28. The king was held to be endowed with a special measure of divine wisdom; cf. viii 14–16; Isa xi 2.

11. See NOTE on xi 1. It seems that sets of stone *weights* of one, two, four, and eight shekels were kept in a *bag* or pouch; with these four weights any number of shekels up to fifteen could be weighed (cf. D. N. Freedman, in *Scripta Hierosolymitana* VIII, 1961, p. 12, n. 25). A shekel equaled about ⅖ oz. avdp. Stone weights of much larger multiples of the shekel were in use also; one representing eight minas or four hundred shekels (ten lbs.) came from Tell Beit Mirsim.

14. *heralds death.* Literally "messengers of death." Cf. xix 12, xx 2, and *Ahiqar* ix, "The wrath of a king is a burning fire" (ANET, p. 428b).

15a. Literally "In the light of a king's face." For the idiom, cf. the "Aaronic blessing," Num vi 24–26.

15b. The king's *favor* gave hope of good things to come, as *a cloud promising spring rain* gave hope of harvest. In a land where rainfall is barely sufficient at best and where there are periodic droughts, spring showers are of great value in bringing on the crops, and clouds are watched for eagerly (cf. I Kings xviii 44; Prov xxv 14).

18. The first line may be a popular saying, from its brevity and sarcastic tone.

20. *understands what he is taught.* Or, "knows the truth of a thing," or, "heeds the word [of his teacher]."

24. *Felicitous.* Or, "apt," "pleasant," i.e., suiting the occasion.

25. Identical with xiv 12.

26. The striking figure, wordplay and brevity indicate a popular saying; the sentiment may be either mocking or pathetic.

27. He is, as we say, "breathing fire and smoke."

29. Cf. i 10–19.

30. Cf. vi 12–14, x 10.

33. Throughout the Bible the casting of lots was a much used method of ascertaining the divine will (Lev xvi 8; Num xxvi 55; Jon i 7; Acts i 26), as well as simply for reaching decisions without religious reference (i 14; Ps xxii 18 EV).

18. THE WISE SAYINGS OF SOLOMON (*continued*)
(xvii 1–28)

XVII

1   Better a dry crust with an easy mind,
     Than a houseful of feasting and quarreling.

2   A knowledgeable servant will have authority over a
          shameless son,
     And will share the inheritance as one of the brothers.

3   Like a crucible for silver and a smelter for gold,
     The Lord is a refiner of the thoughts of men.

4   An evildoer listens to mischievous proposals,
     And a liar[a] lends his ear to greedy talk.

5   He who mocks a poor man insults his Maker,
     And one who makes fun of calamity will not
          escape punishment.

6   Grandsons are the garland of old men,
     And fathers are the pride of their sons.

7   Honest[b] speech is not to be expected from a knave,
     Still less is falsehood from a worthy man.

8   A gift is a lucky stone in the eyes of him who receives it,
     Wherever he turns, he will prosper.

9   One who overlooks a fault does so for love's sake,
     For harping on the matter will break up a friendship.

10   A word of remonstrance to an intelligent man
      Has more effect than a hundred blows on a fool.

11   An outlaw is surely looking for trouble,
      And a merciless emissary will be sent after him.

---

[a] *mᵉšaqqēr*, for MT *šeqer*, "lying."
[b] *yōšer*, for MT *yeter*, "excellence"(?).

12   Better to meet a she-bear robbed of her cubs
       Than a senseless man engaged in his folly.

13   If one returns evil for good,
       Trouble will never depart from his home.

14   "The beginning of a quarrel is like the opening of a sluice
             gate";
       So before the dispute breaks out, let the matter go.

15   To absolve the wicked and to condemn the innocent
       Are equally hateful to the Lord.

16   What good does it do a fool to come fee in hand to buy
             wisdom,
       When he has no mind?

17   At all times a friend is devoted,
       And a brother was born to share adversity.

18   A man has no sense who makes a [rash] bargain
       And mortgages himself in his neighbor's presence.

19   "One who is fond of crime must be fond of trouble,"
       And to make one's doorway inaccessible is to invite
             destruction.

20   A man of perverted mind will come to no good,
       And the double-tongued will meet disaster.

21   He who begets a fool finds much grief,
       And the father of an ill-natured youth has no
             happiness.

22   A cheerful spirit is good for the health,
       But a gloomy outlook makes the bones lean.

23   A corrupt man gives a secret bribe
       To divert the course of justice.

24   The discerning man sees the wise choice right in front of
             him,
       While the fool is looking to the ends of the earth.

25   A senseless son is a vexation to his father
       And bitterness to her who bore him.

26   Even to fine the innocent is reprehensible;
       To flog honorable men is against all right.

27   A learned man is restrained in speech,
       And the judicious man keeps a cool head.

28   Even a simpleton who remains silent may be thought
       wise,
       And his closed lips be taken as a mark of intelligence.

NOTES

xvii 1. An adage of popular wisdom, like the French proverb, "Better an egg in peace than an ox in wartime." Possibly it was expanded from a terse alliterative proverb, *ṭôb pat ḥᵃrēbāh mibbēt rīb,* "better a dry crust than a house of strife." Cf. xv 17.

feasting. Literally "sacrifices"; cf. NOTE on vii 14.

2. Normally the father's property was divided among his sons, the eldest receiving a double share (Deut xxi 15–17). If there were no sons, daughters might inherit, but not the wife; if a man died childless the property went to his male next of kin (Num xxvii 8–11), or to an adopted son who might be a former slave (Gen xv 2–3; cf. the practice in Nuzi, ANET, pp. 219b–220a). The precise situation contemplated here, where a slave takes the share of a renegade son, is not provided for in the Mosaic Law.

5. In the Wisdom writings, belief in retribution rests on the thought of God as the Creator of all, rather than as the divine champion of his covenant people, as in the prophets. Cf. viii 22–36; Job xxxviii 1–xl 18; and cf. Isa iii 13–15. Amen-em-ope says, "Do not laugh at a blind man nor tease a dwarf" (ANET, p. 424a).

7. *knave.* Or, "reckless fool." The rhyming form of the proverb is noticeable, *lō' nā'wāh lᵉnābāl śᵉpat yōšer, 'ap kī lᵉnādīb śᵉpat šāqer.*

8. The translation of this verse is uncertain, though its text is well preserved. *'eben ḥēn* may mean either a charm or a beautiful jewel, *šōḥad* may be a gift or a bribe, *bᵉʿālāw* may refer either to the giver or to the recipient, and the subject of the verbs in the second line is undetermined. Hence other possible renderings of the verse are, "A gift is like a jewel in the eyes of its recipient, every way he turns it, it appears superb," and "A bribe is like a charm in the eyes of the giver."

9. *for love's sake.* I.e., either, "through loving forbearance" or, "to win love."

10. The frequent references to the beating of children and fools (x 13, xiii 24, xix 25, 29, xxiii 13–14, xxix 15) throw a glaring light on the

educational methods of the time. xxvi 3 presumably refers to beating of a stupid or disobedient servant (cf. Luke xii 45–48).

11. *outlaw.* Literally "rebellion."

emissary. Like Saul's messengers sent to arrest David, I Sam xix 14; cf. II Kings vi 32.

13. As Nabal, whose name could be taken to mean "reckless fool," is said to have done to David, I Sam xxv 21.

14. *sluice gate.* In an irrigation ditch for the watering of gardens, cf. xi 25; Isa lviii 11. Brevity, picturesqueness, alliteration, and rhyme suggest that the first line is a popular proverb, *pōtēr máyim rē'šīt mādōn*. Cf. the Akkadian, "If it is really your own quarrel, extinguish the flame" (ANET, p. 426b).

16. This sarcastic comment of a teacher dealing with refractory material shows that fees were brought to the Wisdom teachers. Cf. the English proverb, "An ounce of mother wit is worth a pound of learning."

18. *mortgages himself.* So that he may lose his property, his freedom, or both. The reiterated warnings on this subject (vi 1–5, xi 15, xx 16, etc.) show that many were being ruined by such rashness.

19a. *'ohēb pešaʻ 'ōhēb maṣṣāh.* Literally "He who loves transgression loves strife," a popular saying of the type x–y, x–z; for example, "Who steals an egg will steal an ox."

19b. The proud or unfriendly man's *inaccessible* (literally "high up") *doorway* provokes enmity, as a door easy of access invites friendship.

21. *ill-natured.* The special brand of fool, stubborn and surly, exemplified in the man Nabal, I Sam xxv 2–42.

23. Literally "A bribe from the bosom of a corrupt man is received (*yuqqāḥ* for MT *yiqqāḥ*). Or, "A corrupt (judge, witness) takes a bribe. . . ."

24a. Literally "Face to face with a discerning man is wisdom."

26. Refers to judicial beating (cf. Deut xxv 1–3); see NOTE on vs. 10, above.

27. Cf. x 19, xi 12, xiii 3, for the wise man's reserve and self-control, an ideal shared with Egyptian Wisdom teachers (*Ani*, vii; *Amen-em-ope*, chs. 4, 9; in ANET, pp. 420b, 422a, 423a).

19. THE WISE SAYINGS OF SOLOMON (*continued*)
(xviii 1–24)

XVIII

1 An unsociable man cares only about his selfish concerns,
   He rails against every sound enterprise.

2 The fool finds no pleasure in reasoning,
   But only in airing his views.

3 When wickedness[a] appears, shame comes with it,
   And disgrace is the companion of scorn.

4 The words of a man's mouth are deep water,
   The well of wisdom is a flowing stream.

5 It is not right to favor the guilty,
   Or to deny justice in court to the innocent.

6 A fool's talk lands him[b] in a dispute,
   And his mouth calls out for a beating.

7 A fool's mouth is his ruin,
   And his lips are the snare which traps him.

8 The words of a slanderer are swallowed greedily,
   They go down to the innermost belly.

9 One who is slack in his work
   Is own brother to the wrecker.

10 The name of the Lord is a strong tower
    To which the just man may run and be safe.

11 A rich man's wealth is his strong city,
    It shields[c] him like a high wall.

12 Pride is the precursor of ruin,
    And humility must precede honors.

---

[a] MT "a wicked man."
[b] *yᵉbī'ūhū*, for MT *yābō'ū*, "come."
[c] *massēkātō*, "is his covering," for MT *bᵉmaśkītō*, "in his imagination."

13 When a man answers before hearing what is said,
   He is both stupid and insulting.

14 A [brave] spirit sustains a man when he is ill,
   But when the spirit is sick, who can cure it?

15 A discerning mind acquires knowledge,
   And wise men's ears are alert for it.

16 A man's gift clears the way for him,
   And brings him into the presence of the great.

17 He seems right who states his case first,
   Until his opponent comes and cross-examines him.

18 Casting the lot will settle lawsuits,
   And decide between powerful contenders.

19 A brother offended is harder [to be won] than a strong
      city,
   And his antagonism*d* is like the bar of a castle.

20 A man's stomach will be filled as his speech deserves,
   And he must be satisfied with the crop his lips
      [have sowed].

21 Death or life is in the power of the tongue,
   A man will eat the fruit of whichever he chooses.

22 A man who has found a [good] wife has found
      happiness,
   And has been granted a mark of God's favor.

23 A poor man must speak as a suppliant,
   But the rich man answers roughly.

24 A man has companions for company*e*,
   But a true friend is closer to him than a brother.

---

d *medōnāw* for MT *midyānīm,* "contentions." The ancient versions give a
quite different sense to the verse (reading *nōša'* for MT *nipšā'*), "A brother
saved [becomes] like a strong city, and [LXX adds] is strong as a well-founded
kingdom."

e Reading *lehitrā'ōt,* for MT *lehitrō'ēa',* "to be broken"; cf. xvii 17, xxvii 10.

NOTES

xviii 1. *cares only about his selfish concerns.* Or "wants only to be left alone."

rails against. Or, "bursts out angrily."

4. *deep water.* As in xx 5, suggests obscurity rather than profundity.

5. A legal maxim.

6. *beating.* Here it may be a judicial penalty; cf. Deut xxv 1–3.

8. *are swallowed greedily.* Or, "are like delicious food." This verse is repeated at xxvi 22.

9. For the metaphor of family relationship to indicate related characteristics, cf. Virgil *Aeneid* vi 278, "Death's own brother, Sleep."

10. *a strong tower.* The keep of a fortified city.

11. *shields.* Or, "covers," or "hides."

12. Similar to xvi 18, where the parallelism is synonymous rather than antithetic, as here. The first line may reflect a didactic proverb which has been differently developed in the respective second lines.

14b. Or, "when the spirit is crushed, who can lift it?" Cf. xv 13, xvii 22.

17. A legal maxim, presumably introducing the rebuttal.

18. A legal maxim, calling for settlement of a difficult case, by the casting of a lot. See NOTE on xvi 33.

19. *offended.* Or, "sinned against," though the construction is doubtful.

20. A man must accept the consequences of what he says; cf. vs. 21; xii 14.

22. *happiness.* Literally "good." The x–y, x–z form of *māṣā' 'iššāh māṣā' tōb* suggests a more epigrammatic rendering, "A good wife means a good life." A fortunate outcome of the incalculable risk of marriage is taken as a mark of the Lord's favor, cf. xix 13; and cf. xix 14, xxi 9, 19, xxvii 15–16.

23. *speak as a suppliant.* Literally "utter entreaties."

XIX

1   Better a poor man who lives virtuously
    Than a dissembler who is rich[a].

2   Zeal without knowledge is not a good thing,
    For a man in a hurry makes a slip.

3   It is a man's own stupidity which ruins his life,
    Yet he is bitter against the Lord.

4   Wealth brings many new friends,
    But the needy is parted from the one friend he has.

5   A false witness will not go uncondemned,
    Nor will he escape who breathes out falsehoods.

6   There are many who will praise a noble to his face
    And everyone is the friend of a giver of gifts.

7   All a poor man's brothers shun him,
    Still more do his [former] friends keep him at a
        distance,
    [When he follows them they speak angrily to him][b].

8   He who develops his mind is his own best friend,
    And one who cherishes reason will surely succeed.

9   A false witness will not go uncondemned,
    And one who breathes out falsehoods will perish.

10   It is not fitting that a fool should enjoy comfort,
    Any more than that a slave should rule over princes.

11   A sagacious man is forbearing,
    And it is to his honor when he overlooks a fault.

[a] *'āšîr*, for MT *keşîl*, "fool."
[b] Reading *hû' meraddēp 'omrēhēm lō' hēmāh*, for MT *meraddēp 'amārîm lō' hēmmāh*, "pursuing, words to him are they."

12   A king's rage is like the roaring of a lion,
     But his favor is like dew on the plants.

13   A stupid son is the despair of his father,
     And a wife's grumbling is a constant dripping.

14   A home and wealth are inherited from one's forebears,
     But a sensible wife is from the Lord.

15   [His own] laziness will bring the roof down on the sleeper,
     And the shiftless man will go hungry.

16   "To observe the law is to preserve yourself,"
     To be careless of one's behavior is a fatal error.

17   A benefactor of the needy is lending to the Lord,
     And he will be repaid in full.

18   Discipline your son while there is still hope for him,
     And do not indulge him to his own destruction.

19   A very angry man^e must take the consequences;
     If you intervene with him you will make things worse.

20   Listen to advice and accept correction
     So that finally you may become wise.

21   Many are the plans in a man's mind,
     But the Lord's will determines how things will turn
     out.

22   It is human to desire gain^d
     But "better to be poor than a liar."

23   Reverence for the Lord is life-giving,
     So that one may rest satisfied, untroubled by evil.

24   The lazy man puts his hand into the dish,
     He will not even raise it to his mouth.

25   When you strike an insolent fellow a fool may learn a
     lesson,
     When you admonish an intelligent man, it will add to
     [his] knowledge.

26   One who corrects his father and has no patience with
     his mother
     Is a shameful son and a disgrace.

---

^{c} MT $g^er\bar{a}l$ $\hbar\bar{e}m\bar{a}h$; the first word is unknown and was corrected in tradition to $g^ed\bar{o}l$, i.e., "great in wrath"; cf. xv 18.
^{d} $\hbar osn\bar{o}$, for MT $\hbar asd\bar{o}$, "his kindness."

27 My son, if you will no longer listen to instruction,
       You will [soon] wander away from what you have
          [already] learned.
28 A rascally witness profanes justice,
       And the mouths of wicked men pour out guile.
29 Rods*e* are ready for [beating] the impious,
       And blows for the backs of fools.

e šᵉbāṭīm, for MT *šᵉpāṭīm,* "judgments"; cf. xiii 24.

NOTES

xix 1. *dissembler.* Or, as in xxviii 6, "rogue."

2. *Zeal.* Or, "enthusiasm," Heb. *nepeš.* Cf. Rom x 2.

5. Another example, with vs. 9, of doublets of the same saying.

A false witness is primarily one who makes a false accusation against another, rather than one who gives untrue supporting testimony for or against the accused (Exod xxiii 1–3, 7; Deut xix 16–19).

7. The second and third lines are probably alternatives, representing with line 1 different forms of the same saying.

shun. Literally "hate"; refers to attitude and actions rather than to feelings.

8. *develops his mind.* Or, "obtains wisdom"; literally "obtains mind."

9. Cf. vs. 5.

10. This is not simply an expression of contempt or conservatism, but expresses the sage's belief that the social order should correspond to the moral order established by God (i 29–33, viii 14–21, xxix 2, xxx 21–23; Eccles x 5–7).

12. Cf. xvi 14–15, xx 2; *Ahiqar* vii, "The wrath of a king . . . is a burning fire; . . . noble is his majesty to them that walk the earth (as free men)" (ANET, pp. 428b–429a).

13. *grumbling.* Literally "contentions of."

Constant dripping. Literally "a dripping leak" (which drives one out of the house); cf. xxi 9, 19, xxv 24, xxvii 15.

14. Cf. xviii 22, NOTE.

15. *bring the roof down on the sleeper.* Literally "cause the sleeping-place to fall." So Dahood, PNWSP, p. 40, and cf. Eccles x 18; Prov vi 9–11, xx 4, 13, xxvi 14.

16. Literally "he who observes," "he who disdains." The internal rhyme suggests a common precept.

19. *make things worse.* Or, "have to do it again."

20. *finally.* Literally "at your end."

21. *the Lord's will.* Or, "counsel, decision." *'ēṣāh* means (a) advice given, (b) a decision made after taking counsel. Cf. xvi 9; Gen xlv 8; and *Amen-em-ope,* ch. 18 (ANET, p. 423b).

24. The proverb is found in slightly different form at xxvi 15, with others exhibiting the same kind of sarcastic humor.

25. This seems to mean that though blows cannot teach *an insolent fellow* anything, the sight may be a lesson to a simple fellow, as in vs. 29; cf. xxi 11.

26. *has no patience with.* Literally "drives away."

28. See NOTE on vs. 5 above.

21. THE WISE SAYINGS OF SOLOMON (*continued*)
(xx 1–30)

XX

1   Wine makes men insolent, beer makes them boisterous,
     No one who staggers drunkenly is wise.

2   The dread of a king is like the fear of a lion's roar;
     When he is furious, the offender's life is in danger.

3   It is honorable for a man to avoid a dispute,
     But every fool loves a quarrel.

4   At the onset of winter the idler does not plow;
     So at harvest time he looks for [a crop] and finds none.

5   Sagacity in a man's mind is like deep water,
     The intelligent person will draw from it.

6   Many a man professes[a] good will,
     But where will you find one you can trust?

7   When a man lives a virtuous and honest life
     His sons are fortunate in their inheritance.

8   When a king takes his seat on the judgment throne,
     He sifts out all evil with his eyes;

9   Who can say, "My heart is clean,
     I am free of offense"?

10   Unequal weights and unequal measures,
     Are both of them hateful to the Lord.

11   By his actions a youth makes it clear
     Whether what he is doing is honest and upright.

12   The ear that hears, the eye that sees—
     The Lord is the maker of them both.

13   Do not be fond of sleep lest you lose your inheritance,
     Keep your eyes open and you will have plenty to eat.

---

[a] Literally "calls himself," *yiqqārē'* for MT *yiqrā'*, "he calls."

14 "It is no good, no good!" says the buyer,
But as he goes away he congratulates himself.

15 One may have gold and many jewels,
But a wise man's lips [drink from] a more precious
cup.

16 Take the garment of one who becomes surety for a
foreigner;
And seize the pledge made on account of a "stranger
woman."

17 A man may delight in making his living dishonestly,
But after a time his mouth will be filled with gravel.

18 Through consultation you will make up your mind,
And with firm purpose will conduct your campaign.

19 A gossip is always betraying confidences,
So do not associate with an empty babbler.

20 One who curses his father and his mother—
His lamp will go out in the darkness of night.

21 An estate gained hurriedly at first
Will not be blessed in the end.

22 Do not say, "I will repay a wrong";
Hope in the Lord and he will make you triumph.

23 Unequal weights are abominable to the Lord,
And dishonest balances are wicked.

24 It is by the Lord that a man's steps are directed—
How could a human being know which way to take?

25 A man is trapped who rashly dedicates something,
And stops to consider [only] after making the vow.

26 A wise king sifts out the wicked
And puts them under the wheel.

27 A man's breath is the Lord's lamp,
Illuminating all his inmost being.

28 Graciousness and integrity are a king's defense,
And righteousness[b] supports his throne.

29 Young men are admired for their strength,
And old men are honored for their gray hair.

[b] So LXX. MT reads "with graciousness he supports. . . ."

30 Wounds and bruises will scour the wicked man,
    And beatings will penetrate deep within him.

NOTES

xx 1. The sages' objection to intoxication is that it turns a man into a
fool; cf. xxiii 19–21, xxxi 4–5, and the vivid description of the drunken
man, xxiii 29–35. The use of liquor as a needed stimulant was recognized
(xxxi 6–7; II Sam xvi 2), and also the normal pleasure in its use on
festal occasions (ix 2, 5; Eccles ix 7; Ps civ 15; Job i 13; Sirach xxxi 27–
28, xl 20). However, the possibility of the excesses described in Gen ix
20–23, xix 32–38, and in the prophets (Isa v 11–12, 22, xxviii 1, 7–8;
Jer xxiii 9; Hos vii 5; Amos vi 6) made it necessary to forbid the use of
liquor to priests who were about to officiate, and led to the grave warnings of prophets and sages (Isa v 22; Sirach xix 1–3, xxxi 29–30).

2. Cf. xix 12.

3. *avoid*. Literally "remain seated from a dispute."

4. *winter*. Or, "autumn." Palestine has two seasons, a hot dry summer
from May to September and a cool, moderately rainy season from October to April. These are distinguished in Gen ix 22 as "seedtime and
harvest, cold and heat." Plowing is done as soon as the hard-baked soil
is softened by "the early rain," the first of the winter rains in October
or November.

the idler. He takes the excuse of cold or rain (xxv 23) to omit plowing
before sowing his seed.

5. *deep water*. I.e., in a well; cf. xviii 4.

8, 9. The second couplet is dependent on the first and may have been
added to clarify its meaning. Cf. vs. 26 and xvi 10.

10a. Literally "A weight and a weight, an *'ēpāh* and an *'ēpāh*"; cf.
Lev xix 36; Deut xxv 15; Ezek xlv 10. The *'ēpāh* was the standard dry
measure, equal to three fifths of the U.S. bushel. Cf. vs. 23, xi 1, xvi 11.

12. Therefore man should lend his ear to instruction (xviii 15) and
keep his eyes open to observe; cf. vs. 13.

14. Perhaps this is intended as a counterpart to the condemnation of
the dishonest merchant in vss. 10 and 23; the customer, too, is not sincere
because he pretends what he wants to buy is of no value. The form of
the proverb is unusual in resembling a "Wellerism" ("as *X* said to *Y*").

15. Cf. iii 14–15, viii 10–11.

16. Repeated in xxvii 13. In vi 1–5, there is a warning of the danger
of acting as guarantor. Here the lender is advised to be strict in claiming

the *garment* pledged on behalf of [or, by?] a foreigner [a traveling merchant] or a *"stranger woman"* [see NOTE on ii 16], in contrast to the leniency toward fellow Israelites enjoined in Exod xxii 26–27 EV.

17. *filled with gravel.* Because prostrate on the ground; cf. Lam iii 16.

18. *conduct your campaign.* Literally "make war."

19. Cf. xi 13, xviii 8.

20. Such impiety was regarded as the height of iniquity, not only in Israel (Exod xxi 17; Deut xxvii 16; Matt xv 4) but in Egypt (*Ani* vii–viii, ANET, pp. 420b–421a) and in Assyria, cf. *Ahiqar* ix, "(whosoever) takes no pride in the names of his father and mother, may the sun not shine (upon him), for he is a wicked man" (ANET, p. 429b).

22. *make you triumph.* Or, "save you." Since the wrong has been done already, the former translation is more probably what is intended. Beginning from the multiple retaliation of desert vengeance (Gen iv 24), religious morality first limits vengeance by the principle of justice to "one eye for one eye, one tooth for one tooth" (Exod xxi 23–25), then substitutes divine retribution for personal revenge, as here (cf. Deut xxxii 35; Ps xciv 1), and finally enjoins non-resistance and love as the most effective response to a wrong suffered (xxv 21–22; Lev xix 18; Matt v 38–48). See NOTE on xxv 22.

23. *wicked.* Literally "not good," which in English lacks the force of the Hebrew. "Good" here means what is acceptable to God and expected of men; cf. Mic vi 8.

24. Cf. xvi 9; Jer x 23.

25. *stops to consider.* Or, "tries to get out of it."

vow. A promise to dedicate to the Temple a votive offering in acknowledgment of the granting by God of an earnest wish; cf. Deut xxiii 21; Judg xi 30–31; Lev xxvii 1–25; Ps cxvi 18–19.

26. *under the wheel.* Probably a figurative phrase for "punish," derived from the practice of a victorious king driving his chariot over his prostrate enemies.

27. The conception is difficult, and much can be said for reading *nōṣēr*, "watches, is the keeper of," for *nēr*, "lamp." The verse would then be rendered, "The Lord is the keeper of man's life, the examiner of his inmost being." Cf. Jer xvii 10.

28. Cf. the admonition to a Babylonian prince, "If a king does not heed justice, his people will be thrown into chaos, and his land will be devastated" (BWL, p. 113); and the Egyptian *Instruction for King Merika-re*, "Uprightness of heart is fitting for the Lord. . . . Do justice while thou endurest upon earth" (ANET, p. 415b).

22. THE WISE SAYINGS OF SOLOMON (*continued*)
(xxi 1–31)

XXI

1 The mind of a king is like water channels [under the
    Lord's control];
    He diverts it wherever he chooses.

2 What a man does is right in his own eyes,
    But the Lord weighs hearts.

3 The doing of right and justice
    Is more acceptable to the Lord than sacrifice.

4 Because of their pride and arrogance,
    The vow*a* of evil men is a sin.

5 The plans of the keen man show a profit,
    But all who are too hasty show a loss.

6 He who acquires wealth through deceitful words
    Will find it is a fleeting breath and a deadly snare*b*.

7 The plunder seized by wicked men will drag them down,
    Because they refuse to do justice.

8 The way of the liar*c* is subversive,
    But the just man's action is innocent.

9 It is better to live in a corner of a [flat] roof,
    Than with a quarrelsome woman in a spacious
      house.

10 The mind of a vicious man yearns to make trouble,
    He has no mercy for his fellow man.

---

a neder, for MT *nīr*, "newly plowed land," or *nēr*, "lamp," as in the ancient
versions, neither of which makes sense here.
b mōqēš, for MT *mᵉbaqqᵉšē*, "seekers of."
c kāzāb, for MT *wāzār*, a word whose meaning, if any, is unknown. The
word pair *'īš kāzāb* is found in xix 22.

11   The simple learns a lesson [only] when a scoffer comes
          to grief,
      But the intelligent man understands when a matter is
          explained.

12   A just man reads the thoughts of wicked men*d*,
      And turns such men to ruin.

13   If one shuts his ear to the cry of the poor,
      He too will call out and get no answer.

14   A gift made secretly allays anger,
      And a stealthy bribe, great wrath.

15   When justice triumphs, good men rejoice,
      But this spells ruin for evildoers.

16   The man who wanders from the way of understanding
      Will come to rest in company with the dead.

17   One who loves pleasure will end in poverty,
      And the lover of wine and perfume will not grow rich.

18   The bad man becomes a ransom for the just,
      And the deceiver [is punished], not the upright.

19   It is better to live in a desert land
      Than with a quarrelsome and discontented wife.

20   There is precious wealth*e* where a wise man dwells,
      But the man who is stupid consumes it.

21   He who seeks earnestly what is right and kind,
      Will find life*f* and respect.

22   A wise man attacked a city of warriors
      And humbled the strength in which it trusted.

23   He who watches his mouth and his tongue
      Saves himself from many trials.

24   His names are "Brazen," "Insolent," "Impious,"
      Who acts in arrogant fury.

25   The lazy man's hunger slays him
      Because his hands refuse to work.

d Reading with LXX *libbōt rešā'īm*, for MT *lebēt rāšā'*, "(to) a wicked man's
house."
e Omitting *wāšémen*, "and oil," with LXX. But "oil" may have been the
original reading and *precious wealth* an explanatory gloss.
f Omitting the accidentally repeated *ṣedāqāh*.

26   A sinner^g is always selfish,
     But a good man gives without stint.

27   A sacrifice offered by wicked men is an abomination,
     All the more so if one bring it with a shameful purpose.

28   A lying witness will be discomfited,
     Then one who is well advised^h will speak up.

29   A bad man must put on a bold face,
     But the virtuous is sure of his way.

30   There is no wisdom, no thought, no policy,
     Which can avail against the Lord.

31   The horse may be arrayed for the day of battle,
     But the victory rests with the Lord.

g Reading *ḥōtē'* with LXX, for MT *ta'awāh*, "desire." Cf. xi 24–26.
h *šōmēa' le'ēṣāh*, "heeding counsel," as in xii 15, for MT *šōmēa' lānĕṣaḥ*, "heeding forever."

Notes

xxi 1. The first line combines two forms of the text of this proverb, the second being in brackets; they give different meanings to the saying, since they change the subject of the verb in the second line. The first asserts the sovereign freedom of the king (cf. xvi 10, 15, xxv 3), the second, his subjection to Yahweh (cf. xix 21, xx 27–28; Job xii 24–25).

2. Almost identical with xvi 2.

3. The same sentiment as xv 8; see NOTE *ad loc.*

4. *arrogance.* Or, "ambition," or conceit of knowledge; cf. I Kings iv 29 EV.

5. A slightly expanded version of an alliterative, rhyming, pregnant popular maxim, *hārūṣ 'ak le mōtār, 'āṣ 'ak le maḥsōr.*

6. *deceitful words.* Unkept promises or false witness.
fleeting breath, cf. x 2, xiii 11, xx 21; Eccles i 14.

9. I.e., in a small room or shelter such as was used for guests, cf. II Kings iv 10. It was ironical that the master of the household should be banished there by his wife's tongue. Read *rāḥāb* for *ḥáber,* for sake of parallelism. Cf. vs. 19 and xxv 24.

11. Cf. xix 25.

12. *such.* Literally "wicked."

13. Cf. xxviii 27; James ii 13; *Amen-em-ope,* ch. 2 (ANET, p. 422a), "guard thy self against robbing the oppressed."

14. Cf. xvii 23, xviii 16; possibly a reference to settling a case out of court, or to the bribing of a judge about to condemn the offender. It sounds like a cynical popular adage; cf. "A bribe will enter without knocking."

15. Or, "Good men are happy to see justice done, but it seems ruinous to evildoers."

17. Cf. xxiii 20–21; Sirach xviii 32–33.

18. *ransom.* Or, "substitute," i.e., he gets into the trouble he has planned for *the just;* cf. xi 8. Rashi compares the case of Haman and Mordecai, Esther vii 10.

22. An adage reflecting a true or fictional story now lost to us. A similar story of the defense of (rather than an attack on) a city by a wise man, appears in Eccles ix 13–16, where the conclusion is, as here, that "wisdom is better than might."

23. Probably a developed form of a popular rhyming proverb, *šōmēr pīw šōmēr napšō;* cf. xiii 3.

27. *with a shameful purpose.* Literally "with shameful conduct." They display their bad character even when they engage in religious rites, hence their hypocrisy is even more shocking.

28. *one who is well advised.* Apparently the next witness in a case.

30. *wisdom* here in a sense unusual in Proverbs, i.e., the arrogant claim of secular wisdom; cf. Job v 12–13, xii 2, xxviii 13, xxxix 19–35; I Cor i 20.

23. THE WISE SAYINGS OF SOLOMON—(*continued*)
(xxii 1–16)

XXII

1 A good name is more to be desired than great riches,
   And to be gracious is better than to have silver and
     gold.

2 When a rich man and a poor man meet,
   [Let them remember that] the Lord has made them
     both.

3 A shrewd man sees trouble coming and avoids it,
   While simpletons keep on and pay the penalty.

4 The consequence of humility and reverence for the Lord
   Is wealth and honor and life.

5 Thorns and snares are in the path of the crooked man,
   One who is cautious will give them a wide berth.

6 Give a lad the training he needs for life,
   Even when he is old it will stay with him.

7 A rich man dominates the poor,
   And a borrower becomes the lender's slave.

8 He who sows wrong will reap calamity,
   And the punishment he brings on himself will be the
     end of him[a].

9 A generous man will hear himself blessed
   When he gives of his own food to the needy.

10 Expel the insolent man and discord will leave with him,
   Disputes and name-calling will cease.

11 [The Lord][b] loves a man of pure mind;
   Gracious speech wins the friendship of a king.

[a] *yᵉkallēhū*, for MT *yikleh*, "will cease."
[b] Inserting "the Lord," with LXX.

12   The eyes of the Lord watch over knowledge,
      And he contradicts the words of a deceiver.
13   The lazy man says, "There is a lion outside!
      In the streets I shall be killed!"
14   The speech of harlots is a deep pit,
      He with whom the Lord is angry falls into it.
15   Willful ignorance is ingrained in the mind of a boy,
      [Only] the teacher's cane will rid him of it.
16   One who oppresses the poor to aggrandize himself,
      Will have to yield to the rich and will end in poverty.

NOTES

xxii 1. Cf. x 7; Eccles vii 1; Sirach xli 12–13.

2. This may mean (a) that they share a common humanity, (b) that God has willed their station in life, and may reverse it, or (c) that personal worth is more important than wealth (cf. xix 1, xx 21, xxix 13). Amen-em-ope says, "Man is clay and straw, and the god is his builder. . . . He makes a thousand poor men as he wishes, [or] he makes a thousand men (as overseers)" (ANET, p. 424b).

3. The identical proverb is found at xxvii 12, and a variant at xiv 16. Dahood, PNWSP, pp. 45–46, explains *yistār* as an infixed -*t* form of *sūr,* "turn aside."

4. Material, social, and spiritual rewards.

5. *cautious.* Literally "guarding his life."

8. LXX here adds a variant form of this proverb in which the second line is virtually the same; the first line reads "God honors a cheerful giver," which is the source of the quotation in II Cor ix 7. It is possible that II Cor ix 6, "He that sows sparingly shall reap also sparingly" (where the proverbial form is apparent), is another Greek variant of 8a.

9. *A generous man.* Literally "one whose eye is good." Contrast the "evil eye" or "malevolent expression" of the stingy or avaricious man, Prov xxiii 6, xxviii 22.

11. The subject of *loves* is supplied from LXX. Without it the verse reads literally, "One who loves pureness of mind, grace of speech, his friend is a king." The verse has been damaged in transmission; LXX inserts after *mind,* "all who are blameless are acceptable to him," and another line is missing altogether.

12. *knowledge.* Or, "words of knowledge," as in xiv 7. The divine giver of wisdom cares for those who possess his gift; cf. xv 3.

13. An alternative form of this saying is found in xxvi 13, with other sarcastic comments on "the sluggard."

14. *harlots.* Or, "stranger women," cf. v 3 and see NOTE on ii 16. This is the only mention of this subject in Part II (x 1–xxii 16), in contrast to the emphasis on it in Part I (i–ix).

15. *Willful ignorance.* Literally "Folly."

the teacher's cane. Literally "the rod of discipline." For other references to this method of instruction, cf. x 13, xiii 24, xxiii 13–14, xxix 15. The English proverb "Spare the rod and spoil the child!" is derived from these.

16. The translation and meaning of this verse are doubtful. Literally, it reads, "One who oppresses a poor man to make increase for him, one who gives to a rich man, only for lack." Alternative renderings are, "One man oppresses the poor and makes himself rich, another gives to the rich and makes himself poor"; "One who oppresses the poor man actually exalts him, and one who gives to the rich only makes himself poorer." The general sense is that greed is self-defeating, whatever may be the precise point of the proverb. Cf. xiii 22; Eccles ii 26.

The First Collection of Solomonic Proverbs

The brevity of the proverbs in x 1–xxii 16, their miscellaneous subject matter and the discontinuity of their arrangement militate against the pleasure of reading them consecutively in their traditional order. This order has been retained for ease of reference, but the following classification by topics may be found useful:

A son and his parents—x 1, 5, xiii 1, 24, xv 20, xvii 21, 25, xix 26, xx 20.

Character and its consequences—x 24, 28, xi 27, 30, xii 3, 7, 12, 20, 21, 28, xiii 6, 9, 10, xiv 19, 22, 30, 32, xvi 20, xvii 19, 20, xviii 3, xix 16, xx 7, xxi 5, 16, 17, 18, 21, xxii 5.

Providential rewards and punishments—x 3, 29, xi 18, 21, 23, 25, 31, xii 2, xiii 21, 22, xiv 9, 11, 14, xv 6, 10, 25, xix 29, xx 30 xxii 4.

Poverty and wealth—x 2, 4, 15, 22, xi 4, 24, 28, xiii 8, 11, xiv 20, xviii 11, 23, xix 1, 4, 7, 22, xx 21, xxi 6, 20, xxii 27.

Good and evil men—x 6, 7, 9, 10, 11, 16, 21, 25, 27, 30, xi 5, 6, 8, 19, 30, xii 5, 26, xvi 27, 28, 29, 30, xvii 4, xxi 8, 12, 26, 29, xxii 10.

Wise men and fools—x 8, 13, 14, 23, xii 1, 8, 15, 23, xiii 15, 16, xiv 6, 7, 8, 15, 16, 18, 24, 33, xv 7, 14, 21, xvii 10, 12, 24.

Slander—x 18, xviii 8, xix 5, 9, 28.

The self-disciplined life—x 17, xiii 13, 14, 18, xvi 32.

Foolish talk, temperate speech, and wise silence—x 19, 20, 31, 32, xi 12, 13, xii 6, 13, 14, 18, xiii 2, 3, xiv 3, 23, xv 1, 2, 4, 23, 28, xvi 21, 23, 24, xvii 27, 28, xviii 4, 6, 7, 13, 20, 21, xx 19, xxi 23, xxii 11.

Work and idleness—x 26, xii 11, 24, 27, xiii 4, xiv 4, 23, xv 19, xvi 26, xviii 9, xix 15, 24, xx 4, 13, xxi 25, xxii 13.

Women and marriage—xi 16, 22, xii 4, xviii 22, xix 14, xxi 9, 19.

Family relationships—xi 29, xvii 6, xviii 19, xix 13.

Civic morality—xi 10, 11, 14, 26, xiv 34, xxi 15.

Rash promises—xi 15, xvii 18, xx 16, 25.

Truth and falsehood—xii 17, 19, 22, xiii 5, xiv 5, 25, xvii 7.

Honesty and dishonesty—xiii 25, xv 27, xvi 11, xx 10, 14, 23.

Morality and religion—xiv 2, 27, xxi 3, 4, 27.

A king and his people—xiv 28, 35, xvi 10, 12, 13, 14, 15, xix 12, xx 2, 8–9, 26, 28, xxi 1.

Material and moral values—xvi 8, 16, 19, xx 15, xxii 1.

The administration of justice—xiii 23, xvii 15, 23, 26, xviii 5, 17, 18, xxi 28.

The discipline of education—xv 5, 31, 32, xvii 16, xviii 15, xix 8, 18, 20, 27, xxii 6, 15.

God's oversight of man's life—xvi 1, 2, 3, 4, 5, 6, 7, 9, 33, xvii 3, xix 21, xx 12, 24, 27, xxi 2, 30, 31, xxii 12.

Behavior acceptable to God—xi 20, xv 8, 9, 26, 29.

The nemesis of folly and wrongdoing—xvii 11, 13, xix 19, xx 17, xxi 7, xxii 8, 16.

Happiness—xv 13, 15, 16, 17, 30, xvii 22.

Cruelty and compassion—xii 10, xiv 21, 31, xvii 5, xix 17, xxi 10, 13, xxii 9.

The path of life—xiv 12, xv 24, xvi 12, 17.

Various virtues and vices—x 12, xi 1, 2, 3, 9, 17, xii 9, 16, 25, xiii 7, xiv 17, 29, xv 12, 22, 33, xvi 18, xvii 9, 11, 17, xviii 1, 12, 24, xix 2, 6, 11, xx 1, 6, 11, 22, xxi 24.

The power of religious faith—xiv 26, 27, xviii 10, xix 23.

Sickness and grief—xiv 10, 13, xviii 14.

Quarrels—xv 18, xvii 1, 14, xx 3.

Plans and expectations—xi 7, xiii 12, 19.

Wisdom and folly—xiv 1, xvi 22, xx 5, 18, xxi 22.

Divine omniscience—xv 3, 11.

Old age—xvi 31, xx 29.

Gifts and bribes—xvii 8, xviii 16, xxi 14.

Messengers and servants—xiii 17, xvii 2.

Good and bad company—xiii 20, xxii 14.

III. The Thirty Precepts of the Sages

24. PREAMBLE
(xxii 17–21)

XXII

17
                        Precepts of the Sages

Incline your ear and hear my words,
    And apply your mind to my learning;
18 For it will be a delight to cherish within you,
    It will make your speech firm as with a tent peg*ᵃ*.
19 That your confidence may be in the Lord
    I will now tell you what paths you should follow*ᵇ*;
20 Have I not written for you thirty*ᶜ* precepts,
    Which have in them wise counsel*ᵈ* and knowledge.
21 To teach you to know what is true*ᵉ*
    And so to return a correct report to one who sends you.

ᵃ *keyātēd* for MT *yaḥdāw,* "together."
ᵇ Reading with LXX *'orhōtēkā,* for MT *'ap 'attāh,* "even you."
ᶜ *šelōšīm,* for MT *šilšōm,* "formerly," "three days ago," which was vocalized in tradition as *šālīšīm,* "elite officers," "nobles," and hence translated "excellent things" in KJ. LXX, Vulg., Targ. render the word by "triple" or "three times," a reminiscence of the original meaning "thirty."
ᵈ *bām 'ēṣōt,* for MT *bᵉmō 'ēṣōt,* "with plans."
ᵉ Omitting *'imrē 'ᵉmet,* "words of truth," a gloss on the rare word *qōšt* which apparently has the same meaning.

NOTES

xxii 17–xxiv 22. Precepts of the Sages, or more generally, "words of wise men." That this is a title for xxii 17–xxiv 22 (Secs. 24–27) is evident from the heading in xxiv 23, which begins Section 28. MT has accidentally assimilated the title to *my words* in vs. 17, so that it reads as in RSV "hear the words of the wise." On the relation of Sections 24–27 to the thirty precepts of the *Instruction of Amen-em-ope* (ANET, pp. 421a–424b), see Introduction to Proverbs, above. The preamble and the thirty precepts in Proverbs form the content of the four sections, but the verbal reminiscences of the Egyptian work are confined to xxii 17–xxiii

11. The sages from whose sayings the author has composed his booklet are thus both Israelite and non-Israelite, in the cosmopolitan tradition of the Wisdom movement. In addition to Egyptian, there is evidence of indebtedness to Assyrian-Aramaic Wisdom.

18. *make firm your speech.* I.e., make it well founded in learning. The rather strained metaphor is to be explained as an adaptation of the metaphor in the corresponding line of *Amen-em-ope,* "When there is a whirlwind of words, they shall be a mooring-stake for thy tongue." With vss. 17–18, cf. *Amen-em-ope,* ch. 1 (ANET, pp. 421b–422a).

20. *thirty.* Before the publication in 1923 of the *Instruction of Amen-em-ope* with its thirty "chapters," of which about ten have resemblances in thought and imagery to xxii 17 ff., the meaning of this word had been lost. See textual note [c]. With vss. 20–21 cf. *Amen-em-ope,* ch. 30, "See thou these thirty chapters: they entertain, they instruct," and the preamble, "all precepts for intercourse . . . to know how to return an answer to him who said it" (ANET, pp. 424b, 421b).

25. THE THIRTY PRECEPTS: ONE TO FIVE
(xxii 22–29)

(1)

XXII

22   Do not take advantage of the helpless poor man,
        Nor crush the needy in the public court,
23   For the Lord will take up their cause,
        And will rob those who rob them of life.

(11)

24   Do not befriend a bad-tempered man,
        Nor accompany one given to violent outbursts,
25   Lest you fall into his habits
        And find yourself in a snare.

(111)

26   Do not be of those who make [rash] bargains,
        Who pledge themselves as surety for loans;
27   If you have nothing to pay with,
        Why have your bed taken from under you?

(1v)

28   Do not move back an ancient boundary line
        Which your ancestors established.

(v)

29   Do you see a man who is skillful at his work?
      He will stand in the presence of kings.
      [He will not stand in the presence of the obscure].

NOTES

xxii 22. Literally "Do not rob the destitute because he is destitute."
Cf. xiv 31, xxiii 10–11; Isa iii 13–15; *Amen-em-ope,* ch. 2, "Guard thyself against robbing the oppressed and against overbearing the disabled"
(ANET, p. 422a) and ch. 11, "Be not greedy for the property of a
poor man" (ANET, p. 423a); *The Eloquent Peasant* (ANET, p. 409b).
   24–25. Cf. *Amen-em-ope,* ch. 9, "Do not associate to thyself the heated
man" (ANET, p. 423a).
   26–27. On the emphatic warnings against gambling one's security in
such transactions, see NOTE on vi 1–5.
   28. This theme is represented again in xxiii 10–11, though it corresponds more closely to the law of Deut xix 14. Cf. also Deut xxvii 17;
Hos v 10; Job xxiv 2; *Amen-em-ope,* ch. 6 (ANET, p. 422b).
   Move back. I.e., the stones or cairns (cf. Gen xxxi 52) marking the
boundary. This crime was easy to accomplish and difficult to prove; hence
the strong polemic against it on moral grounds in law, prophecy, and
Wisdom.
   29. *skillful.* Literally "quick." Competence in a particular trade or profession was a special kind of "wisdom"; cf. the metalworker (I Kings
vii 14); the artistic craftsman (Exod xxxv 30–35); the farmer (Isa
xxviii 23–29); the sailor (I Kings ix 27); the soldier (I Chron v 18);
the lumberman (I Kings v 6 EV); and the scribe (Ezra vii 6). The third
line appears to be a variant of the second.

26. THE THIRTY PRECEPTS: SIX TO EIGHTEEN
(xxiii 1–21, 23, 22, 24–35)

(vi)

XXIII

1   When you sit down to dine with a ruler
      Pay attention to your table manners;
2   Use a knife to eat with^a, if you are a man of
          hearty appetite.
3   Do not be greedy for his delicacies
      For it is deceptive food.

(vii)

4   Do not wear yourself out in pursuit of wealth,
      No longer let your thoughts dwell on it.
5   When you look for it, will it not have vanished?
      It will have grown itself wings
      And like an eagle will have flown away into the
          heavens.

(viii)

6   Do not eat the food of a stingy man
      Nor desire his delicacies,
7   For as he estimates his own appetite, so he will yours^b,
      "Eat and drink," he says to you, but his mind is not
          with you.

---

^a *b^ebil'^akā*, literally "in your swallowing," for MT *b^elō'ékā*, "to your throat."
^b Inserting *l^ekā* after *ken-hū'*.

8   After eating your portion you will vomit it up,
     And falsify his° pleasant words.

(IX)

9   Do not talk to a stupid fool,
     For he will scorn your intelligent words.

(X)

10   Do not move back an ancient boundary line,
     Nor intrude on the lands of orphans;
11   For their Champion is powerful;
     He will take up their cause against you.

12   [Submit your mind to instruction,
     And your ears to words spoken with knowledge.]

(XI)

13   Do not hesitate to discipline a youth;
     Though you beat him with a stick, he will not die;
14   Indeed, you should beat him with a stick,
     And so save his life from Sheol.

(XII)

15   My son, if your mind be wise,
     My own mind will be content;
16   You will make my inmost being rejoice
     When your lips speak what is right.

(XIII)

17   Do not envy sinners in your thoughts,
     But rather think constantly on religious faith;

° dᵉbārāw, for MT dᵉbārēkā.

18   If you possess that*d*, there is a future [for you],
        And your hope will not be disappointed.

(xiv)

19   Hear now*e*, my son, and gain wisdom,
        Give attention to following the right path;
20   Be not of those who drink wine to excess,
        Who indulge themselves in devouring meat;
21   For the heavy drinker and the glutton will be disinherited,
        And sleep will clothe a man in rags.

(xv)

23   Buy truth, and do not sell
        Wisdom, instruction, and understanding.

(xvi)

22   Listen to the father who begot you,
        And do not despise your mother when she is old;

24   The father of a just man is filled with joy,
        And the begetter of a wise man is happy on his
           account;
25   So may your father be happy,
        And the mother who bore you rejoice.

(xvii)

26   Give me your attention, my son,
        And may your eyes admire my ways;
27   For a harlot is a deep pit,
        And a strange woman is a narrow well;

d Supplying *māṣā'tā*, "you possess, obtain," from xxiv 14b, where the second
line of this verse is repeated.
e *'attāh* for MT *'attāh*, "you"; cf. vii 24, viii 32.

28   Moreover, she will rob you like a bandit,
      And be worse than' the most treacherous of mankind.

(xviii)

29   Who groans "Alas!"? Who cries "Woe is me!"?
      Who gets into quarrels? Who has complaints?
      Who suffers needless wounds? Whose eyes are
          bloodshot?
30   Those who linger over wine,
      Who drain the mixing bowl.
31   Do not gloat over the redness of wine,
      When it sparkles in the cup,
      When it goes down easily.
32   Afterwards it will bite like a snake,
      It secretes the venom of a viper;
33   Your eyes will see strange apparitions,
      And your mind and speech will be confused;
34   You will be like one prostrated far at sea,
      [Or] who rolls drunkenly likeᵍ the top of the mast,
35   [Saying] "They hit me but it didn't hurt!
      They beat me but I didn't know it!
      As soon as I can wake up
      I shall want another drink!"

ᶠ *ūmibbōgᵉdīm* or *ūbᵉbōgᵉdīm* for MT *ūbōgᵉdīm,* "and treacherous men."
ᵍ *ūkᵉšōkēr kᵉrō'š,* for MT *ūkᵉšōkēb bᵉrō'š,* "as one who lies down on the top."

Notes

   xxiii 1–3. *your table manners.* Literally "what is in front of you"; the
translation is implied by vss. 2–3.
   3. *deceptive food.* Literally "food of lies," i.e., pretentious food, or
more probably, false hospitality; cf. vss. 6–8. *Amen-em-ope,* ch. 23, reads,
"Do not eat bread before a noble . . . false chewings. Look at the cup
which is before thee" (ANET, p. 424a). Ptah-hotep says, "If thou art one
of those sitting at the table of one greater than thyself, take what he

may give. . . . Thou shouldst gaze at what is before thee" (ANET, p. 412b). Sirach xxxi 12–22 deals with the topic at length.

5. *grown.* Literally "made." In Jer xvii 11 the thought and imagery are similar, but the bird is a partridge. Cf. *Amen-em-ope,* ch. 7, "Cast not thy heart in pursuit of riches . . . they will not spend the night with thee . . . they [will] have made themselves wings like geese and are flown away to the heavens" (ANET, p. 422b). Cf. also the Sumerian proverb, "Possessions are sparrows [or, locusts] in flight which can find no place to alight" (Gordon, p. 50).

7. Cf. *Amen-em-ope,* ch. 11, "a blocking to the throat" (ANET, p. 423a).

9. Cf. i 22, ix 7; Matt vii 6; *Amen-em-ope,* ch. 21, "Empty not thy belly [i.e., inner thoughts] to everybody" (ANET, p. 424a).

10. *an ancient boundary,* the phrase has perhaps been assimilated to xxii 28a and *'ōlām* substituted for *'almānāh,* "widow," a better parallel to "orphans." Cf. xxii 28; Exod xxii 22; Deut xxiv 17; *Amen-em-ope,* ch. 6, "Do not carry off the landmark at the boundaries of the arable land . . . nor encroach upon the boundaries of the widow" (ANET, p. 422b).

12. Brackets serving as a secondary preamble (cf. xxii 17) to xxiii 13–xxiv 22.

13–14. Cf. xxii 15. There is a close parallel in *Ahiqar* vi, "Withhold not thy son from the rod, else thou wilt not be able to save [him]. . . . If I smite thee, my son, thou wilt not die, but if I leave thee to thine own heart . . . (ANET, p. 428b).

13. *youth.* Or, "boy."

23. Transposed with vs. 22, which belongs with vss. 24–25.

instruction. mūsār, usually translated "discipline," but which also has the more general sense, "instruction, education."

22, 24–25. A theme which recurs in every division of Proverbs; cf. i 8, x 1, xv 20, xxix 3, etc.

26–28. Cf. the repeated treatment of this theme in Part I (chs. i–ix).

29. *bloodshot.* Or, "dull."

30. *drain.* Literally "come to search," i.e., looking for more wine.

34. The text of MT is translated literally in KJ and RSV, resulting in a completely absurd image. On the other hand, the prostration of the seasick landsman and the rolling mast of a small ship in even a moderate sea, are vivid images of the behavior of a drunken man.

27. THE THIRTY PRECEPTS: NINETEEN TO THIRTY
(xxiv 1–22)

(xix)

XXIV

1   Do not envy bad men, nor wish for their company,
2   For they think of nothing but creating havoc,
     And their whole talk is about causing trouble.

(xx)

3   Through wise skill a house is built,
     And by understanding it is set firm on its foundation;
4   Through knowledge its rooms are furnished
     With all manner of precious and beautiful things.

(xxi)

5   A wise man is superior to a strong one,[a]
     And a learned man is better than one who is physically
          powerful.
6   For planning is necessary to conduct a war,
     And victory follows from [the advice of] many
          counselors.

---

[a] *gābar ḥākām mēʿāz*, with LXX, Syr., Vulg., Targ., for MT *geber ḥākām bāʿōz*, "a man is wise in strength." Cf. xxi 22. Or *bāʿōz* may preserve the archaic comparative *b*.

(XXII)

7   Wise sayings are beyond the understanding of the fool,
    [Where men assemble] in the gate he does not open his
      mouth.

(XXIII)

8   He who is [always] scheming to create trouble
    Becomes known as a master of trickery.
9   Sin is the scheme of a fool,
    And an impious man is an abomination.

(XXIV)

10   If you show weakness in a crisis,
    Your strength is small.

(XXV)

11   Rescue prisoners from death,
    And protect those who are prostrate[b] from being slain.
12   If you say, "See, this is none of my business,"
    Will not he who weighs men's hearts take note of it?
    He who keeps watch on your life will know,
    And will requite a man according to his acts.

(XXVI)

13   My son, as you eat honey because it is good,
    And as wild honey is sweet to your taste,
14   So is knowledge [sweet], and wisdom [good] for your
      soul,

b *muṭṭîm* for MT *māṭîm*, "staggering."

If you possess that you will have a future, and your
hope will not be disappointed.

(xxvii)

15   Do not plot evil against the home of a just man,
    Do not despoil his dwelling;
16   Though a just man should fall seven times he will get
    up again,
    Whereas wicked men will stumble on into ruin.

(xxviii)

17   Do not rejoice at the fall of your enemy,
    Nor be exultant when he stumbles,
18   Lest the Lord see it and be displeased
    And suspend his anger against him.

(xxix)

19   Do not fret yourself about wrongdoers,
    Nor be envious of the wicked,
20   For the bad man has nothing to look forward to,
    And the lamp of the wicked will go out.

(xxx)

21   Reverence the Lord, my son, and also the king,
    And do not be rebellious against either,*
22   For overthrow may come from them at any moment,
    And who knows what calamity either one may send?

---

* 'im šᵉnēhem 'al tit'abbar, with LXX, for MT 'im šōnīm 'al tit'ārāb, "with
those who change have nothing to do."

NOTES

xxiv 3. *house*. Cf. ix 1, where the word is figurative.

6. The second line is identical with xi 14b.

7. *Wise sayings*. *ḥokmōt*, which in i 20, ix 1, xiv 1 is the Canaanite form of Heb. *ḥokmāh*, "wisdom," is here an intensive plural of the Hebrew form. The Canaanite form is used in Proverbs, apparently, only of personified wisdom.

10. *small*. Literally "narrow."

11. *protect*. Literally "restrain."

prostrate. Literally "spread out," as the wounded after a battle.

12. *weighs men's hearts*. Cf. xvi 2, NOTE, and xxi 2.

17–18. To be glad at the discomfiture of an enemy is to express hatred of him, and to provoke God by assuming prematurely that God is on one's side. Cf. xxv 21–22; Exod xxiii 4–5; Matt v 43–45; and the Akkadian *Counsels of Wisdom*, "Unto your opponent do no evil; your evildoer recompense with good; unto your enemy let justice [be done]" (ANET, p. 426b).

19. This verse is identical with Ps xxxvii 1.

fret. I.e., at their present well-being, which seems to contradict the doctrine of divine reward and punishment. Cf. iii 31–32, xxiii 17, xxiv 1.

20. The prosperity of the wicked is only temporary, because they are detested by Yahweh (iii 32), are dangerous (xxiv 2), and are doomed (xxiv 20; Ps xxxvii 2; cf. Ps lxxiii 17–20). Verse 20b is identical with xiii 9b.

21–22. The motive is prudential, and the tone resembles that of Eccles v 1–2, 4–6 EV, and viii 2–5, where God and king are remote omnipotent powers over man's life. Cf. the Assyrian proverb, "When you have seen the profit of reverencing (your) god, you will praise (your) god and salute the king" (Lambert, BWL, p. 133).

28. FURTHER SAYINGS OF THE SAGES
(xxiv 23–34)

XXIV

23 These also are sayings of the sages:
    "To show partiality in a judicial decision is wrong":
24 He who says to a guilty man, "You are innocent,"
    Peoples will curse him and nations revile him.
25 But those who rebuke [the guilty] will be well regarded,
    And on them will come the blessing of prosperity.
26 He kisses the lips who answers honestly.
27 Do thoroughly your work outside,
    Make ready in the field;
    After that, go[a] and build your house.
28 Do not for spite give evidence against your neighbor,
    Nor slander him with your lips;
29 Do not say, "What he did to me, I will do to him!
    I will repay the man for his act!"

30 I walked through the field of the indolent,
    And through the vineyard of the dull-witted,
31 And found them all overgrown with thornbushes,
    The surface covered with weeds, and the stone dike
        broken down.
32 I looked, and took it to heart,
    I saw and learned a lesson—
33 "A little more sleep, a little more slumber,
    A little longer with hands folded in repose"—
34 And poverty will overtake you like a vagabond,
    And your destitution like a beggar.

a lēk for MT lāk, "for you."

Notes

xxiv 23–25. See xxii 17, Note. The short prosaic line in 23b appears to be a legal maxim which is incorporated also in xviii 5 and xxviii 21. With vss. 24–25 cf. xvii 15.

25. *will be well regarded.* Or, "it will be pleasant for."

of prosperity. Or less probably, "of a good man." Cf. Deut xvi 19.

26. One who *kisses the lips* is a friend, *who answers honestly* in giving evidence. Possibly an alliterative adage underlies the verse: *nōšēq sᵉpātáim mēšīb nᵉkōḥīm.*

27. The meaning appears to be something like "count the cost," or "first catch your hare"; i.e., "don't start building your house until thorough preparations have been made." Cf. Luke xiv 28–32. Like the English sayings, this is figurative, and applicable to various situations.

28. Literally "Do not be a witness for nothing," i.e., "without good reason." The OT has many condemnations of "false witness," which meant unjust accusations as well as lying evidence by a witness; cf. Exod xx 16; Deut xix 16–19; Prov vi 19.

29. Counsel against retaliation (as in the story of Samson, Judg xv 10–11) becomes a negative form of the "Golden Rule." On various approaches to this "Golden Rule," cf. xx 22, xxv 21–22; Matt v 38–45; Tobit iv 15; and the Akkadian *Counsels of Wisdom* (see Note on xxiv 17–18).

30–34. Cf. vi 6–11 where vss. 33–34 are found in almost identical form. Note the Akkadian proverb, "As long as a man does not exert himself, he will gain nothing" (ANET, p. 425a).

IV. The Second Collection
of Solomonic Proverbs*

---

* The proverbs found in xxv 1–xxix 27 are classified by topics at the end of Part IV.

29. FURTHER WISE SAYINGS OF SOLOMON
(xxv 1–28)

XXV

1 These are further wise sayings of Solomon transmitted
by the men of Hezekiah, king of Judah.

2 The glory of God lies in what he conceals,
The glory of kings in what they bring to light.

3 As the heavens above are high and the world below is
deep,
The mind of kings is unfathomable.

4 By the removal of impurities from silver
It becomes bright for the silversmith's vessel;

5 [So] by the expulsion of a wicked man from the king's
presence
His throne is firmly founded in right.

6 Do not give yourself airs at a royal court
Or take up your position where the great belong;

7 It is better to be told, "Come up here,"
Than to be humiliated before a noble.

8 Do not hastily take to court what you have witnessed,
For what will you do if the other man later confounds
you?

9 When you are disputing with your neighbor
Do not betray another man's confidences,

10 Lest someone who hears it denounce you
And you get a bad reputation.

11 Like gold inlay^a in objects of wrought silver
Is a secret which has been whispered in the ear^b.

─────────────

^a *pittūḥē* for MT *tappūḥē*, "apples."
^b *'ōzen* for MT *'opnāw*, meaning unknown and probably a scribal error.

12 Like a gold ring or an ornament of fine gold
    Is a sage's reprimand to an ear that listens.
13 Like the coolness of snow in the heat of harvest time
    Is a reliable messenger to him who sends him.
    [He is refreshing to his master.]
14 Like towering clouds and wind which bring no rain
    Is the man who promises a gift but fails to give it.
15 With patient persistence a high official may be persuaded,
    And a soft tongue can break a bone.
16 When you find honey, eat just enough for you,
    Because too much may make you vomit;
17 [So] be infrequent in visiting your neighbor's home,
    Lest he see too much of you and begin to dislike you.
18 [Like] a mace, a sword, or a sharp-pointed arrow
    Is the man who gives false evidence against his
        neighbor.
19 It is like having a loose tooth or a palsied foot
    To rely on a deceiver in time of trouble.
20 Singing gay songs to a heavy heart is like
    Disrobing a man on a cold day,
    Or adding sour wine to soda.
21 If your enemy be hungry, give him food,
    If he be thirsty, give water to drink;
22 For thus you will heap hot embers on his head,
    And the Lord will recompense you.
23 As surely as the north wind brings rain
    A whispering tongue brings angry looks.
24 It is better to live in the corner of a roof
    Than with a quarrelsome woman in a spacious
        house.
25 Good news from a distant land is
    Like a drink of cold water to a weary man.
26 Like a spring fouled by animals, or a polluted well,
    Is a just man who quails before a wicked one.

27 "It is a bad thing to eat too much honey,"
   So consider the words of one who compliments you.[c]
28 Like a city overthrown because it has no wall
   Is the man who cannot control his anger.

[c] Reading *ḥᵃqōr dᵉbār mᵉkabbdékā*, for MT *ḥēqer kᵉbōdām kābōd*, "the searching of their glory is glory."

NOTES

xxv 1. *further wise sayings of Solomon.* See NOTES on i 1 and x 1, and Introduction to Proverbs.

transmitted by. Or "transcribed, published by."

the men of Hezekiah. In the sense "professional servants," cf. "David's men" (I Sam xxiii 3, 5; II Sam ii 31); here a school or scribal establishment under royal patronage, where literary records of the past were assembled and new literature was produced. Hezekiah was the first Judean king since Solomon to reign without a rival king of Israel in the north, and he appears to have organized the assembling and uniting of historical, prophetic, poetical, and Wisdom materials from north and south.

2. Mystery is integral to the idea of God (Exod iii 14; Deut xxix 29 EV; Isa xl 18; Job xi 7, xxvi 14), and wisdom to that of a king (II Sam xiv 17; I Kings iii 9; Isa xi 3).

3. *world below.* Or, "earth," may refer to the netherworld or Sheol.

5. Cf. the Babylonian *Advice to a Prince*, "If [a king] heeds a rogue, the *status quo* in his land will change" (BWL, p. 113).

6–7. Cf. Luke xiv 7–11. The last words of vs. 7 in MT, "what you have seen," belong to vs. 8.

8. The admonition means "Things are not always what they seem."

9–10. *betray.* I.e., by quoting someone who has spoken to you in confidence. Cf. *Ahiqar* ix, "Reveal not thy [secrets] before thy friends, lest thy name become despised of them," (ANET, p. 429b).

11. I.e., a secret is to be treasured.

13. Possibly a reference to the cooling of drinks with snow from Lebanon, but more likely to a change from heat to abnormally cool weather (though not snow!) during the June harvest, as experienced by the author in 1959 in the Judean hills.

14. Towering clouds are cumulonimbus, watched hopefully in a time when rain is needed, but which may pass without giving precipitation.

15. Cf. xv 1; *Ahiqar* vii, "Soft is the tongue of [a king], but it breaks a dragon's ribs" (ANET, p. 429a).

20. *adding sour wine to soda.* I.e., one bitter thing to another.

22. *heap hot embers.* A form of torture; but to return good for evil will be more effective in overcoming enmity, and so the enemy. (Cf. Exod xxiii 4–5, and NOTES on xx 22, xxiv 17–18.) Another possibility is that the figure was derived from an Egyptian repentance ritual i.e., "you will make your enemy repent." Cf. W. Klassen, *N. T. Studies* 9 (1963), 337–50. The admonition is quoted in Rom xii 20 and explained as meaning "overcome evil with good."

23. *north wind.* Here probably means "northwest," if the setting of the saying is Palestine. The true north wind is uncommon and is normally a winter wind bringing clear, cold weather (Job xxxvii 21–22).

24. See NOTE on xxi 9. Cf. the Italian proverb, "Three things drive a man out of his house: smoke, rain, and a scolding wife."

28. Cf. xvi 32.

30. FURTHER WISE SAYINGS OF SOLOMON
(*continued*)
(xxvi 1–28)

XXVI

1 To honor a fool is as unfitting
   As snow in summer or rain at harvest time.

2 Like a fluttering bird or a swooping swallow,
   A causeless curse does not alight.

3 A whip for the horse! A bridle for the ass!
   A stick for the back of fools!

4 Do not answer a fool in his own foolish terms,
   Lest you put yourself on his level.

5 Answer a fool in his own foolish terms
   So he will not think himself wise.

6 One chops off his own feet*a* and invites violence
   Who sends a message by a fool.

7 A maxim quoted by fools
   Is as limp as a lame man's legs.

8 To give a fool a place of honor
   Is like tying a stone firmly in a catapult.

9 A maxim quoted by fools
   Is like a thornstick in a drunkard's hand.

10 To hire a fool or a drunkard
   Is to wound all passers-by with a sword.*b*

11 A fool repeats his folly
   As a dog returns to his vomit.

a raglāw, "his feet," for MT *ragláyim*, "feet."
b Reading *ḥereb meḥōlēl kōl 'ōberīm śōkēr kesīl weśikkōr*, for MT *rab meḥōlēl kōl weśōkēr kesīl weśōkēr 'ōberīm*, literally, "much wounds all and he who hires a fool and he who hires passers-by." One suspects that the confusion has resulted from combining two popular sayings with the same theme, viz., "he who hires a fool [drunkard] hurts all."

12 Have you observed the man who thinks he is wise?
 There is more hope for a stupid fool than for him.
13 The indolent says, "There is a young lion in the road,
 A lion abroad in the streets."
14 As a door turns on its pivot,
 So a lazy man turns on his bed.
15 The lazy man puts his hand into the dish
 But he is too weary to raise it to his mouth.
16 The indolent is wiser in his own eyes
 Than seven men who can give an apt answer.
17 One who mixes in a quarrel which is none of his business
 Is taking a mad dog by the tail^c.
18 It is like madly hurling firebrands and deadly arrows
19 To deceive another and then say, "I was only joking."
20 If no wood is added a fire goes out,
 So "No calumny, no quarrel."
21 Like charcoal to embers and wood to a fire
 A quarrelsome man rekindles a dispute.
22 The words of a slanderer are swallowed greedily,
 And go down to the innermost parts of the body.
23 Like glaze^d on the surface of earthenware
 Is smooth talk concealing an evil intention.
24 A man filled with hate disguises it in his words,
 While inwardly he plots to betray you;
25 When his speech is ingratiating, do not trust him,
 For seven abominations are in his mind;
26 Though his hatred be craftily hidden,
 His wickedness will be shown up for all to see.
27 "He who digs a pit [for another] will fall into it [himself].
 And a stone will come back on the one who rolls it.
28 A lying tongue is a man's own worst enemy^e,
 And smooth talk leads to downfall.

^c So LXX; MT "by the ears."
^d Reading k^esapsāg, for MT kesep sīgīm, "unrefined silver," cf. W. F. Albright in WIANE, pp. 12–13.
^e Reading d^erakāw, for MT dakkāw, "its oppressed ones."

NOTES

xxvi 1. *honor.* Means here to be accorded dignity and the respect of society.

unfitting. To the sage there is a right order of things, and "all things have their appointed time" (Eccles iii 1). The disturbance of this order not only leads to, but is, confusion and evil.

Though *snow* never falls *in summer* in Palestine proper, a rare frost has been recorded as late as April, when crops are well advanced; *rain* (and cold) *at harvest time* in June are unusual but not unknown. See NOTE on xxv 13. Cf. xvii 7, xxvi 8; I Sam xii 17–18.

2. *curse.* Pictured (like the prophetic "word," Isa ix 8 EV, lv 11) as having a quasi-independent existence, once it is uttered it *does not alight* on its innocent intended target, since it is *causeless* and therefore without substance. For the rooted conviction of the power of the curse over persons and events, cf. Gen iii 14, 17, ix 25; Deut xxvii 14–26; Josh vi 26; I Kings xvi 34.

3. Cf. *Ahiqar* vi (ANET, p. 428b).

4–5. Contradictory proverbs are quite common, not only because "circumstances alter cases" but because they are rules for guidance and not absolute commands. Cf. Eccles iv 5–6, ix 16, 18, and the English pair: "Marry in haste and repent at leisure," "Happy the wooing that is not long in doing." The objectives of vss. 4 and 5 are different: vs. 4 means "Do not demean yourself" and vs. 5 "Show the fool his mistake in language he can understand."

6. *invites violence.* Literally "drinks of violence," cf. iv 17. Instead of adding the messenger's feet to his own, what happens is the opposite, and trouble rather than advantage is the result.

7. Literally "As legs dangle from a lame man." Cf. vs. 9.

8. *catapult.* Or, "sling," a guess at the meaning of a word which occurs only here in the OT and is from a verbal root meaning "to throw stones." To tie firmly or bind the stone in it would be absurd because incongruous with its purpose; cf. vs. 1.

9. An alternative form of vs. 7. A drunkard cannot use a weapon effectively.

11. A characteristic of fools and dogs which has not changed with the centuries. II Pet ii 22 suggests that the saying about the dog was a traditional adage which could be variously applied.

12. Cf. xxix 20; the conceited and the impetuous are worse than the dull-witted.

13. A variant of xxii 13.

14. Wooden doors were pivoted in stone sockets.

15. Almost identical with xix 24.

17. *mad*. Or, "angry."

20. Literally "a quarrel becomes silent." The rhyme and structure of the second line suggests that it is a popular proverb of the type: No-this, No-that; cf. "Nothing seek, nothing find"; xiv 4.

21. *charcoal*. For *peḥām*, some read *mappūᵃḥ*, "bellows." Cf. *Meri-ka-re*, "The contentious man is a disturbance to citizens" (ANET, p. 415a).

22. Identical with xviii 8.

26. *for all to see*. Literally "in the congregation," cf. Ps xxii 22 EV.

27. The principle of "the biter bit" or "hoist with his own petar" (*Hamlet* iii 4) is a favorite of proverb makers; cf. xxviii 10; Eccles x 8–9; Ps vii 15 EV; Sirach xxvii 25–27.

31. FURTHER WISE SAYINGS OF SOLOMON
(*continued*)
(xxvii 1–27)

XXVII

1   Do not boast of what you will do tomorrow,
     For you do not know what may happen in a day.

2   Let a stranger, not your own mouth, praise you,
     A foreigner, rather than your own lips.

3   A stone may be heavy, or a load of sand,
     But a provoking fool is harder to bear than both
        together.

4   O, the cruelty of anger and the overflowing of wrath!
     But who can withstand jealousy?

5   Open rebuke is better than concealed approval.

6   The blows of a friend are well meant,
     But like knives*a* are the kisses of an enemy.

7   A well-fed man will disdain*b* honey,
     But to the hungry man even the bitter tastes sweet.

8   Like a bird straying from its nest
     Is a man who wanders from his home.

9   As perfume and incense gratify the senses
     So a friend's cordiality strengthens*c* one's spirit.

10   Do not forsake your friend and your father's friend
     [To go to your brother's house on your day of trouble]:
     "Better a near neighbor than a distant brother."

11   If you gain wisdom, my son, you will make me happy,
     And I shall be able to answer whoever taunts me.

---

a *kite'ārōt* for MT *na'tārōt,* "entreated."
b *tābūz* for MT *tābūs,* "trample."
c *meḥazzēq* for MT *mē'aṣat,* "from counsel."

12   A shrewd man sees trouble coming and avoids it,
       Whereas simpletons go right ahead and must pay the
          penalty.

13   They take*d* his garment who has become surety for a
          stranger,
       And hold him to his promise who has done so for
          foreigners*e*.

14   When a man in a loud voice calls out a blessing on his
          friend
       [Rousing him in the morning],
       To the friend it seems like a curse.

15   A constant dripping on a day of winter rain—
       That is what a quarrelsome woman is like;

16   To try to restrain her is like trying to restrain the wind;
       One cries out that "his hand is slippery."

17   As one iron implement is sharpened by another,
       So a man sharpens the perception of his companion.

18   One who tends a fig tree will eat its fruit,
       And he who guards his master will gain honor.

19   As a face is reflected in water
       So a man's thoughts are reflected in the man.

20   As Sheol and Abaddon are never satisfied,
       Man's desire is insatiable.

21   As a crucible for silver and a smelter for gold,
       Flattery will show what a man is.

22   Though you pound a fool in a mortar
       [Into fragments, with a pestle],
       You will not rid him of his foolishness.

23   Know well the condition of your flocks,
       Pay close attention to your herds—

24   For possessions are impermanent
       And no treasure*f* lasts for generations—

25   Then, when the hay has been cut and the second growth
          appears,
       When the crop has been gathered in from the hillsides,

d See NOTE to xx 16 on indicative for the imperative verbs.
e nākrīm, with LXX, for nākrīyyāh, "a foreign woman."
f Reading wᵉ'ēn 'ōṣār, for MT wᵉ'im nēzer, "nor a crown."

26   There will be lambs' [wool] to clothe you,
         And goats will provide profit from the land,
27   There will be enough goats' milk to feed you,
         Food for your household and sustenance for your
         maidservants.

NOTES

xxvii 1. A reminder that it is God, not man, who directs the course
of events, cf. xvi 1, xix 21; James iv 14. Ptah-hotep says, "One does not
know what may happen, so that he may understand the morrow," and
Amen-em-ope, "Man knows not what the morrow is like; . . . Man is
clay and straw, and the god is his builder" (ANET, pp. 413b, 423b,
424b). Cf. also *The Eloquent Peasant,* ANET, p. 409b.

3. Cf. *Ahiqar* viii, "I have lifted sand, and I have carried salt, but
there is naught which is heavier than [rage]" (ANET, p. 429a).

5. *approval.* Literally "love."

7. Cf. *Ahiqar* xii, "Hunger makes bitterness sweet" (ANET, p. 430a).

8. Referring probably to the restlessness of the traveler rather than to
the infidelity of a husband.

10. The form of the third line suggests a popular saying. The first
two lines may be an expansion of this, or the second line [in brackets]
can be taken as a variant of the third or as an explanatory gloss. Cf.
xviii 24.

12. Almost identical with xxii 3.

13. Identical with xx 16.

14. The words in brackets apparently are a variant of *in a loud voice.*

15. Cf. xix 13b.

16. *his hand is slippery.* Literally "oil of his right hand," so that he can
not hold on. This curious figurative saying is like our "butterfingers."

19. Literally "As [in] water the face to the face, so the mind of the
man to the man."

20. *Sheol and Abaddon.* See NOTE on xv 11; for the thought, cf. Eccles
i 8.

21. The first line repeats xvii 3a.
Flattery will show. Literally "According to his praise," which some take
to mean "according to his reputation."

22. The words in brackets seem to be a variant; the word for *fragments* may be another word for *mortar.*

26. *profit from the land.* Literally "price of a field."

32. FURTHER WISE SAYINGS OF SOLOMON

(*continued*)

(xxviii 1–28)

XXVIII

1   A rogue runs away when no one is chasing him,
      But just men are braver than lions.

2   When a land is in revolt it has many [would-be] rulers;
      Only with an intelligent*ᵃ* one will it endure.

3   A wicked*ᵇ* man who oppresses the needy
      Is like a devastating rain which ruins the harvest.

4   Those who have forsaken morality praise a wicked man,
      But the law-abiding oppose him.

5   The evil faction do not understand justice,
      But the Lord's servants know all about it.

6   A poor man who maintains his integrity is better
      Than a dishonest man who is rich.

7   He is a wise son who observes what he has been taught,
      But a companion of gluttons humiliates his father.

8   He who grows wealthy through usury and rents
      Accumulates to benefit a patron of the poor.

9   If one shuts his ears against moral instruction,
      Even his prayer becomes an abomination [to God].

10   The man who leads upright men into a wrong path
      Will himself fall into a pit,
      [While the innocent will become prosperous].

11   A rich man may pride himself on his wisdom,
      But a discerning poor man can expose him.

12   When good men are in the ascendant*ᶜ* everything is
      splendid,

ᵃ Omitting *yōdēaʿ*, a variant of *mēbīn*.
ᵇ *rāšāʿ* for MT *rāš*, "poor."
ᶜ *baʿⁱlot* for MT *baʿⁱlōṣ*, "when they rejoice."

But when the wicked rise to power one keeps out of
    their way.

13   He who conceals his transgressions will not prosper,
    But he who confesses and forsakes them will find
        mercy.

14   Blessed is the man who continually trembles [before
        God];
    One who hardens his heart [against him] will fall into
        calamity.

15   The wicked ruler of a poor people is
    Like a growling lion or a prowling bear.

16   A great oppressor^d lacks perception,
    But one who abhors unjust gain will live long.

17   A man burdened with the guilt of murder
    Will come quickly to the grave with no one to
        intervene.

18   He who lives blamelessly will be delivered,
    But the corrupt man will fall to destruction^e.

19   A man who works his land will have plenty to eat,
    But one of frivolous pursuits will have plenty of
        poverty.

20   A trustworthy man will be amply blessed,
    But he who is in haste to get rich will be held
        accountable.

21   To show partiality [in a judicial decision] is wrong;
    A man may be at fault [even] over a morsel of food.

22   An avaricious man is concerned about his possessions;
    He does not know when want will overtake him.

23   The one who rebukes a man will later have his thanks
    Rather than the one who flatters him.

24   He who robs his father [and his mother]
    And says he has done nothing wrong—
    He is next thing to a parricide.

---

^{d} Omitting *nāgīd,* "leader," which may belong to one of two forms of the
saying which have been conflated.
^{e} *bᵉpaḥat* for MT *bᵉ'eḥāt,* "in one."

25   A greedy man stirs up contention,
         Whereas he who trusts the Lord will prosper.

26   He who relies on his own ideas is a fool;
         It is the one who lives by [the rule of] wisdom who
            survives.

27   He who gives to the poor will himself lack nothing,
         But one who shuts his eyes [to their need] will be
            roundly cursed.

28   When the wicked rise to power, one takes cover;
         When they fall, the just [once more] flourish.

NOTES

xxviii 1. "Conscience does make cowards of us all" (*Hamlet,* iii 1).

2. *land is in revolt.* As in Isa iii 4–5; Hos viii 4.

3. *which ruins the harvest.* Literally "and there is no food."

4. *morality.* Here translates *tōrāh,* "teaching," "the law of God."

5. *The evil faction.* Literally "evil men"; cf. "the men of Hezekiah," xxv 1.

6. The first line is identical with xix 1a.

8. *usury and rents.* A standard phrase for extortion; cf. Ezek xviii 8, xxii 12. Yahweh will see to it that a charitable rich man (cf. xiv 31) takes the wealth of a wicked rich man! It seems never to have occurred to the Wisdom teachers that society might not always be sharply divided into rich and poor. Cf. Matt xxvi 11.

9. *abomination.* See NOTE on vi 16–19. The term refers to particular moral offenses in vi 16–19, xi 1, xii 22, xvi 5, xvii 15, xx 10, 23; to wickedness in general in xi 20, xv 9, 26; and to hypocritical religion in xv 8, xxi 27 and here.

10. *himself fall into a pit.* Has become proverbial for "the destruction he invites" (cf. xxvi 27 and NOTE), resulting in a mixed metaphor. The last line is a fragment of another couplet resembling ii 21.

12. The second line is a variant of 28a.

13. Confession and resultant *mercy* seem here to refer to human relationships; if they refer to man's relationship with God, the sentiment recalls the religion of the Psalms (cf. Pss xxxii 5, li 1–17).

15. Cf. NOTE on xix 12.

17. *to the grave;* see NOTE on i 12. But the image is forced, and the

Heb. *'ad bōr* may be a corruption of *mēhéreb*, "[will free] from the sword" (cf. Lev xxvi 36).

intervene. Literally "grasp him," cf. Isa xli 10.

19. Identical with xii 11 except for conclusion of second line. Cf. *Amen-em-ope* ch. 6, "Plow in the fields, that thou mayest find thy needs" (ANET, p. 422b).

20b. Or, "He who is in a hurry to become rich will not be acquitted." Cf. vs. 22; i 16, xx 21.

21. The first line repeats the legal maxim found in xxiv 23–25; cf. xviii 5. Neither poor nor rich are to be favored (Lev xix 15; Deut i 17, xvi 19–20). Here the severity of the law is illustrated, on the principle that the degree of fault makes no difference to the law.

22. This may mean either that he worries so much about gain that he does not realize that he may later lose his possessions; or, that the fear of loss is his constant worry.

24c. Literally "is companion to a man who destroys." Cf. Exod xxi 17; Mark vii 9–13.

25. *greedy.* Or, "ambitious," "arrogant."

33. FURTHER WISE SAYINGS OF SOLOMON
(*continued*)
(xxix 1–27)

XXIX

1   The one who resents*a* rebukes and becomes stubborn
    Will be crushed suddenly and finally.

2   When just men are numerous a people is happy,
    When a wicked man rules, a people groans.

3   He who loves wisdom makes his father happy,
    But one who associates with harlots consumes his
      patrimony.

4   A king by justice makes his land*b* secure,
    But a negligent one*c* ruins it.

5   The man who cajoles his companion
    Is spreading a net for his feet.

6   The sin of an evil man sets a snare,
    But the good man runs away*d*, happy to escape.

7   One who knows what is right*e* pleads the case of the
      poor,
    But an evil man has no such knowledge.

8   Insolent men put the city in an uproar,
    But wise men assuage popular anger.

9   When a wise man goes to law with a fool
    [The fool only] rages and laughs immoderately.

10   The bloodthirsty detest a blameless man
    But the upright are concerned for*f* his welfare.

---

a Reading *śōnē'*, for MT *'īš*, "a man"; cf. xii 1.
b *arṣō* for MT *'ereṣ*, "a land."
c Or "deceitful," reading *remiyyāh* (cf. Jer xlviii 10) for MT *terūmōt*, "offerings."
d Reading *yārūṣ*, for MT *yārūn*, "shouts for joy."
e Reading *ṣédeq*, for MT *ṣaddīq*, "a righteous man."
f *yebaqqerū napšō* for MT *yebaqqešū napšō*, "seek his life."

11 A fool holds nothing back,
    But a wise man is reticent.

12 When a ruler pays attention to false reports
    All his servants become wicked.

13 The poor man and his oppressor have this in common—
    The Lord permitted both to see the light of day.

14 A king's throne will be established in perpetuity
    When he is faithful in judging the rights of the poor.

15 Punishment and rebuke produce wisdom,
    But the boy who gets his own way will shame
        his mother.

16 When wicked men are numerous, crime is rampant,
    But good men will see their collapse.

17 Instruct your son and he will gratify you,
    He will delight you in many ways.

18 Without inspired guidance a people falls into anarchy;
    Hence a law-abiding people is fortunate.

19 A slave cannot be instructed with words [alone],
    Though he understands he will not respond.

20 Do you notice the man who speaks too soon?
    There is more hope for the stupid than for him.

21 If one pampers his slave from his youth up,
    In the end he will prove refractory⁹.

22 An angry man stirs up strife,
    And a bad-tempered man causes much mischief.

23 A man's pride will bring him low,
    But the modest will attain to honor.

24 A thief's accomplice is his own enemy,
    When he hears the curse uttered and does not confess.

25 A man's own fear sets a trap [for him]
    From which the believer in the Lord is protected.

26 Many seek the presence of a ruler,
    But [only] from the Lord may one expect justice.

27 A depraved man is abominable to the just,
    As an honest man is abominable to a wicked one.

⁹ The meaning of MT *mānōn* is uncertain; the translation follows Vulg.

NOTES

xxix 1. From xii 1 and xv 10 it may be inferred that a youth who resists educational discipline is referred to.

3. *consumes his patrimony.* Literally "destroys property." Cf. Luke xv 30.

6. Presumably this means that one man's transgression is a temptation to another. Cf. xxii 24–25.

9. *immoderately.* Literally "and there is no quiet," i.e., for deliberation.

11. *holds nothing back.* Or, "reveals everything he thinks [feels]."

12. *become wicked.* I.e., all engage in slander, or, none escapes it.

13. *have this in common.* Or, "meet at this point"; literally "meet together."

18a. The well-known rendering of KJ "Where there is no vision, the people perish" suggests wrongly that the vision is the imagination or foresight of the people. *hāzōn* means a prophetic vision or oracle (cf. Isa i 1), in which the will and purpose of Yahweh are made known; it is given *to* the people. The reference is either to oracles of the prophets, or more probably, to utterances of the sages for which the same divine inspiration and authority is claimed (cf. Sirach xxiv 32–33). Cf. xi 14; I Sam iii 1.

19. Cf. *Ahiqar* vi, "A blow for a bondman . . . and for all thy slaves discipline" (ANET, p. 428b).

21. On spoiling a son, cf. Sirach xxx 7–13.

24. *is his own enemy.* Literally "hates himself [his life]."

the curse uttered. On the unknown thief by the victim; cf. Judg xvii 2.

25. *A man's own fear.* Or, "fear of man."

26. Cf. *Amen-em-ope,* ch. 20, "As for justice, the great reward of God, he gives it to whom he will."

The Second Collection of Solomonic Proverbs

This second collection (xxv 1–xxix 27), like the first (x 1–xxii 16), is largely miscellaneous in subject matter and discontinuous in arrangement. The following topical classification is offered as a guide to the contents:

The discipline of education—xxv 12, xxvii 17, xxix 1, 15, 17, 19, 21.

Reward and retribution—xxvi 27, xxvii 18, xxviii 10, 17, 18, 19, 20, 25.

Good and evil men—xxviii 1, 4, 5, 12, 16, 28, xxix 6, 7, 10, 27.

The fool—xxvi 1, 3, 4, 5, 6, 7, 8, 9, 10, 11, xxvii 3, 22, xxix 9.

Wisdom and folly—xxvi 12, xxviii 26.

Gossip and slander—xxv 8, 9, 10, 11, 18, 23, xxvi 22.

Other vices and follies—xxv 20, 26, 27, 28, xxvi 13, 14, 15, 16, xxvii 4, 8, 13, 20, xxviii 22, 23, xxix 22, 23.

Various virtues—xxv 13, 14, 15, 16, 17, 19, xxvii 9, 10, 12, xxviii 27.

Morality and religion—xxviii 9, 13, 14, xxix 25, 26.

Character—xxvii 19, 21.

Rich and poor—xxvii 7, xxviii 3, 6, 8, 11, xxix 13.

The royal court—xxv 2, 3, 4–5, 6–7.

Rulers—xxviii 2, 15, xxix 2, 4, 8, 12, 14, 16, 18.

Foolish speech—xxvi 28, xxvii 1, 2, xxix 11, 20.

Father and son—xxvii 11, xxviii 7, 24, xxix 3.

Enemies—xxv 21–22, xxvii 5, 6.

Women and marriage—xxv 24, xxvii 15, 16.

Good news—xxv 25.

Curses—xxvi 2, xxix 24.

Quarrels—xxvi 17, 20, 21.

Hypocrisy—xxvi 23, 24–26, xxix 5.

The practical joker—xxvi 18–19, xxvii 14.

The diligent farmer—xxvii 23–27.

V. The Four Appendixes

34. DIALOGUE WITH A SKEPTIC
(xxx 1–9)

XXX

1 The words of Agur ben Yakeh of Massa'[a].
  The man solemnly affirmed, "There is no God![b]
  There is no God, and I can [not know anything][c].

2 For I am more brute than man,
  And I am devoid of human understanding.

3 I have not learned wisdom,
  Nor[d] have I knowledge of a divine Being.

4 Who has ascended the sky and assumed dominion[e]?
  Who has gathered the twind in his hands?
  Who has wrapped up the waters in his robe?
  Who has established all the ends of the earth?
  What is his name? What are his sons'[f] names?
  Surely you know!"

5 "Everything God says has stood the test!
  He is their shield who trust in him.

6 Do not add to his words,
  Lest he rebuke you and prove you a liar!"

7 Two things I ask of thee;
  Refuse me not before I die:

8 Keep me far from falsity and lying words;
  Grant me neither poverty nor riches,
  But feed me with food that is my portion;

---

[a] Reading *hammassā'ī*, for MT *hammassā'*, "the solemn word."
[b] Reading *lā' 'ītay 'ēl*, for MT *le'ītī'ēl*, "to Ithiel."
[c] The negative particle is implied.
[d] Negative carried forward from the preceding verb.
[e] Reading *wayyired*, for MT *wayyērad*.
[f] Plural, as in LXX.

9   Lest, being surfeited, I should deny [thee]
     And say, "Who is the Lord?"
     Or lest, becoming poor, I should steal,
     And profane the name of my God.

NOTES

xxx 1–9. Much uncertainty surrounds this passage with respect to (a) its reputed authorship; (b) the translation, especially of vs. 1; (c) whether the skeptic's denial is of the existence of God, or of the possibility of man's knowing God. The view taken here is that the challenge of the skeptic Agur ben Yakeh in vss. 1–4 is answered by an orthodox Jewish believer in vss. 5–6, who then appends in vss. 7–9 a prayer to Yahweh that he himself may never be tempted to such blasphemous denial of God. The reader will observe that there are similarities both to the language and to the theme of the Book of Job.

1. *Massa'.* An Ishmaelite people of northern Arabia; cf. Gen xxv 13–14.

There is no God! There is no God, and I can . . . : translates the Hebrew rendered in RSV by "to Ithi-el, to Ithi-el and Ucal." Neither LXX nor Vulg. recognize proper names here. The words *lā' 'ītay 'ēl* are Aramaic (cf. Dan iii 29, *lā' 'ītay 'elāh*) and are equivalent to Heb. *'ēn 'elōhīm,* Ps xiv 1. Cf. Dan ii 10; Elephantine papyri 8:10; 15:17–18. They may be rendered alternatively "I am not God," but the context favors the translation adopted. Cf. the converse in Ugaritic, *k ḥy 'al'eyn b'l k 't zbl b'l 'rṣ,* "that alive was puissant Baal, existent the prince, Lord of earth" (ANET, p. 140b).

2. The skeptic is ironical, as Job in Job xii 2.

3. *divine Being.* Literally "holy ones," an intensive plural with singular meaning as in ix 10.

4. *Who has ascended the sky.* Cf. Job xxxviii 3–38; Isa xl 12 ff.; *Epic of Gilgamesh,* Tablet III: "Who, my friend, can scale he[aven]? (ANET, p. 79b); *Dialogue of Pessimism,* 83–84: "Who is tall enough to ascend to heaven?" (ANET, p. 438b).

Unless *his name* is known, neither god nor man can be known as real; cf. Gen xxxii 29; Exod iii 13; Isa lii 6.

his sons'. The divine beings of the heavenly host; cf. Ps lxxxii 6; Job xxxviii 7.

Surely you know. Cf. Job xxxviii 5.

5–6. The reply of the orthodox believer to the challenge of the skeptic:

God's self-revelation in his word is confirmed in the experience of the religious man. The language is pedestrian, and sounds like a composite quotation from written scripture; cf. Ps xviii 30 EV; Deut iv 2; Job xiii 10, xxiv 25.

7–9. A prayer of the pious man. Cf. Job's more agonizing petition, Job xiii 20–21.

8. *my portion*. Cf. "our daily bread," Matt vi 11.

9. *Who is the Lord?* Cf. Deut viii 12–17; Isa v 19, xxix 15–16; Zeph i 12.

35. WARNINGS AND NUMERICAL PROVERBS
(xxx 10–33)

XXX

10   Do not inform on a servant to his master,
       Lest he curse you and you incur guilt.

FOUR KINDS OF SINNERS

11   There is one kind of man who curses his father
       And does not bless his mother!
12   There is the kind who considers himself pure,
       But is not cleansed of his filth!
13   There is the kind whose eyes are ever so proud,
       And his glances haughty!
14   There is the kind whose teeth are [like] swords,
       And whose jaws are [like] butcher knives,
       Devouring the oppressed from the land,
       And the poor from the earth[a].

THE IMPORTUNATE LEECH

15a   A leech has two daughters—"Give!" and "Give!"

FOUR INSATIABLE THINGS

15b   There are three things that will not be satisfied,
       Four that will never cry, "Enough!"—

[a] Reading *mē'ᵃdāmāh,* for MT *mē'ādām,* "from mankind."

16   Sheol, a barren womb, a land short of water,
    And fire which never cries, "Enough!"

AN IMPIOUS SON

17   He who mocks his father and scorns his aged[b] mother—
    His eye will be plucked out by the ravens of the canyon,
    And will be devoured by the young eagles.

FOUR MYSTERIOUS THINGS

18   Three things astonish me,
    There are four I cannot fathom—
19   How an eagle soars in the sky;
    How a snake glides across a rock;
    How a ship moves over the sea;
    And how a man wins his way with a girl.

THE ADULTERESS

20   This is how an adulteress acts: she eats and wipes her
    mouth and says, "I have done nothing wrong."

FOUR INTOLERABLE PEOPLE

21   Under three things the earth shudders,
    There are four it cannot tolerate:
22   A slave who has become a king;
    An obstinate fool when he is filled with food;
23   An unpopular woman when she gets a husband;
    And a slave girl when she supplants her mistress.

[b] Reading *lah*ᵃ*qat* for the obscure *līqqᵃhat* of MT.

FOUR REMARKABLE SMALL CREATURES

24 There are four small creatures of the earth
  Which are the wisest of the wise:
25 The ants are a frail species, but they make sure of their
    food in summer;
26 Marmots are a feeble species, yet they make their home
    on a cliff;
27 Locusts have no king, yet they take the field in battalions;
28 The lizard can be caught in the hands, but it [makes
    its way] into royal palaces.

FOUR PROUD BEINGS

29 There are three which stride proudly,
  Four which carry themselves with dignity when they
    walk:
30 The lion, lord of the beasts, yielding to none;
31 The strutting cock; the old ram;
  And the king whom no man dare resist.

FOLLY MAKES TROUBLE

32 If you have been such a fool as to give yourself airs,
  If you have schemed, with your hand to your
    mouth,
33 [Beware!] As the pressing of milk yields curds,
  So the pressure of anger leads to bloodshed,
  [And the pressing of the nostrils leads to strife].

NOTES

xxx 10. Interference in the affairs of another man's household is re-
sented by both servant [slave] and master; the curse may be uttered by
either, and if the accusation is unjustified (literally "if you bear guilt")
the curse will take effect. See NOTE on xxvi 2.

11–14. On numerical or "counting" proverbs, see NOTE on vi 16. In this example the first or "cue" couplet with its "x, x+1" form and its statement of the common characteristic of the items to be enumerated is missing. Through some accident in copying it seems to have been replaced by the otherwise isolated proverb in vs. 10. Its form may be inferred from vi 16 ("Six things which the Lord hates"), with "six . . . seven" altered to "three . . . four."

11. *the kind.* Or, "group," "circle."

12. *cleansed.* Ritually (Lev xv 1–15) or morally (xv 26, xx 9; Isa i 16).

14. *teeth are [like] swords.* Cf. Pss xiv 4, lvii 4 EV; Mic iii 2–3 where oppression and injustice are said to be tantamount to cannibalism.

15a. An anecdotal fable-proverb, sarcastic and semi-humorous, like the Assyrian saying about the insect apologizing to the elephant for stealing a ride (BWL, pp. 217, 219; cf. *Ahiqar* xi, ANET, pp. 429–30). It is a retort to someone who constantly begs favors. There is no connection with vss. 15b–16.

16. *fire.* Either one out of control, or, more probably, one for which the labor of bringing fuel seems endless. A similar Indian proverb is "Fire is not sated with the wood, nor the ocean with the streams, nor death with all the living, nor the beauty-eyed with men."

18–19. In this type of the numerical proverb, as in vss. 29–31, the climactic fourth line points the parallel in man to what is observed in the external world. There has been much debate about the meaning of this proverb; is it that in each case there is movement which leaves no trace? (Cf. Wisdom of Solomon v 9–12.) Or, that the thing named is without visible means of propulsion? In either case the application to the human situation is problematical. Most think of the last line as a reference to the mystery of the act of procreation (cf. the idiom "he went into her," Ruth iv 13, etc.); but there are also the attendant mysteries of the attraction of the sexes in general, and of the love of a particular man for a particular woman.

20. A prosaic comment, apparently inserted here because it begins with the same word *dérek,* "way," which marks the opening of the four preceding cola or half lines. For the metaphor of eating, for sexual intercourse, cf. vi 26.

21–23. Instances of imbalance in the order of social values.

23. *unpopular.* Literally "hated." This becomes a technical term for one of two wives who is rejected by her husband (cf. Deut xxi 15–17; Gen xxix 30–31); here her behavior is intolerable presumably because she stands on her rights though her husband does not love her.

The *slave girl . . . supplants her mistress* probably by bearing her

master a child when the mistress is barren. The contempt of Hagar for
Sarah in such circumstances is noted in Gen xvi 1–6.

25. *species*. Literally "people." The provident *ants* (cf. vi 6) were
observed elsewhere too; Horace speaks of "the tiny ant, a creature of
great industry . . . not careless of the future" (Sat. I i 33).

26. *Marmots*. Or, "rock badgers"; cf. Lev xi 5; Ps civ 18.

27. *take the field in battalions*. Literally "go out (i.e., to war; cf.
Judg iv 14), all divided in groups." The figure of locusts as an invading
army is vividly developed in Joel ii 4–9.

28. *lizard*. The gecko or house lizard, noted for its ability to climb
walls.

31. *The strutting cock*. The traditional translation (LXX, Vulg.) of two
obscure words. Indian jungle fowl were domesticated in Palestine by the
seventh century B.C. and possibly much earlier. See NOTE on i 17.

the king whom no man dare resist. Only a guess at the meaning of
mélek 'alqūm 'immō. Possibly the fourth of those *which stride proudly*
(vs. 29) is another animal whose name is unknown or unrecognizable in
the text as it stands. Cf. vss. 24–28.

32–33. *If you have schemed*. Or (possibly), "if you have made a rude
gesture" like *pressing of the nostrils*.

33. The third line seems to be a variant of the second.

36. A QUEEN MOTHER'S ADMONITION
(xxxi 1-9)

XXXI

1   Words [of advice] to a king acting foolishly,[a]
     A solemn injunction which his mother lays on him:

2   "How now, my son! How now, O son of my womb!
     How now, O son of my vows!

3   Yield not your virility to women,
     Your loins[b] to the destroyers[c] of kings!

4   It is not fitting for a king to play the fool[d]!
     It is not for kings to be wine drinkers,
     Nor for princes to be fond of[e] beer;

5   Lest in drinking he forget his duty,
     And deny the rights of all the afflicted.

6   Give beer [rather] to one who is in extremity,
     And wine to him whose life is bitter,

7   That he may drink and forget his poverty
     And no longer remember his troubles.

8   Speak out for the one who cannot speak for himself,
     And for the rights of all the unfortunate

9   Speak out! See justice done, and defend the
     afflicted poor!"

[a] Reading *dibrē leno'al melek*, for MT *dibrē lemū'ēl melek*.
[b] Reading *yerēkēkā* (cf. Exod i 5), for MT *derākēkā*, "your ways."
[c] Reading *lemōḥōt*, for MT *lamḥōt*, "to destroy"; cf. v 9–11; I Kings xi 1–3.
[d] Reading *leḥiwwā'ēl*, for MT *lemō'ēl*, "Lemoel," a proper name?
[e] Reading *'awwēh*, for the obscure word *'ēw* of MT.

NOTES

xxxi 1. *Words . . . king acting foolishly*. For, "Words of Lemoel [sic], a king"; cf. Isa xix 13. Nothing is known of a King Lemoel or Lemuel, but this is less significant for interpretation of the text here than the tenor of the whole of vss. 1–4. LXX did not recognize a proper name in either vs. 1 or vs. 4, and in the latter verse the translation "play the fool" is clearly suitable.

solemn injunction. Or, "reproach." A queen mother wielded considerable influence at court; cf. I Kings i 11–13, xv 13; II Kings ix 22, xi 1.

2. *How now*. Or, "Now then!"

son of my vows. I.e., a son in anticipation of whose birth the mother had made vows; cf. I Sam i 11, 27.

3. *loins*. Or, "thighs." Cf. v 9–11; I Kings xi 1–3.

4. *kings . . . princes*. On the thought, cf. Eccles x 17; Isa xxviii 1; Hos vii 5.

5. *his duty*. Literally "what is decreed."

8. *who cannot speak for himself*. Literally "who is dumb."

37. THE IDEAL HOUSEWIFE
(xxxi 10–31)

XXXI

10   A capable wife is a rare find,
      Her worth is far greater than jewels.

11   Her husband gives her his confidence
      And he is well compensated [for it];

12   She rewards him with good and not harm,
      All the days of her life.

13   She seeks out wool and flax,
      And delights to work with her hands.

14   She is like the ships of the merchants,
      As she brings her provisions from afar.

15   She rises while it is still night
      To provide food for her household,
      And give instructions to her maids.

16   She examines a field and buys it,
      From her earnings she plants a vineyard.

17   She girds her strong loins
      And goes to work with a will.

18   She samples merchandise to be sure it is good;
      Her lamp burns late at night.

19   She puts her hand to the spindle whorl,
      And her fingers ply the spindle.

20   She opens her hands to the unfortunate,
      And stretches out her arms to the poor.

21   She does not fear for her family when it snows,
      For all of them are doubly[a] clothed.

[a] Reading *šnáyim*, for MT *šānīm*, "scarlet things."

22   She makes her own bedcovers;
        She clothes herself in fine linen and dyed wool.
23   Her husband is well known at the gates,
        Where he sits with the elders of the city.
24   She makes a wrapper and sells it,
        And supplies a sash to the merchant.
25   Her clothing is of good quality and elegant,
        She happily looks forward to the morrow.
26   When she opens her mouth she speaks wisely,
        And kindly instruction is on her tongue.
27   She watches closely what goes on in her household,
        And permits no one to eat*b* food in idleness.
28   Her sons rise to pronounce blessings on her,
        Her husband, too, sings her praises:
29   "Many women have proved their worth,
        But you have surpassed them all."
30   Charm is deceitful and beauty is fleeting;
        The intelligent*c* woman [who reverences the Lord]
            is the one deserving praise.
31   Give her the reward she has earned,
        And let the gates ring with praise of her deeds.

b Reading *ta'ᵃkīl*, for MT *tō'kēl*, "she eats."
c From LXX; the word is omitted in MT.

NOTES

xxxi 10–31. This poem is an acrostic, the initial letters of its twenty-two couplets following the normal order of the Hebrew alphabet. In consequence the sequence and substance of the thought are subordinated to the necessities of the formal structure. The poem develops the thought of xviii 22, and it is interesting, not only for the light it throws on domestic activities of the time, but because of the degree of managerial responsibility evidently assumed by the wife of a well-to-do man in ancient Israel.

10. *capable wife*. Or, "true lady."
11. *well compensated*. Literally "does not lack spoil."

13. *delights to work with her hands.* Or, "of which her hands make beautiful things."

17. Literally "She girds her loins with strength and makes her arms strong."

18. Or, "She judges that her profit is good."

burns late. Literally "does not go out."

23. *city.* Or, "land." Cf. PNWSP, pp. 62–63.

24. *wrapper.* Or, "gown."

25. *of good quality and elegant.* Literally "strength and ornament."

30. The words in brackets are probably an insertion by a pious scribe who had observed the absence of any mention of religion among the lady's many virtues.

ECCLESIASTES
(QOHELETH)

INTRODUCTION

The Strangeness and Fascination of the Work

Ecclesiastes is the strangest book in the Bible, or at any rate the book whose presence in the sacred canons of Judaism and of Christianity is most inexplicable. The Song of Songs with its frankly erotic tone may seem equally out of place in company with the Law and the Prophets, and has seemed so to not a few Jews and Christians in ancient and modern times. The Song, however, can be interpreted as an allegory of the love of Yahweh for Israel, or of Christ for his Church—on the strength of the figure of the marriage relationship used by Hosea and Jeremiah (cf. Hos ii 2–20 EV; Jer ii 2, iii 1). In the case of Ecclesiastes there is no such possibility of allegorization to bring it into line with the tone and teaching of the rest of the Bible. It diverges too radically. In fact, it denies some of the things on which the other writers lay the greatest stress—notably that God has revealed himself and his will to man, through his chosen people Israel. In Ecclesiastes God is not only unknown to man through revelation; he is unknowable through reason, the only means by which the author believes knowledge is attainable. Such a God is not Yahweh, the covenant God of Israel. He is rather the mysterious, inscrutable Being whose existence must be presupposed as that which determines the life and fate of man, in a world man cannot change, and where all his effort and values are rendered meaningless.

Thus, in place of a religion of faith and hope and obedience, this writer expresses a mood of disillusionment and proffers a philosophy of resignation. His ethic has no relationship to divine commandments, for there are none. It arises rather from the necessity of caution and moderation before the inexplicable, on the acceptance of what is fated and cannot be changed, and finally on grasping firmly the only satisfaction open to man—the enjoyment of being alive. The author is a rationalist, an agnostic, a skeptic, a pessimist, and a fatalist (the terms are not used pejoratively!). In most respects his views run counter to those of his religious fellow Jews. The title of a modern autobiography, *Treadmill to Oblivion,* seems to sum up most (though not quite all) of his conclusions about life.

Yet we find this book described by Franz Delitzsch (1875) as "the quintessence of piety," and a more recent critic, Hertzberg, finds in it the most moving Messianic prophecy in the Old Testament. This point of view can be traced back to the earliest Christian commentator on the book, Gregory Thaumaturgus (d. 270). Gregory said that its purpose was "to show that all the affairs and pursuits of men are vain and useless, in order to lead us to the contemplation of heavenly things." Such may be the only possible rationale of the book's inclusion within a canon of Holy Scripture, but it seems a remarkable example of the indirect method.

A second element of strangeness is the language in which the book is written, a kind of Hebrew unlike any other in the Old Testament. It has features which resemble the Hebrew of the Mishnah (A.D. 200), and of the somewhat earlier copper scroll from Qumran; apparently this was a dialect developed in certain circles under Aramaic influence shortly before the beginning of the Christian era. H. L. Ginsberg, in fact, believes that the book was composed originally in Aramaic. On the other hand, the evidence of similarities to Phoenician marshaled by M. J. Dahood ("Canaanite-Phoenician Influence in Qoheleth," *Biblica* 33 [1952]), is impressive. The inclusion of two Persian loanwords—*pardēs,* "park" (ii 5) and *pitgām,* "decree" (viii 11)—strongly suggests that Qoheleth was not composed before the rise of Persia to world power toward the end of the sixth century B.C.

In the third place, the name or designation of the author, Qōhéleth (in vii 27 and xii 8 *"the* Qōhéleth"), is an ancient puzzle. It has the form of an active feminine participle of the verb *q-h-l* (not found in the simple stem in the Old Testament), from which is derived the noun *qāhāl,* "a gathering, assembly, congregation." "Qōhéleth" seems to mean, therefore, "one who assembles a company or congregation." In the context of the Wisdom movement the term or title could designate a teacher or academician who gathers about him pupils or disciples, as indeed (we are told in xii 9) Qoheleth did. The feminine participial form probably is to be explained as an occupational designation which has become a proper name, like "Sophéreth," originally="member of the scribal profession" (Neh vii 57; cf. the English surnames "Penman," "Scribner"). The "Ecclesiastes" of the Latin and English versions comes from the Greek Bible where it is an attempt to translate "Qōhéleth" on the analogy of the rendering of *qāhāl*, "congregation," by the Greek word *ekklēsia*, "assembly, church." *The ekklēsiastes* is then understood as the leader or speaker of the assembly, whence Jerome's *"conciniator,"* Martin Luther's *"Der Prediger,"* and the alternative title "The Preacher" in the English versions. In the current usage of the word "preacher" it could hardly be more unsuitable as a description of the author of this book.

The very strangeness of the work in its literary and religious context in the Bible is part of its fascination. The author's mood of doubt and pessimism is one into which many reflective persons fall from time to time, and in which not a few of the more skeptical remain. At the same time, there is a deep wisdom even in Qoheleth's melancholy reflections, and in the courage with which he affirms life's values in the teeth of its brevity and frustrations, of the unalterable "givenness" of existence, and the surrounding dark. On his premise that God is unknowable by man, his conclusions are not easily proved wrong. Hence it is all the more strange that his book came to be numbered among the sacred writings whose basic premise is the exact opposite of Qoheleth's—that God, the sovereign Creator, not only is knowable but has spoken to man through Moses and the Prophets, and has revealed his will and power in historic events in the life of his covenant people Israel; that he is the source of man's highest aspirations, the support of man's moral struggle, and the only final security in which man's mind can rest. Others besides Qoheleth, such as Jeremiah, faced life's contradictions as resolutely as he did but remained sure of God. After all, it is their testimony and not Qoheleth's doubts which created the Bible.

How Qoheleth Came to Be in the Bible

The story of the making of the "canon" or authorized collection of sacred books is so fragmentary and obscure that one cannot say precisely when or why Qoheleth came to be included. What is certain is that its suitability for inclusion was still a matter of debate among the Jewish authorities toward the end of the first century A.D., as recorded in the Mishnah (Eduyoth 5:3; Yadaim 3:5). It was retained "because its beginning is religious teaching and its end is religious teaching" (Talmud, Shabbath 30b). The Greek-speaking Christian Church took over Ecclesiastes in Greek in the larger and more loosely defined sacred collection of the Alexandrian Jews.

The reasons which led to the admission and retention of Qoheleth-Ecclesiastes in the Hebrew Bible and consequently in the Christian canon, were probably these. In the first place, its heterodox statements are balanced by others of unimpeachable orthodoxy, such as ii 26, iii 17, and viii 12–13. Some of these are in fact quotations which Qoheleth includes only to refute them. In other cases they sound pious, but really are part and parcel of his thought. Some, such as xi 9c, may be marginal notations by a later hand. The summing up of the book in its concluding two verses is clearly editorial, and intended to fix a line of orthodox interpretation which would help to safeguard the faith of the uncritical reader. Nevertheless, the daring originality of Qoheleth's thought and its challenge to traditional teachings could not be concealed, as the continuing objections to the work bear witness. We must remember also the strange capacity of the human mind, unless trained in logic, to entertain incompatible propositions.

A second reason for the acceptance of Qoheleth was the unquestionable intellectual and literary quality of the book, to say nothing of its ethical wisdom. The avoidance of traditional ideas and forms of expression would appeal to the thoughtful layman, to whom the language of official theology and the interests of its professional exponents seemed remote. When this book was written, such a man no longer lived in the closed society of his ancestors, but in a wider world whose doors had been opened by commerce and foreign conquest. The revival of Israel's national feeling in the

Maccabean struggle of the second century B.C. still lay in the future. Qoheleth was speaking to other men as individual human beings in the tradition of the Wisdom movement, but under the new conditions of Jewish life in the early Hellenistic age.

In the third place, as the editorial appendix in xii 9–14 makes plain, the work was sponsored by others of the group of sages influential in the community. The Wisdom teachers were individualists, and there had always been radicals among them—as witness the Book of Job. They were not subservient to the priestly scribes and orthodox theologians. Before the Exile to Babylon in the sixth century, some of their predecessors had come into conflict with the Prophets (cf. Isa v 21, xxix 14; Jer ix 23, xviii 18). Now in post-Exilic days, when prophecy had faded out and the written Torah or Law of Moses had been established as the supreme religious authority, the scribes and interpreters of the Torah gained new prominence. This was matched and at least indirectly opposed by a revival of the more secular learning of a new generation of Wisdom teachers. Many of these undertook the instruction of young men in their own schools (cf. xii 9; Prov i 2–19; Sirach li 23–30), where their title may have been "Qoheleth," that is, "schoolmaster" or "teacher." Evidently one of them was known to his own pupils as *the* Teacher, "haqqōhéleth," his personal name being replaced by this honorific title. His fame apparently was such, and his teachings so widely known in Wisdom circles, that when Wisdom writings were among those appended as a supplement to the Law and the Prophets, his work was carried with them into what was *later* to be accepted as the corpus of canonical scriptures.

By this time the book had come to be associated with the name of Solomon, traditional patron of Wisdom in Israel. This association undoubtedly contributed to the final decision to retain Qoheleth-Ecclesiastes among so many other works with whose teachings it was at variance. Actually, the name of Solomon does not appear anywhere in the book. The author is identified in i 1 simply as "son of David, king in Jerusalem," which claims no more than that he was a king "of the house and lineage of David" (cf. Matt i 1; Luke ii 4). There can be no question, however, that in i 12–13, 16, ii 1–9 the writer pictures himself, for the purposes of his argument, in the role of the Solomon of legendary wealth and wisdom. There is of course no possibility that the Solomon of history composed this book; to claim this is like claiming that a book about Marxism in modern English idiom and spelling was written by Henry VIII. The editor's biographical notes in xii 9–10 do not suggest even remotely that Qoheleth was in fact a king, let alone Solomon. The ascription of Wisdom writings to Solomon was a literary convention. This is proved beyond question by the book known as "The Wisdom of Solomon" in the Greek Bible (and in the English Apocrypha), which was written in the first century B.C. in Greek for Greek-speaking readers. There, as in Qoheleth, the role of Solomon manifestly is assumed for literary effect, and no observant reader could suppose otherwise.

THE NATURE AND ORIGIN OF QOHELETH'S BOOK

What is before us here is primarily a philosophical work rather than a book of religion. It seeks a rational understanding of human existence and a basis for ethics, through the application of human reason to observable data. As already pointed out, the author excludes from consideration, as unverifiable, the special data of revealed religion. His philosophical method, however, is not that of logical argument developing step by step to a conclusion. He begins by stating a thesis: "A vapor of vapors! Thinnest of vapors! All is vapor!" He then proceeds to describe and analyze the various kinds of experience which have led him to this result. He retails his reflections on the unknowability of God. He dilates on the empty and useless efforts of men to achieve anything substantial in their brief span of life. Then he turns to the ethical question of how a man should aim to live, under the intractable conditions of his existence. At this point Qoheleth makes the one positive affirmation of his philosophy—that to relish being alive is man's chief good. Life ought to be enjoyed (if the inscrutable God permit), but always in moderation and with reserve. One's youth is to be prized as the time when life is at its most vigorous, and its enjoyment may be unalloyed by care or weakness. For life is short and passes quickly; it is hemmed in by the near approach of the final darkness. So in conclusion Qoheleth reiterates his thesis concerning life—"A vapor of vapors! All is vapor!"

Some scholars have been sure that there are echoes of Greek

philosophical views in Qoheleth's thought. In chapter i the ceaseless passing of the generations, and the restless cycle of movements of sun, wind, and water, have suggested Heraclitus' view of the perpetual flux in all things. "Whatever has been is what will be" (i 9) recalls the Stoic theory of world cycles perpetually repeated. "Everything has its season and . . . proper time" (iii 1) may be related to the Stoic doctrine that man should "live according to nature" because he is in the grip of fate. Even the much later dictum of Marcus Aurelius that "worldly things are but as smoke, as very nothingness" so closely resembles Qoheleth's thesis that it has been held to confirm the influence on him of an earlier Stoicism. The hedonism of the Epicureans apparently is reflected in his declaration that man's sole good is to eat and drink and find enjoyment in life (ii 24). Parallels in thought and method to the sixth-century Greek gnomic poet Theognis also have been noted.

When these claims of philosophical influence are examined, bearing in mind other unmentioned aspects of the thought of these philosophies and also the long tradition of Near Eastern Wisdom itself, they are unconvincing. The most that can be said is that Qoheleth's thought may have been stimulated by Greek thought reported at second hand. Such ideas may have been talked about in the Phoenician port cities even before Alexander the Great's conquest of the region in 332 B.C. There are some slight indications that Qoheleth had Phoenician connections, and may have visited the region. Certainly his tone of sophisticated disillusionment recalls the atmosphere of cosmopolitan life in seaport cities more than that of an inland provincial town like Jerusalem.

Nevertheless it is the philosophical character of Qoheleth's work rather than its affinities with particular schools of Greek thought that distinguishes it. He displays the philosophic temper in a search for truth. Observation and reasoning take the place of intuition and the data of revelation as the avenues to knowledge. His is a critical work, critical of the traditional teachings of the sages in Israel as well as of theological orthodoxy. This radical wing of the Wisdom movement had had a long history in the Near East before the rise of Greek rationalism, and may well have been one of the original stimulants of the latter. Nevertheless, on linguistic grounds alone—the contamination of classical Hebrew by Aramaisms and Phoenicianisms, the use of two Persian words (but no Greek words and no certain Greek constructions)—Qoheleth is to be dated toward the end of the Persian domination or early in the Greek period, that is, in the fourth century B.C. or the beginning of the third. Greek influence, in fact, was already widespread before Alexander's conquests. It is therefore possible that before his time Greek philosophical ideas had been heard of and discussed by those who, like Qoheleth, were interested in such matters.

Our author's deepest roots, however, are in the skeptical, pessimistic side of Egyptian and Mesopotamian Wisdom on the one hand, and, on the other, in certain basic tenets of Hebrew thought. The former is described above in the General Introduction. The latter has in view such facts as are taken for granted—the real existence of the one God, his creation of the physical universe and of man, and his sovereignty over the course of events in this world. The transcendence and mystery of the divine Being stand over against the physical and moral weakness of man and the brevity of human life. But Qoheleth does not think of creation as the inception of God's relations in historic time with the human race, and in particular with Israel. To him, creation means simply the establishment in the beginning of the unchanging physical and temporal setting for the life of successive generations. "All the world's a stage, / And all the men and women merely players," though in a somewhat different sense from Shakespeare's. Again, the doctrine of divine Providence has become in Qoheleth an arbitrary and absolute determinism. Any possibility of divine intervention in nature or in human affairs is ruled out, because nothing new happens under the sun. Man may catch glimpses of the divine order in the very regularity of physical processes in the natural world and the relentless procession of events; not, however, in any moral order recognizable in experience. What God is doing is his own secret, and whether he is well-disposed or ill-disposed toward man is unknown. Revelation is ruled out because there is no possibility of communication from beyond the impenetrable veil (iii 11). The moral and physical feebleness of man, of which the rest of the Old Testament is well aware (cf. Isa xxxi 3, xl 6–7; Jer x 23, xiii 23, xvii 9), has become for our author the impotence of a captive. Death, for him, is not the end of a life in which knowledge of and fellowship with God had been possible (as, e.g., in Ps vi 4–5 EV). Rather it is just the oblivion which terminates conscious life and all possibility of a temporary emotional satisfaction. Hence Qoheleth's determination to grasp the fleeting enjoyments of life is his version of the life-affirming quality of Hebrew religious thought.

Some echoes are heard of the Prophets' concern for social justice, of their denunciations of oppression, the venality of judges and the self-interest of rulers. But there is a notable difference; Qoheleth only deplores such conditions as among the anomalies and frustrations of human life which it is useless to try to change. He does not identify himself—and certainly not God—with the cause of the sufferers as Isaiah does (iii 13–15), possibly in part because he himself was one of the leisured beneficiaries of the social system. The Prophets' picture of God as the angry champion of the oppressed is totally alien to him. A similar attitude of detachment is observable in their view of temple worship. They declared that cultic sacrifices are worthless apart from moral obedience to God's will in daily life (cf. Isa i 10–17; Jer vii 22–23; Hos vi 6; Amos v 21–24). To Qoheleth the thoughtless participants in temple worship are fools; the wise man will participate only in the spirit of respectful inquiry.

Though Qoheleth begins and ends with a thesis which the intervening material explicates and illustrates, there is no ordered sequence to his argument. What we find in the book is a series of reflections and soliloquies, interspersed with brief narratives, parables, maxims, and proverbial sayings. Broadly speaking, his philosophy is set out in the first part of the book and the ethic derived from it in the second part. O. Eissfeldt[1] distinguishes four principal categories of material: (a) autobiographical reflections (i 12–18, ii 1–13); (b) admonitions addressed to a pupil (iv 17–v 8, vii 9–14, xi 1–6, etc.); (c) generally valid observations (i 2–11, iii 1–8, vii 1–8, etc.); and (d) individual Wisdom sayings (ix 17–x 20). In addition, it is to be noted that the admonition beginning at xi 7 is continued in xii 1–7 in a brilliant and moving poem which does not resemble anything else in the book. The prose appendix in xii 9–14 is obviously from the hand of an editor.

Who was Qoheleth? All that we know about him comes from the biographical notes in the appendix, plus what can be inferred from his own thoughts and the language in which these are expressed. We learn that he was a professional sage and teacher, and, like the

[1] *Einleitung in das Alte Testament,* 3d ed., 1964, pp. 668–69.

author of Proverbs i–ix, a diligent student of *meš̄alīm,* (a term including proverbs, parables, and gnomic forms of various other kinds). We are told of the care that he took to express himself in felicitous language, and of the impression he made of earnestness and honesty in his search for truth. From his incidental asides and presuppositions it seems that he belonged to the privileged class. He shows little interest in formal religion and most of its customs and traditional beliefs. From the feeling with which he speaks of the rapid approach of old age and counsels young men to make the most of youthful opportunity, we can infer that his own youth lay behind him. It is possible but unlikely that his bitter remarks about women reflect an unfortunate personal experience; more probably they express a traditional dislike of the sages for the opposite sex as tempting men from the way of wisdom (cf. Prov v 1–23, vii 5–27, ix 13–18). We are reminded of Xantippe, the cantankerous wife of Socrates, by the sayings about shrewish wives (cf. Prov xxi 9, 19, xxvii 15).

From the Aramaic and Phoenician coloring of the dialect in which Qoheleth writes it may be inferred that he had connections with Phoenicia or had lived in adjacent North Israelite territory. Ezekiel xxviii 1–19 and Zech ix 2 indicate that the Wisdom movement flourished at Tyre. When Qoheleth composed the material of his book it seems that he was a Wisdom teacher living in Jerusalem, since his casual reference to attendance at sacrificial rites implies that the Temple is nearby. (But cf. v 1 EV, NOTE.) No weight can be attached to the assertion that he had been "king in Jerusalem," for this belongs to the role of Solomon which he assumes in the first two chapters only. He could have written as he did, had he lived elsewhere. But the incidental references to weather phenomena in relation to agriculture (xi 3–4, xii 2) are appropriate to the Palestinian climate, less so to the better-watered Phoenicia, and not at all to Egypt or Mesopotamia where great rivers provide abundant water for the irrigation of crops.

Not much help in determining the date and provenance of the book can be found in references to social and political conditions and events. Its background appears to be a stable and stratified authoritarian society, chiefly engaged in agriculture and commerce. There is no hint of war conditions or of social upheaval. The mention in v 8 of a hierarchy of officials in a "province" under an ap-

parently distant king, and in x 5 of a local authority other than the
king, suggests that he is living under the administrative system of
the Persian empire. It is of course possible that the same language
might have been appropriate in the early Hellenistic period when
Palestine was under the dominion of the Ptolemies. (The Seleucids
are ruled out by the evidence of Sirach and of the second-century
Qoheleth manuscript from Qumran that the work is older than the
second century B.C.) The caution against reviling the king in secret
(x 20) would be pertinent whether the king was near or far away.

Qoheleth's counsel concerning behavior at a royal court, however (viii 2–5, x 16–17), is a different matter. On the face of it,
this is addressed to youths who might expect later to find themselves
in the presence of a king, presumably in an official capacity. Such
instruction to a potential courtier is an old theme of the Wisdom
movement (cf. Prov xvi 13–15, and the Egyptian *Instruction of
Amen-em-ope,* ch. 9, ANET, p. 423a). Although Sheshbazzar,
Nehemiah, and perhaps Ezra had access to the Persian monarch,
and leading Jews appeared at the courts of the Ptolemies and
Seleucids, what Qoheleth contemplates is a circumstance usual
enough to be included in his educational curriculum. Probably "the
king" here means any king, the embodiment of absolute authority
to which one must learn to accommodate himself. Consequently the
situation is typical and illustrative only, like the episode recounted
in ix 13–15 and the rhetorical exclamation in x 16–17. Gordis[2] may
be right in identifying the "Council of Ten" of vii 19 as the ruling
council of a Hellenistic city, but the phrase could equally well refer
to the collective power of a council of elders at any period. The
political conditions portrayed by Qoheleth thus do not enable us to
pinpoint the date of his work any more exactly than does the linguistic evidence, but they are consistent with the latter's indication
of the fourth or the third century B.C.

QOHELETH'S PHILOSOPHY

The principal thesis of the book is found, as already remarked, in
the words with which it begins and ends—"A vapor of vapors! All

[2] Robert Gordis, *Koheleth, the Man and His World* (abbr. Gordis), New
York, 1955, p. 269.

is vapor!" It is echoed in the constantly recurring phrases "a vapor and a grasping at the wind," and "this too is a vapor." The word *hebel,* "vapor" or "breath," connotes what is visible or recognizable, but unsubstantial, momentary, and profitless. The rendering must be varied to bring out the particular shades of meaning in different contexts. Thus the traditional translation "Vanity of vanities, all is vanity" can be freely expanded to read: "Everything in life is hollow and utterly futile; it is the thinnest of vapors, fleeting as a breath, and amounts to nothing." Man's self-conscious existence, his experience of life's struggle and all he tries to accomplish, turns out to be the merest vapor. "What has a man to show for all his trouble and effort during his brief lifetime under the sun?" (i 3). The answer is—nothing!

The evidence which Qoheleth adduces as grounds for his apparent philosophical nihilism is as follows:

(a) The world which is the setting of man's life and man's own experience of life itself show endless movement without change, the perpetual pouring out of effort without *yitrōn,* "profit," anything gained by it. The generations come and go, mankind moves across the stage from darkness to darkness in endless procession—while the stage itself goes round and round. Everywhere there is constant, weary movement, but no real change. Nothing is new, nothing new happens, nothing becomes memorable (i 3–11). The reason for this is that God has decreed that the world should be what it is— from man's standpoint a warped and defective world which no effort of his can alter (i 15, vii 13). Qoheleth had conducted his own experiments to discover the secret of what is happening, but they have been fruitless. All his expenditure of energy has had no tangible result, and he has been left clutching at the empty air (i 12–14). When he tried to discover the nature of wisdom itself, and what it is that distinguishes wisdom from folly, the cost cancelled out the gain (i 17–18, vii 23–viii 1). He sought through rational self-indulgence to isolate and define the good derived from pleasure and possessions. But all that he could find was the ephemeral happiness of the passing moments (ii 1–11, v 18). The value of wisdom and the fruits of effort were both alike cancelled by the inexorable fact of death (ii 14–16, 18–26, v 11–17 EV).

(b) Everything that happens to man appears to be predetermined, and fitted to its uniquely appropriate time. But *why* it happens this way and not in some other way, and what it all means (if anything) is an impenetrable mystery (iii 1–15, vii 23–24, viii 16–17, ix 11–12). God has put an insoluble enigma, a darkness, in the human mind (iii 11), and man is in no position to dispute with omnipotence (vi 10–12, vii 13). Hence it is useless to try to combat the wickedness and social injustice one sees and regrets; evil (in the language of the moral impotence of today) "is just one of those things" (iv 1–3, v 8 EV, viii 10–15).

(c) The theological theory that retribution inevitably overtakes wickedness, and goodness brings prosperity, is contradicted in experience. A man's character and accomplishments apparently make no difference to his fate. The righteous and the wicked, the wise man and the fool fare much the same, and meet the same inevitable and imminent doom (iii 16, vii 15, viii 14). No one can tell whether or not God will favor him (ix 1). Indeed, men and animals die the same death, and who can say with assurance that man's spirit goes up to God and the animal's downward to the earth? (iii 18–21.) Here Qoheleth seems to be rejecting for lack of proof a claim that some of his contemporaries were making.

(d) As life is cancelled by death, so all values are negated by their opposites. Greater knowledge brings with it only more distress (i 18). Every kind of excellence is overcome by some predetermined misfortune (ix 11–12). Other men's indifference to worth and wisdom make these ineffective (ix 13–16), and "a small folly may outweigh wisdom [and] honor" (x 1). Arbitrary power in human hands plays havoc with social values (x 5–7). A famous man is soon forgotten (iv 13–16). The fruits of a lifetime of toil and anxiety may be lost through a single error in judgment (v 13–17 EV). Death is the final and universal negation of values (ii 16, vi 6, viii 8, ix 3, xii 1–7).

All this sounds like an argument for suicide. H. Wheeler Robinson comments: "It was fitting enough that such an un-Hebraic philosophy of life should reach its climax in an eloquent and sombre picture of death. The book has indeed the smell of the tomb about it."[3] Yet, curiously enough, that is *not* the over-all impression

[3] *Inspiration and Revelation in the Old Testament,* Oxford, 1946, p. 258.

that the book makes on most readers; and the rejection of life, let alone self-destruction, is *not* the practical conclusion Qoheleth derives from his philosophy. He has followed the relentless arguments of reason to stark theoretical conclusions. But his *practical* conclusions, and the counsel he gives because of them, are affirmative. They have the joy of life rather than the odor of death about them. He himself is better than his philosophy. His soul affirms what his reason would lead him to deny, and it is on a positive note that he lays stress as he tells young men how to live.

The Ethical Wisdom of Qoheleth

Despair was indeed the initial conclusion to which Qoheleth was driven: "So I came to hate life, because it depressed me that all man's activities beneath the sun are only vapor" (ii 17; cf. ii 20). The reason for his despair was that he had been thinking of life in terms of what a man could accomplish during his lifetime through planning and effort, driven by desire. He had found the stuff of life beyond his power to mold. It rolled on like an irresistible flood, carrying all before it. Nothing he could do left a definite residue, whether of material wealth, fame, wisdom, or even satisfaction. What happened seemed to happen inevitably, because the unseen and unknown God had so decreed for reasons known only to himself. At this point Qoheleth paused to ask a second question: Why, then, do men want to go on living? How is it that they do in fact find in it at least temporary satisfactions and some measure of happiness? Does any *relative* good remain to man?

Yes, indeed! he answers: more than enough to make life worth living. This is his wisdom:

(a) *One must face facts,* and not go on asserting or accepting as true what will not stand up under examination in the light of the evidence. The traditional teaching that virtue is rewarded in this life and vice is punished is the first bastion he carries by assault (viii 14). It simply *is not true,* he declares, that dedication to wisdom and virtue, *or* the pursuit of pleasure, *or* the accumulation of wealth, adds up to happiness. The conservative wing of the Wisdom movement had claimed that "Right will protect the blameless life, but sin overturns the wicked" (Prov xiii 6). "It just is not so!" says Qoheleth.

(b) *One must learn to live with what cannot be changed,* and bow to the inevitable. What is bent cannot be straightened by man's efforts, and what is wrong cannot be righted. As the corruption of government officials is the responsibility of their superiors, not that of ordinary citizens, so what seems wrong with the world is God's responsibility (i 15, v 8 EV, ix 1–2). At this point the Teacher is almost Muslim in his counsel of submission to the mysterious decrees of God. The world appears to roll on, heedless of man. What God is about is *his* affair, and he has not admitted man to the secret.

This amounts to a denial of divine revelation, and of the belief that man was created as an almost divine being, to care for and exercise dominion over the other creatures and all the works of God's hands (cf. Ps viii 5–8 EV; Gen i 26). But man is too limited in wisdom and power to do this, says our author. In the final analysis man is *like* the animals rather than superior to them, because both are subject to the same quirks of fate and to the same death. All man's efforts to transcend his mortal existence through wisdom or creative effort are doomed to defeat from the beginning, because God has so decreed.

(c) To the qualities of honesty in facing facts, and of courage to accept life on its own terms, Qoheleth adds a further and equally fundamental virtue—*the capacity to find enjoyment* in work and wisdom and in the very experience of living. Accept, he says, the happiness which can be yours when you realize that you cannot bend the world to your will! Do not miss the present joy, which must be savored in the passing moment or be lost forever! Do not give up your chance of happiness through a restless dissatisfaction that is forever straining after what it cannot have (ii 24–25, iii 12–14, ix 7–10, xi 7–10)! But let a man remember that if God permits him to enjoy the fulfillment of his desires, that is his good fortune. He must not count on it, so he should appreciate it when it comes. Life can be sweet—never sweeter than in the vigor of one's youth. For old age comes apace, when men may be left to look back with anguished regret on a life which has been consumed in fretful anxiety and profitless ambition (xi 7–xii 1).

Thus the good of life is in the living of it. The profit of work is in the doing of it, not in any profit or residue which a man can exhibit as his achievement or pass on to his descendants. The fruit of wisdom is not the accumulation of all knowledge and the understanding of all mysteries. It lies rather in recognizing the limitations of human knowledge and power. Man is not the measure of all things. He is the master neither of life nor of death. He can find serenity only in coming to terms with the unalterable conditions of his existence, and in enjoying its real but limited satisfactions.

QOHELETH AND THE RELIGION OF THE BIBLE

In spite of his philosophy of negation, and in the face of frustration, transience, and the insoluble enigmas of human experience, Qoheleth has discovered a key to happiness. He has found that the stream which runs in the confined channels of a man's brief life on earth may be cool and refreshing. Here speaks the voice of the human spirit, affirming values which unaided reason cannot discover, and reverent before them. This is his religion. It is not the religion of his fathers, nor by any means what the religion of the Bible has meant to Jews and Christians, ancient or modern. That is why this is such a strange book to be found in the Bible.

Everywhere else—except in the words of another agnostic inquirer in Prov xxx 1–4—the Bible affirms, not only that God is knowable, but that he has in fact made himself, his will, and his salvation known to man. Yet the Bible of Jews and Christians would be poorer without this book that in many ways seems alien to it. The author's stern and unrelenting honesty as he faces facts and questions a doctrine which will not face them is a moral tonic. He forces his readers to examine the basis of their own beliefs and to say where he is wrong. He points to the possibility of serenity and happiness on the basis of resignation, as Jesus Christ was later to do on the basis of faith in the goodness of God. To those who have found faith, resignation would be a poor substitute. But at least it is better than frustration and despair.

Again, what Qoheleth has to say *is* the truth about life, as seen from one side. This is indeed the way the world appears, if the fact and even the possibility of revelation through religious experience is ruled out by definition. If what Moses and the Prophets tell us, if what the New Testament affirms when it declares that the God of Israel has drawn near to men in Jesus Christ—if these are illusions, then Job heard no voice in the whirlwind and the heart of the Bible is Qoheleth. The significance of the Book of Job, however, does not lie chiefly in its declaration that at long last the wrestler with life's darkness hears God speak. It lies rather in Job's final realization that a thoughtful religious man will live always on a knife-edge between belief and doubt. The voice he hears, and the knowledge of God he comes to in consequence, are concealed alike from conventional belief and from dogmatic rationalism. The man in agony to whom at last God has spoken cannot doubt the reality of revelation, though now he knows that it is a revelation of a mysterious One, whose purpose for man is good but whose ways man can never fully understand.

> Lo, these are but the outskirts of his ways!
> How small a whisper do we hear of him!
> Who could understand the thunder of his omnipotence?
>
> (Job xxvi 14)

Qoheleth's book is needed in the Bible as a counterweight to smug assurance and unreflective belief. Because it forces the reader of the Bible to look straight at the darkness which surrounds him, it is a component of true religion. Yet it is only one component, as the sensitive Bible reader is made aware by the chorus of its voices, joyously witnessing to the experience of God as truth and justice, goodness and everlasting mercy.

FURTHER READING ON QOHELETH

The best book available in English for further study of Ecclesiastes-Qoheleth is Robert Gordis, *Koheleth, the Man and His World,* New York, 1955. It is scholarly, perceptive, and interesting, and the present author is much indebted to it. *Studies in Koheleth,* by H. L. Ginsberg, New York, 1950, is a smaller scholarly study without detailed commentary, distinguished by the author's contention that the work was composed originally in Aramaic. (The same author's most recent book on the subject, *Koheleth,* Tel Aviv/Jerusa-

lem, 1961, is in Hebrew.) The introduction to and exegesis by
O. S. Rankin in *The Interpreter's Bible,* Vol. V, New York, 1956,
is reliable and eminently useful, as is that of E. T. Ryder in *Peake's
Commentary on the Bible,* London and New York, 1962. Of older
works, M. Jastrow's *The Gentle Cynic,* Philadelphia, 1919, provides an interesting translation. G. A. Barton, *Ecclesiastes* (International Critical Commentary), 1908, and A. L. Williams, *Ecclesiastes* (Cambridge Bible for Schools and Colleges), 1922, are
standard works still of great value. Much of the best recent work on
Qoheleth has appeared in scholarly journals.

Students who read French and German may consult: K. Galling,
Der Prediger, 2d ed., 1963; H. W. Hertzberg, *Der Prediger,* 2d ed.,
1962; E. Podechard, *L'eccclésiaste,* 1912; and W. Zimmerli, *Das
Buch des Predigers Salomo,* 1962.

1. TITLE OF THE BOOK; THE THESIS OF THE WRITER
(i 1–2)

I

1   The Words of Qoheleth, son of David, king in
       Jerusalem.

2   Breath of a breath! (says Qoheleth). The slightest breath!
       All is a breath!

NOTES

i 1. *Qoheleth*. Not a proper name, as is evident from its use with the definite article in vii 27 and xii 8, though its form was doubtless intended to suggest an occupational surname like the English "Smith." It is a pen name like those sometimes adopted by modern journalists to conceal their identity and at the same time to hint at the standpoint from which they write. The most probable meaning is "one who assembles" (an audience, or group of pupils), so "teacher, academician"; but the term is suggestive rather than precise. (See further, Introduction to Ecclesiastes pp. 192–93.)

son of David, king in Jerusalem. In the first two chapters *only*, the author assumes the role of a king like Solomon; in v 8–9 EV and viii 2–4 he clearly is not the king.

2. The first phrase is a literal translation, the second gives the *meaning* of the same words which are repeated in the Hebrew text; *hébel* denotes a breath, empty of substance and also transient. The writer's thesis is that everything in man's experience of life in this world ("under the sun" [*passim*]) is empty of meaning or worth, both in itself and because of its transience. Hence all man's restless activities, his efforts to achieve something, are ultimately futile. This thesis he attempts to demonstrate from experience, and at the end of this collection of his reflections he reiterates it (xii 8). This is not, however, the sole theme of the book. Having stated his philosophical premise, Qoheleth goes on to consider the ethical question of how men should live in a world where all experiences are fleeting and all effort without permanent result.

2. THERE IS NOTHING NEW UNDER THE SUN
(i 3–11)

I ³ What has a man to show for all his trouble and effort during his brief lifetime under the sun? ⁴ One generation goes, another generation comes, but the earth always remains the same. ⁵ The sun rises and the sun sets; and returning*ᵃ* to its place, it rises there once more. ⁶ Blowing toward the south and veering toward the north, ever circling goes the wind, returning upon its tracks. ⁷ All the rivers flow continually to the sea, but the sea does not become full; whither the rivers flow, they continue to flow. ⁸ All words fail through weariness, a man becomes speechless; the eye cannot see it all, nor the ear hear the end of it. ⁹ Whatever has been is what will be, and whatever has been done is what will be done. ¹⁰ There is nothing new under the sun. When there is something of which one says, "Look now, that is new!", it has been already in the ages before us. ¹¹ As there is no memory of former things, so even of later things which have yet to be there will be no recollection among men of a still later time.

ᵃ Reading *šāb 'ap*, for MT *šō'ēp*, "panting"; cf. vs. 7b.

NOTES

i 3–11. The first evidence for Qoheleth's thesis is that neither the ceaseless round of motion in the natural world nor the toil and effort of men changes anything, or leaves any permanent mark.

3. Literally "What *remainder* is there to man?" *yitrōn* is the surplus or profit of a transaction, the difference which it makes, and hence its value (cf. ii 11, iii 9). Qoheleth says there is none.

trouble and effort. Cf. ii 21, v 13 EV.

under the sun. I.e., "on earth," "during his lifetime" (cf. xi 7). The expression is not found in the Bible outside Qoheleth, but occurs in Elamite and Phoenician writings.

5–8. The generations of men rise and pass away with the same monotonous regularity and ceaseless motions visible in the natural world, and with an equal lack of novelty.

8. *All words . . . speechless.* I.e., it is beyond man's powers to compass with word or thought the endless, intricate movement. Another possible rendering is, "All things are more wearisome than words can tell."

9. *Whatever has been.* I.e., in the natural world.

whatever has been done. I.e., by (or, "happens to") man.

10. *There is nothing new under the sun.* A statement found also in an inscription of the Elamite Untasgal, and similar to Pythagoras' saying, "The things that happen once happen again, and nothing is absolutely new." (See J. Levy, "Rien de nouveau sous le soleil," *Nouveau Clio* [1953], 326 ff.)

11. *former . . . later things.* Or, "generations."

3. THE FUTILITY OF HUMAN EFFORT AND WISDOM
(i 12–18)

I 12 I, Qoheleth, was king over Israel in Jerusalem. 13 And I applied my mind to search and investigate by wisdom all that is done beneath the sky—a grievous affliction God has put on human beings to afflict them. 14 I observed all the deeds done under the sun, and saw that all was an empty breath and a grasping at the wind. 15 What is bent cannot be straightened[a], and what is missing cannot be made up. 16 I said to myself, "Well now, I have increased and added to my wisdom more than any who preceded me in Jerusalem, and my mind has had much experience of wisdom and knowledge. 17 So I turned my attention to the nature of wisdom and knowledge [on the one hand], and of foolish behavior and vulgarity [on the other]. I learned that this too was a grasping at the wind. 18 For with more wisdom comes more worry, and he who adds to his knowledge adds to his pain.

[a] *lᵉhittāqēn*, for MT *litqōn*, "be straight"; or read *lᵉhittākēn*, "be estimated."

NOTES

i 12–18. The author now assumes the role of a Solomon, not only because that king was the legendary exemplar of true wisdom, but because "a king . . . can do as he pleases" (viii 2–3; cf. ii 12) and hence is free from the inhibitions and obstacles that beset ordinary men in their search for wisdom. The conclusion is reached that man is destined by God to ceaseless effort without result, since the setting of his life cannot be altered. Even the quest for understanding is futile.

12. *I, Qoheleth, was king over Israel.* The regular formula for begin-

ning a royal declaration; cf. "I am Mesha . . . king of Moab" (ANET, p. 320b).

15. *be made up.* Or, "be counted." Cf. the Old Babylonian version of the Gilgamesh epic, Tablet III, "As for mankind, numbered are their days, whatever they achieve is but wind" (ANET, p. 79b).

16. *any who preceded me.* This is either a slip by the author, or is a reference to pre-Davidic kings of Jerusalem like Melchizedek (cf. ii 7; Gen xiv).

17. *to the nature of.* Literally "to know."

4. THE ILLUSORY SATISFACTIONS OF PLEASURE-SEEKING
(ii 1–11)

II ¹ I said to myself, "Let me experiment with pleasure and have a good time!", but this also turned out to be [unsubstantial as] a vapor. ² Merrymaking, I concluded, is foolishness; and as for pleasure, what does it accomplish? ³ I investigated by stimulating my body with wine while my reason remained in control, and by putting my hand to folly—so that I might discern whether this is good for men to do beneath the sky, in the brief span of their lives. ⁴ I carried out great undertakings, I built myself houses, I planted vineyards, ⁵ I made for myself gardens and parks and planted in them trees bearing all kinds of fruit. ⁶ I constructed reservoirs from which to irrigate the plantation of young trees. ⁷ I bought slaves and slave girls, in addition to my household retainers; my possessions of cattle and sheep also were greater than those of all who had preceded me in Jerusalem. ⁸ I amassed also silver and gold, such private treasure as kings and satraps have. I provided myself with male and female singers, and with the pleasures of the flesh, concubine after concubine. ⁹ As I became greater than any who had been before me in Jerusalem, still my wisdom stayed with me. ¹⁰ Nothing my eyes desired to see was denied them; I did not inhibit my thoughts from any kind of pleasure. Indeed, my mind drew delight from all my activities, and this was what I got from it all. ¹¹ For when I considered all the things that I had done and the energy I had expended in doing them, it was clear that the whole of it was futility and a grasping at the wind, and none of it was profitable [for a man's life] under the sun.

Notes

ii 1–11. Qoheleth imagines the unrestrained pleasure-seeking open to a king of Solomon's legendary wealth (I Kings x 10–27). He concludes that, while it is enjoyable for the moment, nothing of lasting value is gained by it.

1. *experiment*. Literally "test thee" [addressing himself].

5. *parks*. Heb. *pardēsīm*, a loanword from Persian which appears also in Greek as *paradeisos*, and in English as "paradise." The occurrence of the word here has some bearing on the date of Qoheleth (see Introduction to Ecclesiastes).

7. *in addition to my household retainers*. Or, "and I had retainers who were born in my household."

8. *satraps*. Literally "provinces, satrapies."

pleasures of the flesh. Literally "the delights of the sons of mankind." The meaning of the words following is uncertain.

11. *futility*. Or, "an empty breath."

5. THE WISE MAN IS NO BETTER OFF THAN THE FOOL
(ii 12–17)

II ¹² Then I turned my attention to a comparison of wisdom with foolishness and stupidity. [For what can a man do who comes after a king but what he (the king) has done already?]ᵃ ¹³ It had seemed to me that wisdom surpasses folly as light surpasses darkness; ¹⁴ the wise man has eyes in his head, while the fool goes forward blindly. But then I realized that the same chance happens to them both. ¹⁵ I said to myself, "Since I shall meet the same fate as the fool, how then is wisdom an advantage?" So I concluded that this too was futility. ¹⁶ For of the wise man, as of the fool, there is no lasting memory; soon in days to come everything will have been forgotten. How alike in death are the wise man and the fool! ¹⁷ So I came to hate life, because it depressed me that all man's activities under the sun are only a vapor and a clutching at the wind.

ᵃ Supplying *ya'ᵃśeh* after *māh,* and reading *'āsāhū* with LXX for MT *'āsūhū.*

NOTES

ii 12–17. In comparing wisdom and folly, Qoheleth concludes that the intrinsic superiority of the former is cancelled by the common fate of all.

12. The bracketed words are difficult to interpret in their present position; they may have been accidentally displaced from after vs. 11, and refer to the argument of vss. 1–11. Elsewhere Qoheleth concludes a meditation with such a rhetorical question; cf. iii 22, v 6 EV, v 17 EV, vi 11–12, etc.

14. *chance.* Or, "fate." "If in relation to God who causes all things, it is destiny, as having no relationship to man's conduct it is pure contingency or chance" (O. S. Rankin, *Israel's Wisdom Literature,* New York, 1936, p. 96).

6. DEATH ROBS A MAN OF THE FRUITS OF HIS LABOR
(ii 18–26)

II 18 Thus I came to detest all that I had achieved under the sun, which I would leave to the man who comes after me. 19 Who knows whether he will be a wise man or a fool? Yet he will be in command of all the fruits of my toil and wisdom during my lifetime. Here again is futility. 20 So once more I fell into despair about all that I had achieved under the sun, 21 since a man who has labored with wisdom, knowledge, and skill must hand over what he possesses to one who has not worked for it. This, too, is futility and a great evil. 22 For how does a man benefit from all the toil and stress of his lifelong struggle? 23 He spends all his days in the pains and vexation of his business; even in the night his mind has no rest. This too, is futility. 24 There is nothing better for a man than to eat and drink and find satisfaction in [doing] his work; even this, I came to see, is in God's hands. 25 For who can eat and rejoice apart from him*a*? 26 Indeed, to a man whom he favors God assigns wisdom, knowledge, and happiness; whereas to one who offends him, he gives the task of gathering and collecting what the man must [then] hand over to the one God favors. This also is futility and a grasping at the wind.

a mimmennū for *mimmennī,* "from me."

NOTES

ii 18–26. Not only does death treat alike the wise man and the fool; it cancels the lasting value of the wise man's achievements, because a fool may be the one to profit by what the wise man leaves behind. The most he can hope for is to be able to enjoy living, and to find a present satisfaction in the doing rather than in the product of his labor. But even this is uncertain, for it is determined not by a man's worth, but by the inscrutable will of God.

18. *all that I had achieved.* Or, "all the fruits of my toil for which I had toiled."

19. *during my lifetime.* Literally "under the sun."

25. *rejoice.* The meaning of the verb here is uncertain.

26. *one who offends him.* Literally "a sinner." This verse has been taken by some to be an orthodox addition to Qoheleth's words, on the grounds that it savors of conventional teaching about the consequences in this life of moral and immoral behavior. Rather, it is simply a fuller statement of what has already been said about the inscrutable will of God, and is to be understood in the light of ix 1–2. *Why* God favors one and regards the other as a sinner is to Qoheleth another of the baffling phenomena of life, as the concluding words of the verse show.

7. EVERYTHING HAPPENS AT THE TIME GOD
DECREES FOR IT
(iii 1–15)

III

1 Everything has its season, and there is a proper time for
every happening under the sun—

2 A time to be born and a time to die,
A time to plant and a time to uproot [what has been
planted],

3 A time to kill and a time to heal,
A time to wreck and a time to build;

4 A time to weep and a time to laugh,
A time to lament and a time to dance for joy;

5 A time to scatter stones and a time to gather them,
A time to embrace and a time to shun embraces;

6 A time to seek and a time to give up,
A time to keep and a time to throw away;

7 A time to tear apart and a time to sew together,
A time to be silent and a time to speak;

8 A time to love and a time to hate,
A time for war and a time for peace.

9 What does the doer [of these] add by his effort? 10 I see
the sore task that God assigns to men to afflict them; 11 [and
I see too] that God makes each event right for its time. Yet
he has put in their minds an enigma, so that man cannot
discover what it is that God has been doing, from beginning to
end. 12 I do know that man's only satisfaction is to be happy
and find pleasure in living. 13 Indeed, when a man can eat and
drink and find satisfaction in his occupation, he has a gift from
God. 14 I know that whatever God does will endure; to it
nothing can be added, and from it nothing can be subtracted.

God acts, and men must stand in awe of him. 15 That which was, now is; and that which is to be, has already been. God will see to what requires [his] attention.

NOTES

iii 1–15. In the endlessly repeated round of human experience, each event occurs at its proper time in God's scheme of things, and man's effort to make what happens conform to his own desires is fruitless. What it is that God has predetermined is hidden from man, who can only live in awe of the inexorable progression of "time," and enjoy such passing happiness as God may grant him.

1. *happening.* Or, "phenomenon," a developed meaning of *ḥēpeṣ*, "desire, desirable thing," as in vs. 17, v 8 EV, viii 6. Cf. the saying attributed to Aesop, "It is a great thing to do the right thing at the right season."

2. *to be born.* Literally "to give birth"; but the Qal may be used loosely in a passive sense. Cf. Sirach xxxiii 15, "The works of the Most High . . . are in pairs, one the opposite of the other."

9. Literally "What is the profit to the doer in that at which he toils?" Qoheleth argues that, since everything must happen at the right moment according to God's plan, nothing man can do makes any difference.

11. *an enigma* (or "darkness," "obscurity"); Heb. *'ōlām,* a word which has caused difficulty to translators here because its use in this sense is unique in the OT. The root meaning is "that which is hidden," as in the common phrase *'ad 'ōlām,* "until the distant, hidden future," "forever." The meaning here is defined by the second part of the verse. Cf. The Babylonian Theodicy, line 256, "The mind of the god, like the center of the heavens, is remote . . . his knowledge is difficult" (ANET, p. 440a).

12. *man's only satisfaction.* Literally "there is no good in them."
in living. Or, "while he lives."

15. Literally "God seeks what has been [or, has to be] pursued."
God . . . attention. The literal translation is clear enough, but what it means is not. Gordis renders "God always seeks to repeat the past."

8. THE FACT OF INJUSTICE PROVES THAT MAN IS ONLY A MORTAL ANIMAL
(iii 16–22, iv 1–3)

III ¹⁶ Another thing I observed about man's life in this world is that where justice should be found, there wickedness is; and where the just man*ᵃ* should be, there is an evildoer*ᵃ*. ¹⁷ I quoted to myself, "God will judge between the just man and the evildoer," since there is a destined time for every experience and an appointed moment for every deed*ᵇ*. ¹⁸ Then I said to myself, "It is *ᶜ*on men's own account*ᶜ*, that God may show [them] that they are only animals.*ᵈ* ¹⁹ For the fate of men and the fate of animals is the same; as one dies, so dies the other, for all have the same breath of life. Man has no superiority over the beast, for all are a breath that vanishes. ²⁰ All are bound for the same place. All have come from the ground, and all are returning to the ground. ²¹ Who can be sure that the life of man ascends on high, and the life of beasts goes down to the underworld? ²² So I saw that there is nothing better for man than to be happy in what he is doing, since that is his lot; for who can enable him to see what will be after him?

IV ¹ Next I turned to consider all the acts of oppression which are done under the sun; I witnessed the tears of the oppressed who have no one to comfort them; their oppressors have power in their hands, but they themselves have no avenger*ᵉ*. ² I

ᵃ Reading with LXX and Targ. *haṣṣaddīq* for *haṣṣédeq*, and *hārāšā'* for MT *hārēša'*.

ᵇ *šīm*, "appointed," for the anomalous *šām* of MT.

ᶜ⁻ᶜ *lᵉbaddām* for MT *lᵉbārām*, "to purify [or] test them."

ᵈ *ūlᵉhar'ōt 'ᵉlōhīm lāhem šᵉhēm-bᵉhēmāh*. The order of words has been disarranged in MT, apparently because the scribe was copying from a manuscript in which some words had been written above the line. *hēmmāh* is to be omitted as a dittograph.

ᵉ *mᵉnaqqēm* for MT *mᵉnahēm* "comforter," though MT may be right in repeating latter word.

thought the dead who are already dead more fortunate than the living who are still alive. 3 Better off than either is he who has not yet been, and has not witnessed the evil that is done under the sun.

NOTES

iii 16–22, iv 1–3. The twin problems of the corruption of justice and the oppression of the helpless lead Qoheleth to somber reflections about death. He first considers the orthodox answer to these problems—that God's judgment will eventually set things right—since this too must have its appropriate moment. But then he reflects that man's wickedness and suffering are related to the fact that he is no different from the animals in life and in death. In this case the dead and the yet unborn are better off than the living.

iii 17. *quoted*. Literally "said." Qoheleth echoes the standard answer to the problem of injustice, only to discard it. Many have taken the saying to be a note by a later reader, because of its orthodox tone.

19. *breath of life*. Or, "spirit."

a breath that vanishes. Qoheleth's favorite word *hebel*, which in different contexts means what is "fleeting," "futile," "vain," "empty."

20. A reference to the stories in Genesis of creation and man's ejection from the garden; cf. Gen ii 7, iii 19.

21. *be sure that*. Or, "know whether."

the underworld. Literally "the earth," as in Isa xxvi 19.

9. A LIFE OF SHEER TOIL IS PROFITLESS
(iv 4–16)

IV 4 I saw that all a man's toil and skill is expended through the desire to surpass his neighbor; this, too, is an empty thing and a clutching at the wind. 5 [They say] "The fool folds his hands and consumes his own flesh." 6 I say, "Better one handful in peace, than two handfuls won by toil and reaching for the wind." 7 I saw still another example of futility in this world — 8 a lone and solitary man, with no son and no brother, but who toiled endlessly without ever satisfying his yearning for wealth [nor asking himself], "For whom am I toiling and depriving myself of contentment?" His was an empty and miserable life.

9 Two are better than one, for they get a better return for their labor. 10 If either one falls, his companion helps him up; but what if one falls and there is no one to help him up? 11 Further, if two sleep together, they keep warm; but how can one be warm alone? 12 Where one may be overpowered [by an enemy], two can resist attack, and "a cord of three strands is not quickly broken."

13 "Better to be a youth poor but wise, than to be a king who is old and foolish"—[like the] one who no longer had the wits to heed a warning, 14 though he had risen from a prison to the throne in the very kingdom where he was born in poverty; 15 I watched all the living under the sun throng to the side of a second youth who was to replace him. 16 [But] the endless numbers of the people in the past and in the future would care nothing about him. This again is an example of futility and grasping at the wind.

NOTES

iv 4–16. Qoheleth returns to his first question, "What has man to show for all his trouble and effort . . . ?" (i 3). The motives which drive him are emulation, greed, and ambition, but their results are only loss of contentment, isolation from one's fellows, and a quickly vanishing fame.

5. A sarcastic popular saying about the typical indolence of "the fool," who goes hungry and grows thin because he will not work; cf. Prov vi 10–11, xix 15, xxi 25. Qoheleth quotes it only to refute it by quoting another proverb in the opposite sense; cf. Prov xxvi 4–5.

6. Or, "Better to eat in peace what you can hold in the palm of one hand, than what both hands cupped will hold, won by toil and reaching for the wind." Cf. Prov xvii 1.

8. *solitary*. Literally "with no second one."

contentment. Or, "good things."

an empty and miserable life. Literally "futility and an evil task."

9–12. Three examples of the value of human companionship, concluding with what the shift to metaphor indicates is a popular saying. Cf. the Icelandic proverb, "Two are an army against one."

13–15. Another common proverb is expanded by reference to what seems to have been an actual episode illustrating the transience of fame. The sentence structure is surprisingly clumsy for Qoheleth.

16. Literally "All the people are endless, all who had preceded them, and those too who would come after him." This seems to mean that a man's importance is only momentary in the perspective of endless generations; cf. i 3–4, 9–11.

10. ADVICE ABOUT RELIGIOUS OBSERVANCES
(v 1–7 EV)

V ¹Be circumspect when you go to the house of God. Approach in order to learn, rather than to offer a sacrifice like that of fools who know nothing ᵃexcept how to doᵃ wrong. ²Do not speak impetuously, nor think of uttering a hurried word before God. Since God is in heaven and you are on earth, let your words be few. ³"A dream follows on much busyness, and a fool's speech on too much talk." ⁴When you make a vow to God, do not be slow in paying it, for he has no liking for fools. Pay what you vow to pay. ⁵It is better that you make no vow, than that you make a vow and fail to keep it. ⁶Do not allow your tongue to put you in the wrong; and do not say to the messenger [who comes to collect it], "It was just a mistake." Why should God be angered by your speech, and destroy what you have accomplished? ⁷"Like so many empty dreams are so many empty words." Simply show respect to God!

ᵃ–ᵃ *milla'ᵃsōt* for MT *la'ᵃsōt,* "to do."

NOTES

v 1–7 EV. Qoheleth was a teacher as well as a thinker and writer (cf. xii 9), and here his views on the outward observances of religion are cast in the form of admonitions. He deprecates the glib utterances and unthinking vows of "fools" who have never given a thought to the philosophical problems of religion, and he counsels a grave reserve when participating in worship and the making of vows. His God is not the Yahweh who had revealed himself and his will to his chosen people Israel, but the unknown and unknowable Being who has predetermined all that happens in the natural world and in human experience. One should not speak rashly to, or of, such a Being; nor, having made a vow to him, should one presume to neglect its fulfillment.

1. *Be circumspect*. Or, "Watch your step!"

house of God. A temple, probably but not necessarily the Jerusalem Temple: see Introduction to Ecclesiastes, pp. 199–200. The sage is expressing his contempt for thoughtless participation in cultic worship. This view is to be compared with that of the Hebrew Prophets that temple worship, apart from the self-dedication to God's service which it professes to represent, is worthless (cf. Isa i 10–17; Jer vii 22–23; Hos vi 6). The Egyptian *Instruction of Ani* vii includes an admonition which resembles Qoheleth's: "Make an offering to thy god, and beware of sins against him. Thou shouldst not enquire about his [affairs]. Be not free with him" (ANET, p. 420b).

3. *on much busyness*. Or, "after much preoccupation." The writer is quoting a popular adage, though for his purpose only the second line is apposite.

6. *tongue*. Literally "mouth."

to the messenger. LXX reads here, "in God's presence." If the Hebrew text is right the messenger was the priest or perhaps the priest's servant who came to collect what had been vowed; cf. Mal ii 7. In the *Instruction of Ani* v the messenger is death (ANET, p. 420b).

Why should. Or, "Lest."

7. A second, similar proverb is now quoted to underscore Qoheleth's advice.

11. THE HIERARCHY OF EXPLOITERS
(v 8–9 EV)

V 8 If you see oppression of the poor and denial of justice
and right in a province, do not be shocked at the sight: for each
official is being watched by his superior, and over them all
is the king*a*. 9 [The real wealth of a country is in its cultivated
land.]

a wᵉgābōᵃh mē'ᵃlēhem bakkōl hammélek, for MT *ūgᵉbōhīm 'ᵃlēhem* (vs. 7,
MT) . . . *bakkōl hū' mélek,* "and greater than them . . . in all is a king."

NOTES

v 8–9 EV. Qoheleth thinks that the rapacity of government officials
is not to be wondered at, since each in turn suffers under the one above
him, all the way up to the king.

8. *province.* Or, "state."

8–9. The last two lines of these verses have been damaged in manuscript transmission and no attempt at their reconstruction has been wholly
successful. It seems clear that the word "king" belongs at the end of vs.
8. The bracketed words are little more than a guess at the meaning of the
Hebrew.

12. WRONG AND RIGHT ATTITUDES TO WEALTH
(v 10–20 EV)

V   10 He who loves money never has enough money, and whoever cares most about making money thinks his profits are too
small. This is futility. 11 The more the provisions, the more
there are who consume them; what benefit accrues to the owner,
except that he can look on?

12 Sweet is the sleep of the laborer, whether he eat little or
much; but the full stomach of the rich man will not let him
sleep. 13 A painful misfortune which I have observed beneath
the sun was this—wealth was hoarded by its owner at great cost
to himself, 14 and then that wealth was lost through a bad investment; he had sired a son and [now] he had nothing [to
leave him]. 15 As he had come naked from his mother's womb,
he must return as he came, with nothing salvaged from his toil
which he could take with him. 16 This surely is a grievous
calamity; since he went exactly as he came, what did he gain by
toiling for wind, 17 while all his days he ate his food in darkness, in constant vexation, misery and anger?

18 So I reached the conclusion that what is satisfying and
suitable is to eat and drink and enjoy oneself in all one's struggle
under the sun, during the few years which God grants a man;
that is what one gets out of it. 19 Furthermore, every man to
whom God grants riches and possessions, and enables him to
benefit from them, and to possess his share and be happy in his
work—he has a bonus from God. 20 Such a man will not brood
over the shortness of his life, when God keeps his mind occupied with happy thoughts.

NOTES

v 10–20 EV. From the greed of officials, Qoheleth passes to the subject of private greed, and the price in happiness which is paid by those who make possession of wealth their goal.

10. *whoever . . . small.* Or, "whoever loves wealth has not enough revenue."

11–12. Cf. the Sumerian proverbs, "Stomach added to stomach, the house of a man is destroyed," and "He who eats too much will not [be able] to sleep" (Gordon, pp. 97, 271).

13. *hoarded.* Or, "guarded."

14. *bad investment.* Or, "ill-fated enterprise."

17. *in darkness.* Either literally—because he grudged a lamp, or metaphorically—"in gloom."

constant. Literally "much."

18. *struggle.* Or, "toil."

few years. Literally "numbered days."

what one gets out of it. Literally "his portion."

19. *bonus.* Literally "gift."

20. *brood . . . life.* Literally "he will not much remember the few days of his life."

13. CONTENTMENT IS LIFE'S HIGHEST GOOD
(vi 1–9)

VI ¹ One misfortune which I have observed under the sun, and which bears heavily on men [is this]—² a man to whom God grants riches, possessions, and an honored place [in the community], so that he lacks nothing that heart could desire, but whom God has not given the power to enjoy it—rather a stranger enjoys it instead. This is a hollow mockery and a sore affliction. ³ If a man fathers a hundred children and lives many years and is prominent all his life, but does not find happiness— I declare that a stillborn child is better off than he. ⁴ Though its coming is futile and it departs in darkness, though its name is hidden in darkness and it has no burial place; ⁵ though it never saw the sun nor knew anything—it rests more peacefully than he. ⁶ Even if a man should live a thousand years twice over, but find no contentment—does not everyone have the same destination?

⁷ All a man's toil is for his mouth, but his wants are never satisfied. ⁸ How then is a wise man better off than a fool? [Only] in knowing*ᵃ* how to conduct himself during his life. ⁹ "Better is what you can see than what you can imagine." That, too, is futility and a grasping of the wind.

ᵃ *mibbil'ᵃdē yōdēᵃ'*, literally "apart from his knowing," for MT *mah-le'ānī yōdēᵃ'*, "what does the poor man have who knows. . . ."

NOTES

vi 1–9. The converse of what has just been said is the case of a man who has everything that heart can desire, but is prevented by circumstances, or by his own attitude, from enjoying life. The stillborn child is better off than the man who lives a long life of discontent. To be driven by unsatisfied desire is to deprive oneself of the happiness which is near at hand.

2. *a hollow mockery*. Heb. *hebel*, "a vain, empty, and fleeting breath."

3. *is prominent all his life*. Or, "many though his days may be."

4. *futile*. Or, "with an empty breath."

and it has no burial place. This clause has been displaced in MT where it appears in vs. 3 after "happiness."

6. The hiatus before the concluding rhetorical question suggests spoken rather than written style. The meaning is clear enough—without happiness a man might as well die soon as late.

7. Cf. the similar proverb in Prov xvi 26.

9. A popular adage quoted.

what you can imagine. Literally "the going of the self," or "the wandering of desire."

14. MAN'S LIFE IS BOTH FATED AND
INCOMPREHENSIBLE
(vi 10–12)

VI ¹⁰ Whatever is was decided upon before [it came into existence], and its destiny*a* is known. Man cannot dispute with what is stronger than he is. ¹¹ For the more he talks, the more meaningless it becomes. How does man profit by that? ¹² Who knows what is man's good in life, the few and futile days of his life which pass like a shadow? Or who can tell a man what will be after him under the sun?

a Reading *'ašrēhū*, for MT *'ašer-hū'*, literally "what [man] is" (Dahood, *Biblica* 33 [1952], 208).

NOTES

vi 10–12. Everything that is, is predetermined and foreknown. Man cannot alter his fate, or comprehend the meaning of his brief and fleeting life.

10. *decided upon.* Literally "named."
with what is. Or, "with one who is."
12. *pass like a shadow.* Literally "which he makes them like a shadow."

15. SEVEN PROVERBS, WITH QOHELETH'S COMMENTS
(vii 1–14)

VII ¹ "Better is fame than fine ointment"—hence the day of one's death is more important than the day of one's birth.

² "It is better to go to a house of mourning than to go to a feast"—for that is how all men end, and the living man takes it to heart.

³ "Better is grief than laughter"—it clouds the face but it improves the mind. ⁴[So] the thoughts of the wise turn to the house of mourning, but the thoughts of fools to the place of amusement.

⁵ "It is better to listen to the rebuke of a wise man than to lend one's ear to the singing of fools"— ⁶ for "like the noise of [burning] thorn bushes under a cooking pot is the loud laughter of fools." This, too, is a hollow thing. ⁷ But oppression can turn [even] a wise man into a fool, and take away his courage*ᵃ*.

⁸ "Better the end of something than its beginning," and "Better to be patient than proud." ⁹ Do not be easily upset, for vexation is typical of fools. ¹⁰ Do not say, "How does it come about that former days were better than these?" It is not the part of wisdom to ask such a question.

¹¹ "It is good to have wisdom as well as an inheritance," and it is an advantage to men while they live, for ¹² "the shelter of wisdom is like the shelter of*ᵇ* wealth," with the added advantage of knowing that wisdom gives life to its possessors.

ᵃ Reading *motnāw*, for MT *mattānāh*, "a gift"; (Cf. G. R. Driver, "Problems and Solutions," VT 4 [1954], 229–30). Literally "destroy the heart of his loins."

ᵇ Reading *keṣēl . . . keṣēl* with Vulg., for MT *beṣēl . . . beṣēl*, "in the shadow of" (*bis*). Quite apart from versional support, the former is a typical proverb form (cf. Hos iv 9).

13 Observe how God orders things; for who can straighten what he has made bent? 14 Be pleased when things go well, but when they go badly, look out! God has arranged that one should correspond to the other, so that man may never know what lies ahead of him.

NOTES

vii 1–14. The quotation and adaptation of familiar proverbs was one of the instructional techniques of the Wisdom teachers. The "proverb of comparative value" is a favorite in many cultures. Qoheleth here quotes (or formulates) seven such sayings keyed to the word "good" (in comparisons, "better"), vss. 1, 2, 3, 5, 8 (two), 11, and elaborates on them to illustrate his philosophy.

1. The conciseness, alliteration, and chiasma of the opening words identify it as a colloquial proverb, *ṭōb šēm miššemen ṭōb*. On the principle that one should "call no man happy before he is dead" (Ovid), Qoheleth asserts that one's deathday is more significant than one's birthday. An allusion to the anointing of a newly born infant may be intended.

2. From its structure this aphorism seems to be the author's own composition.

a feast. Literally "a house of feasting"; a scroll of Qoheleth from Qumran reads "house of joy," "place of amusement" as in vs. 4.

3. Qoheleth interprets and comments on another popular adage suggested by his previous remarks.

5–6. The self-conscious didactic tone suggests a dictum of a Wisdom teacher, but the extended comment makes it unlikely that this was composed for this context. The contemptuous comparison, however, with its pun and alliteration—*šir,* "song," *šīrīm,* "thorn bushes," *šīr,* "cooking pot," *kᵉsīlīm,* "fools"—looks like a popular saying.

6. *hollow thing.* Or, "vapor, empty breath" (*hebel*).

8. Two further current adages; cf. I Kings xx 11; Prov xvi 32, xxv 7.

9. *is typical of fools.* Literally "rests in the bosom of fools."

11. This works both ways: a rich fool may squander his inheritance, but a wise man who also is poor is ignored (cf. ix 15).

13. Cf. i 15.

14. *look out!* Or, "consider!"

correspond to. Or, "alternate with." Everything has its opposite (cf. iii 1–8), so that man must not count on the continuance of either good or bad fortune.

16. NO MAN CAN BE PERFECT
(vii 15–22)

VII 15 I have seen it all during my transitory existence—the innocent perishing in spite of his innocence, and the wicked man who lives long in spite of his wickedness. 16 Do not be overscrupulous, or make a fetish of wisdom: why make your life horrible? 17 Do not be very wicked [either], or play the fool: why die before your time? 18 It is best to grasp one thing and not let go the other. He who fears God will consider*a* both sides. 19 [On the one hand], "Wisdom gives more strength*b* to a wise man than a council of ten gives to a city." 20 Yet there is no man so righteous that he [always] does what is best and never makes a mistake. 21 Do not pay too much attention to all the things men say, or you will hear your [own] servant reviling you; 22 for many times, as you know full well, you yourself have reviled others.

a yōṣi', "bring forth [for consideration]," for MT yēṣē', "go forth," "withdraw from."
b LXX and Qumran scroll read "help."

Notes

vii 15–22. It is clear to Qoheleth that men do not receive their just deserts, as the more conventional Wisdom teaching asserted (cf. Prov x 28, xi 21, etc.). Therefore it is as unprofitable for men to exhaust themselves in struggling for moral perfection as it is to hasten their demise through folly. True reverence for God is shown by a moderation which is not moral indifference but the recognition that, while wisdom is important, no man can be perfect.

15. *in spite of.* Or, "because of."

16. *overscrupulous*. Literally "very righteous." Cf. the Greek maxim *mēden agan*, "nothing too much," variously attributed to Solon and others.

make a fetish of wisdom. Literally "make yourself [or, "pretend to be"] excessively wise." Extreme views or fanatic behavior show lack of balance, and hence lack of the common sense which is indispensable in wisdom. Like happiness, wisdom is not self-existent, but is a quality of experience.

why. Or, "lest you"; so also in vs. 17.

18. *one thing . . . the other*. Can hardly mean "wisdom" and "folly" here, but rather both sides of a question.

19. *council of ten*. Or, "the ten rulers," a popular saying, referring to the council of elders in a Hellenistic city (so Gordis, p. 269).

17. THE FRUSTRATING SEARCH FOR WISDOM
(vii 23–29, viii 1)

VII ²³ I sought for wisdom in all this; [I said, I want to be wise], but it was beyond me. ²⁴ What it was, proved remote, and so very deep that no one could find it. ²⁵ So I turned my attention to study and explore and seek for wisdom and meaning on the one hand, and to identify wickedness, stupidity, folly, and madness on the other. ²⁶ More bitter to me than death was my experience with woman, whose thoughts are traps and snares and whose hands are chains; by God's favor one may escape her, but whomever he disapproves will be caught by her. ²⁷ See, this is what I have found, [says Qoheleth], adding one thing to another to reach a conclusion, ²⁸ after searching long without finding anything—one man in a thousand I found, but not one woman in all these did I find [to be wise]. ²⁹ This only, mark you, I discovered, that God had made man upright [?], and they have willfully turned to many reckonings of their own.

VIII ¹ Who can compare with the wise man? Who else understands what things mean? A man's wisdom lights up his face, and the hardness of his countenance is transformed.

NOTES

vii 23–29, viii 1. Qoheleth tells how the ultimate meaning of wisdom proved beyond his reach, so that he turned his attention to the problem of defining the distinction of wisdom from stupidity and folly in human beings. Women seemed to him to embody the latter exclusively, and among men the case was only slightly better. God had made man [upright?] in the first place; but he had not predetermined that man should be evil or foolish because he had predetermined man's fate. Most men had corrupted themselves by their own scheming; but that some men nevertheless were really wise was demonstrated by their obvious intelligence.

vii 23. *I sought for wisdom.* Literally "all this I tested with respect to wisdom." The words in brackets look like a textual variant of the opening clause.

26. *bitter.* Agrees with the subject of the sentence rather than with woman (or, *"a* woman"); hence, *my experience with* instead of the usual translation, "I found more bitter than death is the woman. . . ."

29. *upright.* Heb. *yāšār,* a unique and curious word to be used of man's creation. The context suggests that it is a corruption of *wᵉ'iššāh,* "and woman," but there is no support for this in the ancient versions.

reckonings. Or, "inventions."

18. KINGS SHOULD BE OBEYED BECAUSE OF THEIR POWER OVER MEN
(viii 2–9)

VIII 2 Do what the king commands*a*, because of your sacred oath. 3 Do not hurry from his presence in agitation; nor hesitate to go when the errand is distasteful. For he does as he pleases. 4 Since a king's word is law, who dare say to him, "What are you doing?" 5 He who obeys will avoid trouble, and the wise mind will know when and how to act. 6 For there is a proper time and action in every circumstance. To his great misfortune 7 man does not know what will happen, and who can tell him how it will happen [when it does]? 8 As no man can control the wind [to confine the spirit], so the day of one's death cannot be determined; there is no immunity in the battle, nor can wealth*b* save its owner. 9 All this I realized as I thought about everything men do under the sun, when one man has power to injure another.

a Reading with LXX *'et pi-hammélek*, for *'ᵃnī pī-mélek* of MT, which is untranslatable as it stands.
b *'ōšer* for MT *reša'*, "wickedness," the same three Hebrew consonants in reverse order.

Notes

viii 2–9. The wise man will have a wholesome respect for the absolute power of the monarch, and will conduct himself with discretion in his relations with him. The king has the power of life and death, which ordinary men do not. It is implied that the wise man belongs to the upper classes, with access to the court.

2. Cf. *Ahiqar* vii (ANET, p. 428b).

3. *hesitate to go*. Literally "stand still."

4. *is law*. Literally "is powerful."

6. *in every circumstance.* Or "for everything that happens," "every experience."

great misfortune. Literally "man's evil is great upon him." Cf. vi 1.

8. There is a wordplay here on $rū^a ḥ$, which means both "wind" and "spirit." The words in brackets look like the marginal comment of some reader, explaining the metaphor; cf. iii 21.

immuntiy in. Or, "exemption from." For the thought, cf. iii 19, v 13–17 EV, vi 2.

9. *one man has power.* As a king has.

19. WICKEDNESS GOES UNPUNISHED IN THIS LIFE
(viii 10–15)

VIII 10 Thus I saw wicked men borne to their tombs*a*, and as men returned from the sacred place, they were praised*b* in the very city where they had acted so. This, too, is futility. 11 Because the sentence for wrongdoing is not quickly executed— that is why man's mind is filled with thoughts of doing evil, 12 since a sinner does what is wrong a hundred times, and still survives. I am aware [of what is said], that "it will be well [in the end] with those who reverence God, because of their reverence for him"; 13 and, "that it will not be well with the wicked and their days will not lengthen like a shadow, because they do not reverence him." 14 But there are anomalies in life: there are just men to whom what happens should happen to the wicked, and there are wicked men to whom what happens should happen to the just. I declare that such a thing makes no sense. 15 So I commend enjoyment, for man has no other good in this life than to eat and drink and be happy; this will accompany him in his struggle during the few*c* years which God grants him beneath the sun.

a For MT *qᵉbūrīm wābā'ū,* "buried, and they came," LXX reads *qᵉbārīm mūbā'īm,* "they were brought to [their] tombs."
b wᵉyištabbᵉḥū for MT *wᵉyištakkᵉḥū,* "they were forgotten."
c Inserting *mispar,* as in ii 3, vi 12, and some manuscripts here.

NOTES

viii 10–15. Qoheleth concludes from his observation of life that the traditional teaching that goodness is rewarded and wickedness punished is not in accordance with the facts. When they die wrongdoers may be praised rather than condemned. If God's judgment is delayed, wicked men in the meantime are encouraged to go on sinning. Moreover, it sometimes happens that the wicked are actually rewarded, and the righteous punished. Since a man therefore cannot count on his virtue being recompensed, he must find his only compensation for life's struggle in the daily enjoyment of living.

10. The text of this verse has been damaged in manuscript transmission and any restoration remains doubtful.

the sacred place. I.e., the place of burial. Gordon, p. 285, refers to the suggestion that this is a euphemism for "the unclean place," the cemetery.

12. *I am aware [of what is said].* The words in brackets are necessary to the sense unless Qoheleth is contradicting himself, or unless vss. 12b–13 are an insertion by a later hand.

14. *makes no sense.* Or, "is immoral": these are attempts to catch the particular shade of meaning here of Qoheleth's favorite word *hebel,* "vapor, breath," what is meaningless, vain, empty, and fleeting.

15. *struggle.* Or, "toil"—the sheer expenditure of energy, with no result.

20. MAN'S MYSTERIOUS FATE
(viii 16–17, ix 1–12)

VIII 16 When I set my mind to acquire wisdom and to observe the activity which takes place on earth—for day and night
it never sleeps— 17 I saw that it all is God's doing. Man cannot
discover what it is that is going on in this world; however hard
he may search he will not find out; if even a wise man says he
knows, he cannot discover it all.

IX 1 So I thought about all I had observed*ª*—that just and
wise men and what they do are in God's power; whether he will
favor them or not, no one knows. Anything may happen to anyone; 2 the same chance befalls the innocent and the guilty, the
good and the bad, the [ritually] clean and the unclean, the
one who brings a sacrifice and the one who does not. As it is
with the virtuous, so it is with the sinner; as with the one who
swears, so with him who is afraid to swear. 3 This is the worst of
all the things that happen under the sun—that all meet the
same fate. That is why men's minds are full of evil, and madness
is in their minds while they live—because their [only] future is
to die. 4 It is true that "while one is among the living*ᵇ* one has
hope," for "it is better to be a live dog than a dead lion."
5 The living at least know that they will die, but the dead
know nothing at all; they no longer have any compensation,
when their memory has perished. 6 Their love, their hate, their
ardor have completely vanished, and they have no part forever-
more in all that happens under the sun.

7 So then, eat your bread with cheerfulness, and drink your

ª nātattī 'et libbī lir'ōt kol-zeh, for MT *nātattī 'el libbī wᵉlābūr 'et kol-zeh*,
"I gave to my mind to prove [?] all this."
ᵇ yᵉḥubbar, for MT *yᵉbuḥar*, "is chosen."

wine with an untroubled mind, since already God has approved
what you do. 8 At all times let your clothing be white, and the
oil on your head not be lacking. 9 Enjoy life with the woman
you love all the fleeting days of your life that God grants you
under the sun, for that is your compensation while you live
and toil in this world. 10 Everything your hand finds to do, do
with your full strength; for there is no doing or reckoning or
knowing or understanding in Sheol, whither you are bound.

11 Once more, I saw that under the sun the race is not won
by the swift, nor the battle by the warrior; still less does bread
come to the wise, riches to the intelligent, or favor to the
learned; when the time comes, bad luck overtakes them all.
12 Man never knows when his time of misfortune will come;
like fish caught in an accursed net, like birds trapped in a snare,
so men are caught when the moment of disaster comes suddenly
upon them.

NOTES

viii 16–17, ix 1–12. Qoheleth returns to the theme of the impenetrable mystery which surrounds man's life, since God has kept its meaning
hidden from him (cf. i 17, iii 11, vi 12, vii 23–24), and the fate of all
living creatures is the same death (ii 14–16, iii 18–21, vii 15, viii 8).
However wise he may be, no man knows whether or not the arbitrary
decree of God will favor him. Man's sole certain good is the hope and
happiness he can find from day to day, before the sudden and inexplicable blow of fate strikes him down.

viii 16. *activity.* Or, "work."

it never sleeps. I.e., never ceases. But this line may have been displaced from vs. 17 where it would refer to the sleepless activity of God.

17. See preceding NOTE.

in this world. Literally "under the sun."

a wise man. Of a kind unlike the agnostic Qoheleth. Job accused his
counselors of such overconfidence, cf. Job xii 2, and also Isa v 21; Jer
ix 23.

discover it all. Transferring "all" from the redundant opening phrase
of ix 1.

ix 1. *thought about all I had observed.* Literally "I gave my mind to observe all this."

whether he will favor them or not. Literally "whether love or hate."

Anything may happen to anyone. Literally "everything is before them," with the first word of vs. 2 added and read as *lakkōl*. Cf. the Babylonian proverb, "Anything of a god [is difficult] to find out" (BWL, p. 266).

2. Just as the same fate overtakes man and beast (iii 19–20), so fate makes no distinction among men on moral grounds.

chance. See Note on ii 14.

3. *the worst of all.* Or, "the evil in all."

because their [only] future is to die. Or, "and afterwards [they go] to [be among] the dead."

4. Two popular proverbs are quoted, the first of which appears in many languages and is quoted by Cicero (second century B.C.) with reference to sickness.

5–6. With this unequivocal statement about death, cf. vs. 10 and Pss. vi 5 EV, lxxxviii 12 EV, cxv 17; Job xiv 10–12. Other OT writers speak of the "shades" of men as still possessing consciousness and memory, where they "dwell" in the gloomy, dusty cavern of Sheol beneath the earth (Num xvi 30–33; I Sam xxviii 8–14; Ps cxliii 3; Isa xiv 9–11, 15–17). Job ponders the possibility of resurrection (xiv 14–17, xix 25–27), and in the eschatology of late prophecy and apocalyptic writing resurrection is affirmed (Isa xxvi 19; Dan xii 2).

7. *already God has approved.* As seems apparent from the fact that man is permitted this enjoyment; cf. vs. 1 and ii 24–26. Apparently the picture of domestic happiness in vss. 7–9 follows a traditional form; E. A. Speiser has pointed out to me the remarkable parallel in the Old Babylonian fragment of Gilgamesh X (ANET, p. 90a).

8. *white.* As for a festive occasion.

9. MT repeats "all your fleeting days."

12. *accursed.* Literally "evil."

21. PESSIMISM ABOUT WISDOM IN PRACTICE
(ix 13–18, x 1)

IX 13 Another example of wisdom in this life which I have observed was this, and it struck me as significant: 14 There was a small city, with few men in it; and a great king attacked it, surrounded it, and built great siegeworks against it. 15 Now there was*a* in it a man who was poor but wise, and he might have saved the city by his wisdom. But no one thought of that poor man.

16 So I said, "Wisdom is better than might!", yet the wisdom of the poor man was despised, and his words went unheeded. 17 "The quiet words of wise men are to be heeded rather than the shouting of a king of fools" [and] 18 "Wisdom is better than weapons"; but [on the other hand] "One rogue can ruin a great deal of good"; [and]

X 1 "Dead flies will make a bottle of perfume stink!" A small folly may outweigh wisdom [and] honor.

a wᵉnimṣā', "there was found," for MT ūmāṣā', "and he found."

NOTES

ix 13–18, x 1. An anecdote or parable introduces some gloomy reflections about the vulnerability of wisdom to neglect and folly.

ix 13. *significant.* Literally "great"; cf. Exod. iii 3.

14. There is no way of telling if an actual incident is referred to, or if this is a parable.

15. *might have saved.* Literally "he saved." The former sense is implied by the comment in vs. 16. The point is that *no one* remembered the wise man because he was little regarded, rather than that men were not grateful for his advice which saved the city.

16. The proverb is quoted ironically, since in this case the superiority of wisdom went unrecognized.

18. The first proverb is a variant of that in 16a.

rogue. Literally "sinner," but in the specialized sense of the Wisdom writers who tend to identify sinners as the morally obtuse (cf. Prov v 22–23, viii 33–36). When proverbs are quoted in argument, they can be counterbalanced often by others which contradict them (cf. Prov xxvi 4–5).

x 1. *bottle of perfume.* The apparently verbal form *yabbīaʿ* is more probably (as Gordis, p. 305, suggests) a noun meaning a vessel from which liquid flows. "Bottle" seems more suitable than Gordis' "container." Presumably it was a large jar in which ingredients were mixed. *Perfume* is literally "oil of the perfumer."

22. A MISCELLANY OF PRECEPTS, PROVERBS, AND REFLECTIONS ON LIFE
(x 2–20, xi 1–6)

X

2 The thoughts of a wise man tend to the right,
   But the thoughts of a fool to the left;

3 Even as he walks along the road he shows no sense [of direction],
   But announces to all and sundry that he is a fool.

4 If the anger of a ruler is aroused against you, do not abandon your post,
   For mildness will palliate great faults.

5 There is an evil which I have observed in the world, which seems like a mistake attributable to the Ruler himself—

6 Folly is placed in many high positions, while rich men sit in lowly seats.

7 I have seen slaves mounted on horses, and aristocrats walking on foot like slaves.

8 He who digs a pit will fall into it,
   And one who breaks down a wall may be bitten by a snake.

9 He who dislodges stones may be hurt by them,
   And he must take care who would chop down trees;

10 If the ax is blunt and one does not sharpen it beforehand, he must use more strength; he would succeed better by showing intelligence.

11 If a snake which has not been charmed, bites,
   What is the use of having a snake charmer?

12 The words of a wise man are gracious, but the lips of a fool devour him;

13   He begins by talking nonsense, and ends in an evil
        frenzy.

14   The fool has a lot to say for himself; but no man knows
        what the future holds, and who can tell him what
        will happen after him?

15   The fool's exertions so exhaust him
        That he cannot find his way to town.

16   Woe to you, O land, whose king is a youth,
        And whose princes feast in the morning!

17   Happy are you, O land, whose king is of noble birth,
        And whose princes feast at the proper time,
        For strength and not for dissipation!

18   Because of indolence the roof beams sag,
        And a lazy man has a leaky house.

19   Men make a feast for enjoyment, and wine makes life
        pleasant,
        But money is everyone's concern.

20   Even in privacy do not revile a king,
        Nor in your bedroom abuse a rich man;
        For a bird of the air may carry your voice,
        And some winged creature tell what you say.

XI

1   Throw your bread on the surface of the water,
        For after many days you will find it.

2   Divide what you have into seven, or even into eight parts,
        For you never know what disaster will strike the land.

3   If the rain clouds are full [of water], they will pour rain
        on the earth;
        If a tree is blown down by a south or a north wind,
        where it falls, there it remains.

4   He who is always watching the wind does not sow,
        And one who keeps his eyes on the clouds will
        not reap.

5   Just as you do not know how the spirit enters the bones
        in the womb of a pregnant woman, so you cannot
        know how God works in everything he does.

6   In the morning sow your seed, and until evening give your
hand no rest; for you never know whether this or
that will be successful, or whether both may turn
out well.

NOTES

x 2–20, xi 1–6. Precepts and proverbs were a teaching tool in the
schools conducted by professional wise men, of whom, according to
xii 9, Qoheleth was one. They collected, repeated, and modified popular
adages, and composed sententious sayings of their own. Several distinct
collections of these appear in the Book of Proverbs. At this point in
Qoheleth's meditations, when he had just made use of several proverbs
in commenting on the parable of the poor wise man, there is inserted a
small collection of what may have been some of his favorite sayings. The
adages themselves show no special mark of Qoheleth's distinctive philosophy, but the class-conscious comment in x 5–7 and the concluding admonitions in x 20–xi 2, 5–6 do so. As in the Book of Proverbs, the
proverbs quoted here are in the form of rhythmic couplets of parallel
lines.

x 2. *the right* and *the left* have acquired in many languages a secondary connotation of what is socially approved or disapproved, or morally
right or wrong (e.g., Gr. *dexios, skaios;* Lat. *dexter, sinister;* Fr. *droit,
gauche,* etc.). Cf. Gen xlviii 17; Ps cxxi 5; Matt xxv 33.

3. *shows no sense [of direction],* the difference of right from left, and
so (metaphorically) of wisdom from folly.

4. Cf. Prov xv 1, 18, xvi 14.

your post. Or, "your place"; i.e., do not flee in panic. The translation
of the second line is uncertain.

5. *the Ruler.* Or, "the One in power," i.e., God. Cf. i 15.

6–7. Qoheleth betrays his upper-class viewpoint: to him the anomalies
he complains of are a subversion of the right order of social life.

8–9. *a pit.* To trap wild animals, cf. Ps xxxv 7. These verses are a
longer version of the adage in Prov xxvi 27; cf. Prov xxviii 10. Cf.
the Egyptian proverb, "He who shakes the stone—it will fall on his
foot" (*Instruction of 'Onchsheshonqy,* sec. 22, line 5, in Glanville, *Catalogue of Demotic Papyri in the British Museum,* vol. II).

dislodges stones. To roll them over a cliff upon an enemy.

10. *ax,* or, "knife"; literally "iron [implement]."

he would . . . intelligence. Or, "[More] wisdom would conduce to
[greater] success."

11. A caustic adage on the difference between promise and performance. A reference to the acquisition of wisdom may be intended, i.e., why go to school, if you pay no attention?

14. The first clause may be a proverb, but the verse as a whole is in prose.

15. The indolent is one kind of fool; cf. Prov. xxvi 15 for a parallel saying.

16. *is a youth.* Or, "was a steward." Another example of the upsetting of the social hierarchy, which troubles the aristocratic Qoheleth. Cf. x 5–7, v 8 EV, and Nabal's sneer at David, I Sam xxv 10.

feast in the morning. Cf. Isa v 11.

19. *money is everyone's concern.* Or, "[provides] answers for all." The latter literal translation, if it means simply that one must have money to enjoy life, affords neither a parallel nor a contrast to the first line, though it has some similarity to vii 12. With the preferred translation, cf. i 13, iii 10, and especially v 19 EV. In this case the meaning is that the rich, like all others, cannot be entirely carefree in their enjoyment.

20. *privacy.* Literally "private apartment," an example of metonymy. An alternative translation is "your thoughts," literally "your knowledge." With 20c and d, cf. *Ahiqar* vii, "A word is a bird: once released no man (can recapture it)" (ANET, p. 428b).

xi 1–2. *Throw.* Or, "send away." A precept in metaphor, a kind of involuted proverbial comparison: "Just as when you throw something from the shore into the sea, it later comes back to you, so if you take risks by investment in a trading venture, the returns will eventually come in." The metaphor suggests, though it does not necessitate, a reference to maritime commerce. Cf. the Egyptian parallel, "Do a good deed and throw it into the river. When this dries up, you shall find it" (*Instruction of 'Onchsheshonqy,* sec. 19, line 10, in Glanville, *op. cit.*). At the same time, Qoheleth counsels against "putting all one's eggs in the same basket."

3–4. The first two lines emphasize that what is to happen will happen, and what has happened must be accepted. The third and fourth lines may be a popular saying about the man who makes excuses for not working. On Qoheleth's lips they mean that one must venture, in spite of life's uncertainties (cf. vs. 1).

5–6. The author returns to the subject of the inscrutable activity of God, with which man must come to terms (cf. ii 26, iii 14, vii 13–14, viii 16–ix 1). Verse 6 is a precept of diligence, to be understood as referring back to vs. 4 rather than as a metaphor of sex activity, as some have thought. The idea is that man must do his work to enjoy the present life, though to determine the future is beyond his powers.

23. THE JOYS OF YOUTH AND THE ONSET OF AGE
(xi 7–10, xii 1–8)

XI 7 Sweet is the light of day, and good it is for one's eyes to see the sunshine! 8 Yes, though a man live many years, let him be happy in them all, remembering that the days of darkness will be many, and what lies ahead is oblivion. 9 Be happy, young man, while you are young, and revel in the days of your vigor; go where your thoughts incline you, and do what your eyes fancy. [Yet know that for all these things God will call you to account.] 10 Banish care from your mind, do not burden your body, for dark-haired youth is fleeting.

XII

1 In the days of your youth, remember your grave^a,
   When days of trouble have not come yet,
   Nor have the years approached when you will say,
   "I find no pleasure in them";
2 Before the sunshine turns to darkness,
   The light fails from moon and stars,
   And the clouds return, bringing the rains.
3 When that day comes, the palace guardians will tremble
   And the powerful men will stoop,
   The grinding women will cease work because they are
      few,
   And they will find it dark who look out from the
      lattices.
4 The doors to the street will be shut
   As the sound of the mill becomes low,
   The voice of the birds will be silenced,^b
   And all who sing songs will be hushed.

^a *bōr^ekā* for MT *bōr'ēkā*, "your creator."
^b *w^eyiddōm qōl*, for MT *w^eyāqūm l^eqōl*, "one will arise for the voice," which seems meaningless here.

5   Then men will grow afraid of a height,
        And terrors will lurk on the road;
     The almond tree will blossom, the locust be weighed
        down,
        And the caper berry be impotent.
     For a man is on the way to his long-lasting home
        And the mourners gather in the street, [waiting]—
6   Until the silver cord be cut, and the golden bowl be
        broken,
        The pitcher shattered at the spring,
        And the water wheel broken at the cistern.
7   So [man's] dust will return to the earth where it was
        before,
        And the breath of life will return to God who
        gave it.
8   Breath of a breath!—says Qoheleth—All is a breath!

NOTES

xi 7–10, xii 1–8. Qoheleth has argued that, before life's impenetrable
mystery and under its predetermined conditions, man's only certain good
is the present happiness to be found in being alive. This conclusion he
now repeats with eloquence, with his accent on youth as the time when
life is at its most vigorous, and its joys are at their sweetest. He speaks
as one to whom the fresh morning of life is past, and who watches with
regret the lengthening shadows from the declining sun. His words touch
new heights of beauty and pathos in the famous allegory of the onset of
old age.

xi 7. *good it is. The solum bonum* of man and the one positive result
of Qoheleth's quest as stated in ii 3, 24; cf. also iii 12, 22, v 18 (EV),
viii 15.

8. *oblivion.* Heb. *hebel,* "nothingness," "vapor, an empty breath"; see
NOTE on i 11.

9. The words in parentheses seem to interrupt the flow of the sentence,
and to express the view of the orthodox editor who added xii 13–14,
rather than Qoheleth's own view (cf. iii 17–18, viii 16–ix 1).

10. *dark-haired youth.* Or, "youth and the morning of life." The word
*šaḥ*ⁿ*rūt* occurs only here, and its meaning is uncertain.

xii 1. *your grave.* For MT "your creator." This altered translation of a ciently alike to be easily confused in writing especially from dictation; (b) everywhere else in his book Qoheleth refers to the Deity simply as "God," and there is no special appropriateness here for the alternative term; (c) the word *bōr*, "pit," though it may mean a cistern as in xii 6, is commonly used also metaphorically of the grave or Sheol, the place of the dead (cf. Isa xxxviii 18; Prov i 12, etc.); and (d) the meaning "grave" is consonant with iii 18–22 and is peculiarly suitable to the present context. With the following figurative description of the process of growing old, cf. the Egyptian Ptah-hotep's preface to the *Instruction* for his son: "Feebleness has arrived; dotage is coming. . . . The eyes are weak, the ears are deaf, the strength is disappearing. . . . The heart is forgetful. . . . All taste is gone. . . ." (ANET, p 412a).

2. *The light fails . . . stars.* Literally "and the light and the moon and the stars."

clouds return, bringing the rains. Literally "return after the rains." As is clear from Ruth i 15–16, this means "return in company with"; to overlook this idiom (which is supported also from Ugaritic) produces a meteorological absurdity. The approaching darkness of winter when the heavy clouds of autumn herald the winter rains provides a parallel with the failing light of day.

3. *palace guardians.* Literally "those who watch the house." It seems clear from the references to the guards, the men of power, the women slaves at the mill and the ladies at the lattice windows, that the picture is that of a great man's house.

powerful men. Either physically or in importance.

find it dark. Literally "be darkened." The figures represent a man's increasing decrepitude with the approach of death.

5. The *blossom of the almond tree* is white, suggesting the white hair of the aged, the *locust . . . weighed down*, his labored movements, the useless *caper berry* (a sexual stimulant), his loss of virility.

long-lasting home. Cf. the Egyptian phrase "house of eternity."

6. Figures of death: the ornamental lamp is extinguished when its *cord* is *cut*, and its *bowl* falls and is *broken:* and when the water on which life depends fails, because *pitcher* and *water pot* lie *broken* at the source. Heb. *galgal* usually means "wheel," but the parallelism here requires the meaning "bowl" or "pot"; cf. Ugaritic *gl* (*I Keret* 71–72, 164–65).

7. *dust.* Or, "soil" from which man's body was made (cf. Gen ii 7; Eccles iii 20).

breath of life. Or, "spirit"—not a divine spark which returns to God but the animation of the body through God's act (Gen ii 7), which ends when God so determines.

8. Qoheleth's book ends with the repetition of his opening thesis which, he feels, is now fully demonstrated.

24. BIOGRAPHICAL FOOTNOTES AND SUMMATION BY ANOTHER SAGE
(xii 9–14)

XII ⁹ In addition to becoming a wise man himself, Qoheleth instructed the people in what he had learned, pondering and examining the composition*a* of many wise sayings. ¹⁰ Qoheleth tried to find felicitous language, and honestly to express the truth.

¹¹ Wise men's words are like goads, and like nails driven home with a mallet are those who master the collected sayings of their mentor. ¹² Beyond this, my son, be warned; book learning is an endless occupation, and much study is exhausting. ¹³ The sum of the matter when all has been heard [is this]: Reverence God, and observe his laws. This applies to everything. ¹⁴ For God will judge every deed according to its hidden intention, whether good or evil.

a Reading the noun *tōken* with LXX, for a verb in MT, *tiqqēn,* "he arranged."

NOTES

xii 9–14. The manuscript of Qoheleth's reflections and precepts was edited and published by another professional wise man. He gave the book its title, inserted the words "says Qoheleth" at i 2, vii 27, and xii 8, and then appended some biographical information and comments of his own. Evidently he was an admirer of the author and felt that this collection of his observations and speculations was worthy of study. At the same time he cautioned the reader against becoming confused by the divergent and even daring ideas presented, and provided a safe and simple rule for avoidance of intellectual and moral difficulties—Reverence God, and observe his laws.

11. *mallet.* Or, "pestle."
their mentor. Literally "one shepherd."
12. *book learning . . . occupation.* Literally "much use of books is endless."

KEY TO THE TEXT

PROVERBS

Chapter	Verse	§	Chapter	Verse	§
i	1–33	1	xvii	1–28	18
ii	1–22	2	xviii	1–24	19
iii	1–35	3	xix	1–29	20
iv	1–27	4	xx	1–30	21
v	1–14	5	xxi	1–31	22
	15–20	6	xxii	1–16	23
	21–23	4		17–21	24
vi	1–19	6		22–29	25
	20–21	7	xxiii	1–35	26
	22	6	xxiv	1–22	27
	23–35	7		23–34	28
vii	1–27	8	xxv	1–28	29
viii	1–36	9	xxvi	1–28	30
ix	1–18	10	xxvii	1–27	31
x	1–32	11	xxviii	1–28	32
xi	1–31	12	xxix	1–27	33
xii	1–28	13	xxx	1–9	34
xiii	1–25	14		10–33	35
xiv	1–35	15	xxxi	1–9	36
xv	1–33	16		10–31	37
xvi	1–33	17			

ECCLESIASTES

Chapter	Verse	§	Chapter	Verse	§
i	1–2	1	vii	1–14	15
	3–11	2		15–22	16
	12–18	3		23–29	17
ii	1–11	4	viii	1	17
	12–17	5		2–9	18
	18–26	6		10–15	19
iii	1–15	7		16–17	20
	16–22	8	ix	1–12	20
iv	1–3	8		13–18	21
	4–16	9	x	1	21
v	1–7	10		2–20	22
	8–9	11	xi	1–6	22
	10–20	12		7–10	23
vi	1–9	13	xii	1–8	23
	10–12	14		9–14	24